YEARBOOK IN EARLY CHILDHOOD EDUCATION

Bernard Spodek • Olivia N. Saracho
EDITORS

VOLUME 1
Early Childhood Teacher Preparation
Bernard Spodek and Olivia N. Saracho, Editors

VOLUME 2
Issues in Early Childhood Curriculum
Bernard Spodek and Olivia N. Saracho, Editors

VOLUME 3
Issues in Child Care
Bernard Spodek and Olivia N. Saracho, Editors

YEARBOOK IN EARLY CHILDHOOD EDUCATION
EDITORIAL ADVISORY BOARD

The *Yearbook in Early Childhood Education* is a series of annual publications. Each volume addresses a timely topic of major significance in the field of early childhood education, and contains chapters that present and interpret current knowledge on aspects of that topic, written by experts in the field. Key issues—including concerns about educational equity, multiculturalism, the needs of diverse populations of children and families, and the ethical dimensions of the field—are woven into the organization of each of the volumes.

YEARBOOK
IN
EARLY CHILDHOOD EDUCATION
VOLUME 2

ISSUES IN
EARLY CHILDHOOD
CURRICULUM

Bernard Spodek • Olivia N. Saracho

EDITORS

Teachers College, Columbia University
New York • London

Published by Teachers College Press, 1234 Amsterdam Avenue
New York, NY 10027

Library of Congress Cataloging-in-Publication Data

Issues in early childhood curriculum / Bernard Spodek, Olivia N. Saracho.
     p. cm. — (Yearbook in early childhood education ; v. 2)
   Includes bibliographical references and index.
   ISBN 0-8077-3124-2 (alk. paper). — ISBN 0-8077-3123-4
(pbk. : alk. paper)
    1. Early childhood education—United States—Curricula.
I. Spodek, Bernard. II. Saracho, Olivia N. III. Series.
LB1139.4.I85 1991
372. 19—dc20   91-24966

Printed on acid-free paper

Manufactured in the United States of America

98 97 96 95 94 93 92 91   8 7 6 5 4 3 2 1

To Olivia N. Saracho's father,
Pablo J. Villarreal,
who has shown great determination
and has given wisdom and inspiration to others.

Contents

Introduction: Concepts of Early Childhood Curriculum

Bernard Spodek

Olivia N. Saracho

A curriculum is a repertoire of learning experiences, planned and organized according to the program's educational goals. Each curriculum reflects a vision of what children "ought to be and become" (Biber, 1984, p. 303) based on a view of social values and a structure that translates those values into experiences for learners. Curriculum, as a special area of study within education, emerged from the need to arrange, organize, and translate such visions into educational programs of study. The first formal book in the area of curriculum was not produced until 1918 (Bobbit, 1918). Modern curriculum study in this country dates from the early 1890s, when major committees debated the form and structure of public schooling. Today, curriculum development is an essential component of education at all levels.

Over the years, there have been different conceptions of the term *curriculum*. Caswell and Campbell (1935), two leading curriculum specialists, defined curriculum as "composed of all of the experiences children have under the guidance of the teacher" (p. 66). Their view of curriculum as experiences rather than products was supported by others. Smith, Stanley, and Shores (1957) conceived of curriculum as a sequence of potential experiences set up in the school to discipline children and youth to think and care as a group. Tyler (1957) viewed curriculum as all of the students' learning, as planned and directed by the school to attain its educational goals.

Curriculum is now generally considered to be all of the experiences that learners have under the auspices of the school (Doll, 1970). The study of curriculum includes the historical study of the intents and content of schooling, analyses of curriculum documents, and analyses of the experiences provided to children in school.

The definition of curriculum has changed through the years to respond to social forces and school expectations. However, the process of developing curriculum remains consistent. Curriculum developers establish goals, develop experiences, designate content, and evaluate experiences and outcomes.

CURRICULUM DEVELOPMENT IN EARLY CHILDHOOD EDUCATION

Although curriculum development is a process that extends throughout education, from preschool through higher education, the curriculum development process of early childhood education differs in many ways from that of other levels of education. The most obvious difference is in the students concerned. Making curriculum decisions for young children requires the educator to be more concerned with the individual's level of development. The concern for "developmentally appropriate practices" reflects that.

Early childhood educators sometimes have different conceptions of educational goals. While some early childhood educators are concerned with specific learning outcomes, others advocate global outcomes, such as supporting the child's overall development. In addition, the methods and materials of early childhood education are different from those of education at other levels.

Perhaps the study of early childhood curriculum needs to be distinct from the study of curriculum at other levels. This does not suggest that there are no common elements. Indeed, the view presented earlier, that curriculum reflects social values and translates those values into experiences for learners, is true for curriculum at all levels. It is also true that early childhood curriculum is concerned with arranging, organizing, and translating that vision into educational programs. But the structure, process, and content of the programs that are developed in early childhood education are unique and have been unique throughout the history of early childhood education.

This volume seeks to illuminate many of the issues related to early childhood curriculum development as it exists today and as it has evolved over time. Chapter 1 reviews the history of early childhood curriculum. It describes how different concepts of knowledge that were held at different times have influenced the various historical curriculum models. In the twentieth century, knowledge of developmental processes has also influenced curriculum. Different concepts of human development inspired a variety of early childhood curriculum models in the 1960s and 1970s. Recently, there has been a move away from the acceptance of variety in early childhood curriculum models toward an implicit acceptance of a single curriculum model.

The next two chapters focus on the nature of the child and the importance of knowledge of young children to curriculum planning. Herbert Zimiles's chapter focuses on the wide range of diversity found within the child population in school today. Although early childhood educators have always attended to the individual needs of children, attention must be paid to group differences as well. The call for multicultural education and the various programs designed for at-risk, gifted, and other identifiable groups of children reflect that attention. An understanding of young children also needs to be grounded in concepts of human growth and development. In Chapter 3, Anthony D. Pellegrini and Janna Dresden identify some of the current concepts of human development and demonstrate how these can be addressed in early childhood programs.

The next three chapters focus on early childhood classroom processes. Harriet K. Cuffaro analyzes the materials used in early childhood classrooms. These materials are analogous to the textbooks provided for older children. As different conceptions of curriculum have evolved, different materials have been provided to young children, and materials have been used differently. Olivia N. Saracho analyzes play as a medium for teaching and learning in early childhood programs. She identifies the various kinds of play teachers can use in fostering learning and describes the various ways teachers can influence children's play to enhance that learning. Douglas H. Clements reviews our knowledge about the use of computers in programs for young children. He provides guidelines that teachers can use for integrating computers into classroom programs.

Sharon L. Kagan, in the chapter that follows, reminds us that most young children today attend more than one early childhood program, either serially or concurrently. She describes the educational continuity among programs as well as the consistency of program structures needed to address the educational needs of young children.

Joseph H. Stevens, Jr., addresses a concern for parent programs in the early childhood curriculum. His chapter reports on research related to parent support programs connected to early childhood programs. These support programs enhance classroom programs for young children and extend learning to include the family.

The next two chapters deal, in different ways, with the issue of evaluation in early childhood curriculum. Lorrie A. Shepard describes the influence that evaluating children through standardized tests has had on early childhood curriculum. Children are sorted out by these tests in the hope that a narrower range of individual differences can be addressed in a classroom. One consequence of this testing is that the curriculum has been narrowed to conform to the limited area of learning assessed by these tests. Douglas R. Powell and Irving E. Sigel explore problems in evaluating programs for young children, focusing especially on the validity of evaluation instruments and designs. If we are to judge the educational worth of programs for young children, we need to be able to evaluate their outcomes. The problems of evaluation, especially in relation to the education of young children, must be considered.

Our concerns for the education of young children must go beyond the education of children within our country. Increasingly, programs of early childhood education, care, and development are being established throughout the world. Such programs are especially important in developing nations. Cassie Landers identifies the arguments that support such programs and the critical issues in implementing them.

The final chapter looks to the future of early childhood curriculum. The field of early childhood education has always been a dynamic one. New models of early childhood education have evolved through the years in response to new educational ideologies, new social demands, and new knowledge. The issues that are identified in this book are ones that can guide early childhood curriculum development in the future. Ultimately, our programs for young children will have to change. Early childhood educators will need to be sensitive to changes in the cultural context as well as changes in our knowledge about children's development in creating new programs for children. They must also be sensitive to the new social and educational structures and institutions that will be evolving.

REFERENCES

Biber, B. (1984). *Early education and psychological development.* New Haven: Yale University Press.

Bobbit, F. (1918). *The curriculum.* Boston: Houghton Mifflin.

Caswell, H. L., & Campbell, D. S. (1935). *Curriculum development.* New York: American Book Co.

Doll, R. (1970). *Curriculum improvement.* Boston: Allyn & Bacon.

Smith, B. O., Stanley, W. O., & Shores, H. J. (1957). *Fundamentals of curriculum development.* New York: Harcourt Brace Jovanovich.

Tyler, R. W. (1957). The curriculum then and now. In *Proceedings of the 1956 Conference on Testing Problems.* Princeton, NJ: Educational Testing Service.

CHAPTER 1

Early Childhood Curriculum and Cultural Definitions of Knowledge

Bernard Spodek

The content of all education is culturally defined—traditionally, in terms of how a society defines knowledge of truth, virtue, and beauty. As conceptions of truth, virtue, and beauty change, so does the content of education. For most of the history of Western civilization, the transmission of the culture's notions of truth, virtue, and beauty was limited to an elite sector of the population. Only in the last 100 years or so has there been a move toward more universal education.

Our nation supports the ideal of universal education. But while education may be universally available in our society, there is no universal form of education. Schools perpetuate class differences in society by providing wealthier children with a more classical education and working-class children with a more technical education (Kleibard, 1985). Some recent critics have suggested that even the elite in colleges and universities receive a vocationally oriented technical education and that the classical definitions of the educated person are being ignored (Bloom, 1987).

Seldom are similar arguments raised about the differences in early childhood education programs offered to low-income children as compared to those offered to affluent children. Nor are arguments typically heard about the content of early childhood education, though it is a form of general education. One possible explanation is that early childhood educators are more concerned with the effects of early childhood education on a child's development than with what a child comes to know as a result of that education.

In reality, however, the content of early childhood programs is similarly embedded in the ideals of truth, virtue, and beauty that are held by a particular community. As conceptions of knowledge and social demands have changed, so has the content of early childhood education. A review of the history of early childhood education programs illustrates this point.

1

CONCEPTIONS OF EIGHTEENTH CENTURY
EARLY CHILDHOOD PROGRAMS

In the schools of colonial America, from their establishment in the seventeenth century and continuing through the first third of the nineteenth century, no distinctions were made between programs for young children and those for older children. Common, or primary, schools had no entrance age. In 1826, for example, when school records began to be kept, 5 percent of all children below the age of four, including 20 percent of all three-year-olds, were enrolled in the common or primary schools of Massachusetts (May & Vinovskis, 1977).

During the American colonial period, young children were expected to learn to read as early as age three or four. The early primary schools essentially taught the rudiments of reading to enable people to gain access to the Bible, so they could live a proper religious life. The Bible was considered the source of all knowledge and morality. Being able to read the Bible was considered all the formal education needed by most persons.

The first basic school text in America was the horn book, a paddle-shaped board covered by a thin transparent layer of an animal's horn. These books contained the alphabet, short prayers, and excerpts from the Scriptures. Children learned the sounds of the letters, which were then combined to make words. Once the children learned these simple reading skills, they could read the Bible themselves. A more extensive school curriculum, including writing and arithmetic, became more important as the commercial life of the colonies expanded and knowledge of the three Rs was necessary in even the simplest businesses (Good & Teller, 1973).

Schools for children in Europe were similar at that time. However, new approaches to early childhood education and care began to appear toward the end of the eighteenth century. These included church day nurseries and the "knitting school" of Jean Frederick Oberlin, established in the Alsace region of France during the 1770s. In this school children were taught language and handicrafts and were provided with exercise and play. Content was transmitted mainly by showing pictures about natural and social history and the Scriptures. The children learned the names of things that were portrayed in the pictures presented to them. They were first taught in the local Alsatian dialect, then in French (Deasey, 1978).

Language education was becoming important in Europe as modern European nations were being created through the integration of smaller states. A single common language maintained the integrity of each new nation. Similarly, Noah Webster's *Blue-Backed Speller* provided a common language and spelling for the newly established United States of America.

NINETEENTH CENTURY EARLY CHILDHOOD PROGRAMS AND THE AGE OF REASON

Greater distinctions were made among young children, older children, and adults during the nineteenth century, and greater investments were made in young children by their families. Productive work moved from the handicrafts of cottage industries to industrial factories. Child labor in the home was supervised by parents and was considered relatively safe from abuse. As children worked in mines and factories, reformers began to fear that children were performing beyond their capabilities and under unsafe and unhealthy conditions. Industrialization and urbanization brought with them new social problems.

At about this time, the "age of reason" evolved, with logic and experience overshadowing faith and religion as the source of truth. Scientific knowledge was being created and discovered in the world at large as well as in the laboratory. Empiricism, with its dependence on personal experience and observation as a source of knowledge, and rationalism, with its dependence on reason and intellect as a source of knowledge, became legitimized as a basis for the school curriculum. Schools modified their programs as lectures and recitations gave way to direct experiences and exercises in reasoning.

Owen's Infant School

One of the first educators to design programs especially for young children was Robert Owen, a factory owner and social reformer (Harrison, 1968). Owen concluded that early education was needed to prepare people to live in the ideal society. A rational education would develop the proper character needed for the ideal society. The focus on rationality and the use of experience characterized Owen's Institute for the Development of Character and its section for younger children, called the Infant School.

Owen assumed that society should be concerned with promoting the maximum happiness for the greatest number of persons. Knowledge was viewed as being derived from objects surrounding the individual, while truth could be determined reasonably from what is consistent with nature. Children could learn to distinguish right from wrong by becoming aware of the natural consequences of their actions rather than through the imposition of rewards and punishments. Owen also assumed that each individual's character was the result of the education received and the conditions under which one lived. He believed that the early years of life were the best time to develop character (Owen, 1857).

Owen's Infant School had a short history in the United States. The infant schools established in the 1820s competed with the common schools of that period. Education of young children outside the home was also opposed by family educators who believed that the best education for young children took place in the home, at the hearth, on the knee of the child's mother—a form of education characterized as "fireside education." Whether the idyllic conditions of the home actually existed for most children is questionable (Strickland, 1982).

Froebel's Kindergarten

The kindergarten, originally established by Friedrich Froebel, has had the longest history and the greatest impact on the field of early childhood education. Froebel was a philosophical idealist, like Plato, who believed that ideas could be validated abstractly, without recourse to experience. Experience illuminated ideas rather than created them. Froebel's basic ideas were religious in nature; the ultimate ideal was the unity of man, God, and nature. Each man, for example, reflects the whole of his culture, just as each tree reflects the totality of nature (Kilpatrick, 1916). Froebel's ideal represented a dialectic. The unity of nature was the thesis, the diversity within nature was the antithesis, and the idea of each diverse element representing the totality of the universe was the synthesis.

Froebel viewed development as a process of unfolding. Education should follow each child's nature in order to attain the beauty of the individual's mature power (Froebel, 1896). Education should follow development, guarding and protecting children who learned through self-activity. Children's knowledge resulted from their contact with materials (gifts) and activities (occupations) that symbolized these ideas. Froebel's first gift was a ball that, with its single external surface, symbolized unity (of man, God, and nature). The second gift included a ball as well as a cube, symbolizing diversity (the diversity found in nature), and a cylinder, representing the mediation of these two opposites (the diversity of individual things reflecting their essential unity). The meanings reflected in these symbols represented the knowledge that children were to achieve by manipulating materials and engaging in activities.

Froebelian kindergarten education, which arrived in the United States in 1856, flourished. Unlike the infant school, the kindergarten did not separate the education of children from their life in the family. Froebel viewed the mother as central to the proper education of the young. This was consistent with views embodied in fireside education noted above.

Froebel's philosophy was also consistent with transcendentalism, a philosophic movement that proposed to discover the nature of reality through the process of spiritual intuition. Elizabeth Peabody, a leader in the early kindergarten movement, was allied with the transcendentalist movement in Boston, as were other leaders (Shapiro, 1983).

Froebelian kindergarten education changed very little during the nineteenth century, though it had many different uses. Churches incorporated kindergartens into their parish and missionary work. American missionaries in Brazil, Rhodesia, Turkey, China, Japan, and many other countries established kindergartens while converting the native population to Christianity. Kindergartens were also established by the Women's Christian Temperance Union, settlement houses, labor unions, and businesses (Vandewalker, 1908). Often, however, practices in these kindergartens reflected the concerns of the particular program's sponsors as much as they did Froebel's philosophy.

Empirical Models of Early Education

During this same period, an empirical approach to early education was evolving in Europe. This approach served as the basis for educating handicapped children and was also adapted by Maria Montessori to educate "normal" young children. The earliest pioneer of this approach was probably Jacob-Rodrigues Pereire, who also influenced Rousseau in his educational thinking. Pereire had fallen in love with a deaf-mute woman and developed a method to teach her language (Boyd, 1914). Speech was taught by imitation, using vision as a guide while the deaf-mute individual touched the face and neck of the speaker to feel the vibrations of speech. One also spoke to the deaf-mute through touch by putting one's lips against the ear, face, or some other sensitive part of the body so that impressions could be gained by the movement of air formed by speech. Signs were also used (Lane, 1976).

Jean-Marc-Gaspard Itard, in his effort to educate Victor, the wild boy of Aveyron, used Pereire's approach to language education, along with the educational approaches of others. Victor had been found in the woods of Aveyron in France in 1800. He walked on all fours, had no language, and shunned most cooked food. Itard took over the education of Victor after his capture. Building on the work of Pereire, Itard devised an educational regimen designed to socialize Victor, develop his language skills, and provide him with an understanding of the physical world.

Itard's program of instruction was a caring, nurturing one. It assumed that people gained knowledge of the physical world through their experiences as perceived through the senses. Itard's approach to education was first to awaken Victor's senses of touch, taste, and smell, and later to train the senses of hearing and vision. Attempts were made to teach communication through gesture. Victor was also taught the names of things and learned to categorize things broadly.

Through this program, Victor learned to match sketches to the objects they represented and to distinguish shapes and colors. He learned to write and read, understand simple grammatical structures, and identify parts of speech. He also was provided with moral training. While Victor did gain some aspects of language, he never learned to speak. In the final analysis, Victor was considered a child suffering from deficiencies, possibly retarded and/or autistic as well as mute, rather than simply a child of nature (Lane, 1976).

Itard's contribution to the field of education was significant. His method was adopted by Edouard Seguin, an educator of mentally handicapped children, who created a systematic approach to sensory pedagogy. His educational model reflected the stages of the mental act. The first phase, impression, resulted from the sensory experience with an object; the second required the child to consider the sensory impression; the third phase required the child's expression related to the sensory experience. Each act contains both a motor function and a sensory function. Seguin used the physiological exercises of the senses and muscles to construct and reconstruct complete circles of acts, from impression through expression. The exercise of one sense was used to corroborate the action and verify the acquisition of another sense (Talbot, 1964).

Seguin used music to develop controlled behavior and oral expression, physical and gymnastic training to develop intelligent behavior, and art for symbolic training. He developed a wide range of manipulative sensory materials for children, including form boards, lacing and buttoning frames, pegboards, and texture boards. Other materials for sensory training, such as word-matching sets, syllable cards, and charts for teaching reading, were also developed (Talbot, 1964).

Today, the focus on sensory training, derived from an empirical theory of epistemology, is still an important part of both special education and early childhood education. Contemporary theory suggests that individuals come to know the world as a result of their experiences. The sensations gained from these experiences, and the way in which these sensory impressions are organized, give meaning to the world. These literally help children "make sense" of it.

Systematic sensory training, however, was not addressed in the education of normal children. Perhaps normal children's senses are trained adequately during the typical process of maturation and the normal experiences that children have. When the maturation process is disturbed, systematic training might need to be provided. Sensory education, however, did become part of Montessori education.

EARLY CHILDHOOD EDUCATION
IN THE TWENTIETH CENTURY

The twentieth century saw the development of new approaches to early childhood education that had their roots in the early childhood education initiatives of the prior century. Each, however, was also influenced by changes in knowledge about children, in knowledge about knowledge, and in the social context. Each new or modified approach, including Montessori education, nursery school education, and the reformed kindergarten movement, resulted in a different early childhood curriculum.

The Montessori Method

After graduating from medical school at the turn of the century, Maria Montessori worked with mentally defective children in the Orthophrenic School in Italy. Not content with caring for their physical needs, Montessori sought keys to unlock their intellectual potential. In doing so, she explored the works of earlier philosophers and educators, including Rousseau, Pestalozzi, Froebel, Itard, and Seguin. Montessori began testing the educational strategies and approaches to materials that had been developed by Seguin and devised a system of education that proved to be effective with handicapped children (Kramer, 1988).

Montessori left the Orthophrenic School and created her own *Casa dei Bambini,* or Children's House, in Rome for working-class children. She extended her educational approach to normal children, evolving a systematic education of the senses. While Montessori viewed development as a process of unfolding, she felt that environmental influences also played an important role.

Montessori's curriculum was designed to influence sensorimotor, intellectual, language, and moral development. It included exercises in practical life, education in basic academic skills, language education, muscular education, and the education of the senses. These diverse elements were interrelated, for even the learning of basic academic skills was embedded in sensory education. The Montessori curriculum was based on assumptions about how children gained knowledge about the surrounding world, what children needed to know to function independently, and what children needed to succeed in traditional schools (Montessori, 1964, 1965).

Montessori's educational methods and her conception of development owed more to the study of physical anthropology than to the developing field of child development. This influence is seen in her use of physical measurements as indices of educational development as well as in her educational philosophy (Spodek, 1973).

The Nursery School

At the same time the Montessori method was created in Italy, the nursery school was established in England. Nursery school education reflected a desire to provide social justice for children, as had the infant school a century earlier. The nursery school was designed for the education and nurturance of children between the ages of two and seven. A concern for health, hygiene, nutrition, and exercise was combined with a concern for the proper education of poor and working-class young children. Starting in the slums of London, the idea of the nursery school spread throughout England in the early 1900s and soon attracted educators and child development specialists from the United States. Nursery schools were first founded in the United States around the time of World War I.

Nursery school education was based on the play of young children. Both indoor and outdoor play was encouraged, and a range of new play materials was created or adapted for use by groups of children. The nursery school valued the development of creativity in young children. Creativity would serve the needs of children in their present lives and prepare them for their future lives, helping them become scientists, artists, and managers as well as workers. In support of creativity, the program included a variety of art, music, and movement activities, in addition to play. Self-caring skills, perceptual-learning skills, and science were also taught through activities that included gardening and nature study. Academically oriented readiness activities were also provided (McMillan, 1919).

The nursery school was influenced by a number of educational philosophers, including Montessori and Dewey. New conceptions of development and new theories of psychology, including the Freudian and maturationist views of child development, were also major influences (Owen, 1920). The nursery school became closely associated with the child development movement in the United States, at least in part because of its association with the child study centers that were developing in universities throughout the nation.

Reforming the Kindergarten

The progressive education movement effected a reconstruction of kindergarten theory and practice in the first quarter of the twentieth century. Froebelian theory was directly attacked by progressive kindergarten educators who could accept neither the goals of the Froebelian kindergarten nor its basic assumptions of symbolic education. However, it was some time before the majority of kindergarten educators abandoned the Froebelian philosophy. Many retained their early beliefs about the value of traditional kindergarten education, while others sought to accommodate Froebelian philosophy to the newer progressive ideas. Meetings of the International Kindergarten Union (IKU) were held, seeking ways of rectifying the two approaches to early childhood education. The IKU established a committee of distinguished kindergarten educators to accomplish this task. Committee members worked long months to develop a common view of kindergarten education, a task that turned out to be impossible. The committee finally issued three diverse reports, one taking a Froebelian approach, a second taking a progressive approach, and a third attempting a conciliatory approach (Committee of Nineteen, 1913).

The progressive kindergarten, following Dewey's ideas, saw the social life of the community as the source of children's education. Kindergarten educators became concerned with children's reconstruction of knowledge and built their teaching methods on Dewey's theory of instrumentalism or pragmatism to achieve this aim.

Dewey rejected Froebel's approach to symbolic education in the kindergarten. Play, in Dewey's conception of education, was embedded in the child's natural impulses rather than in the need to manipulate materials in order to abstract the symbolic meanings in them. Children were given direct experiences with both physical and social phenomena. They were to reconstruct those experiences through play in the kindergarten (Dewey, 1938). Both Patty Smith Hill and Alice Temple, leaders in the kindergarten movement during the first third of the twentieth century, were heavily influenced by Dewey's progressivism. They worked consistently toward reconstructing the American kindergarten.

The Emerging Influence of Child Development

During the twentieth century, increased attention was given to theories of child development as the basis for early childhood programs, and less concern was shown for theories of knowledge. The child study movement was closely allied with the early childhood education field. G. Stanley Hall, founder of the child study movement, was instrumental in moving kindergarten educators from a Froebelian view of the child based on philosophic idealism to a more scientific view of the child based on empirical study.

In the early stages of the progressive kindergarten movement, behavioral theory, more a theory of learning than of development, was applied to the kindergarten curriculum as habit training became the basis for young children's learning. This is evident in the writing of Edward Thorndike (1903) and in the conduct curriculum that was developed in the laboratory school kindergarten and first grade of Teachers College, Columbia University (Burke, 1923).

The "child development point of view," based on a maturationist conception of development (see Gesell, 1943), seemed to represent the consensus of early childhood educators in the 1940s and 1950s (e.g., Hymes, 1955). Young children were provided with safe, supportive environments in which they could explore their developing competencies without being frustrated by unrealistic expectations that might be set by teachers.

Psychoanalytic theory had a great impact on the development of early childhood curriculum. Art was used less as a form of representation and more as a form of expression of feelings. Play was seen as a medium for emotional catharsis, allowing children to rid themselves of fears, anxiety, and other negative feelings that might otherwise lead to adult neuroses. Children could explore their inner selves and express feelings in ways that might not be allowed in their homes. Teachers were admonished to observe and record children's behavior rather than intervene in their activities. The progressive early childhood curriculum, designed to allow children to reconstruct their experiences in order to create shared meanings in a community, gave way to a curriculum designed to provide a warm, nurturing environment that allowed children's development to unfold and also provided an outlet for the expression of affect.

Variations in Early Childhood Curriculum

The 1960s saw a convergence of social concerns in our nation and the use of new theories of child development as the basis for early childhood education. J. M. Hunt's (1961) volume, *Experience and Intelligence,* synthesized a great deal of the evolving child development theory and research that challenged the maturational point of view. Hunt suggested that human development, including intellectual development, was modifiable through environmental experiences. The work of Jean Piaget, a developmental epistemologist, and B. F. Skinner, a learning psychologist, served as the inspiration for many of the new programs.

Many of the curriculum models that evolved were originally developed in university research centers and funded by private foundations. Some of these approaches to early childhood education became the "Planned Variations" curriculum models of the Head Start and Follow Through programs. These programs were different in their developmental orientations and in their conceptions of what and how to teach young children. Programs differed in their goals as well as in the means used to achieve those goals. Different areas or kinds of knowledge were postulated by the various curriculum developers. These were reflected in what was taught in each program (Day & Parker, 1977; Evans, 1975; Spodek, 1973).

These newer approaches became popular during the 1960s and 1970s. Unfortunately, neither private early childhood centers nor local public school systems adopted them as their standard curricula, partly because they required greater resources than were available or training that teachers did not have. It is hard to find examples of these various curriculum models reflected in early childhood programs either within or outside the pubic schools today. The one exception might be the High/Scope model (Hohmann, Banet & Weikart, 1979). Though this model has been characterized as a Piaget-based curriculum, it has been suggested that it was more inspired by Piagetian theory than grounded in it (Sylva, 1986).

The diversity among these Planned Variations models was great. As noted, there was no agreement about program methods, goals, or objectives. The comparative evaluation made of these diverse programs raised a number of issues. Many program sponsors argued that the traditional tests used to evaluate the programs were too narrow to measure all program contents and thus favored some narrowly conceived programs over others. Some programs were faulted for teaching specifically for the tests used in the evaluation. In addition, program implementation was inadequate, and there were great variations in outcomes among the various sites for each program model (House & Hutchins, 1979).

With all the problems in sponsoring and evaluating alternative approaches to early childhood education, the idea of supporting a variety of programs for young children and allowing them to compete in the marketplace of ideas has great merit. Throughout the history of early childhood education we have seen new program models, based on new conceptions of learning and development and responding to changes in society, challenge and sometimes replace established models that have been supported by the education establishment. Nurturing of alternative approaches to early childhood education has kept the field responsive to the emerging needs of children, families, and communities.

Developmentally Appropriate Practices: The New Orthodoxy

During the 1960s and 1970s, alternative early childhood education programs were created and disseminated among schools, teachers, and children. The optimistic spirit of these decades was reflected in the establishment of new programs, a search for new knowledge, and an acceptance of many different ways of developing good programs. In contrast, the 1980s became a period of program constriction in early childhood education. The field backed away from the spirit of optimism that had characterized it. The 1980s brought a new conservatism in the field of early childhood education as well as in the country as a whole.

It is difficult to identify the reason for the change in the field. Perhaps it was the result of shrinking social programs in the United States. Funds for programs for young children became scarcer, and providing *any* kind of program was considered valuable. Early childhood programs became more universal and were increasingly sponsored by public schools. Perhaps there was a fear that public school systems were rigid and that the new programs for young children would be designed to be like existing public school programs for older children. Indeed, there is evidence to support both explanations. Perhaps there were other forces both within and outside the field of early childhood education—forces that have not yet been identified—that were influencing the field. Whatever the cause, as a field, early childhood education now seems less disposed to nurturing program diversity and more disposed to establishing narrow standards for early childhood programs.

An example of the narrowing of standards can be seen in the National Association for the Education of Young Children's (NAEYC) established guidelines for developmentally appropriate kindergarten practices, which were later expanded to include the entire age range from birth through age eight (Bredekamp, 1987). These guidelines were issued after a yearlong deliberation by a broad-based commission of early childhood educators, though they do not reflect the report of the commission (Spodek, 1985). The document has become the conventional wisdom of early childhood curriculum: that early childhood education programs are based upon developmental theory alone.

Although the NAEYC document has been widely disseminated as a guide to determine an appropriate curriculum for young children, it has also been criticized. The exclusive use of developmental guidelines for judging programs has been criticized as inadequate. In addition, the guidelines' examples of appropriate and inappropriate practices have made the meaning of "developmentally appropriate practices" even more narrow.

Jipson (1990) has raised questions about whether the document actually represents the accumulated knowledge of the field of child development and whether it reflects an appropriate knowledge base for recommending early childhood curriculum. She suggests that the guidelines reflect a narrow range of knowledge seen from a positivist perspective and project a cultural bias. Kessler (1991) also suggests that the developmental "inappropriateness" of some of the practices criticized in the document cannot be substantiated if one uses children's ability to learn as the criterion. The fact that a young child has mastered some learning is prima facie evidence that the practice is appropriate to the developmental level of that child, even though the practice might be judged inappropriate by NAEYC's guidelines.

Even under the best of circumstances, developmental theory can provide information only on the appropriateness of educational method—the how of what we teach—not on educational content—the substance of what we teach. The fallacy created by making developmental appropriateness the only criterion for judging an early childhood curriculum is that no attention is being given to the content of the programs. At best, the guidelines might help teachers to teach their materials well. Yet, as Eisner (1990) has suggested, "if something is not worth teaching, it is not worth teaching well" (p. 524).

BEYOND DEVELOPMENTAL APPROPRIATENESS

Spodek (1986) has suggested that, in addition to the developmental dimension of programs, the cultural context dimension and the knowledge dimension should be considered in judging a program's worth. No program of early childhood education should be judged worthwhile on one dimension alone.

Analyzing the Developmental Dimension

In analyzing the developmental dimension of early childhood curriculum, it is important to note that there is no one theory of development that is accepted by all. Kohlberg and Mayer (1972) identified three streams of curriculum, each driven by a different ideology and each consistent with a different view of human development. The romantic ideology reflects the work of Rousseau, Froebel, Gesell, Freud, and others who viewed development as maturation and education as the unfolding of inner virtues and abilities. The cultural transmission ideology conceives of education as the passing of knowledge, skills, values, and social and moral rules from one generation to the next. Behaviorism provides the psychological principles for a technology of education, offering a variation on direct instruction within this stream. The progressive ideology, built upon the work of Dewey, Piaget, and others, views education as helping the child achieve higher levels of development through structured, though natural, interactions with the physical and social environments. The idea of education as the attainment of higher levels of development reflects this relationship between human development and education that has resulted in a conception of the teacher as a child development specialist.

Determining whether a program is developmentally appropriate requires first identifying the ideological stream within which the program is embedded. Programs within the *romantic* stream reflect a concept of readiness. Children may be given developmental tests to determine their readiness for a program. If they are judged not to be ready, they may be withdrawn and allowed to mature before being enrolled. Within the *cultural transmission* stream, children are tested to determine whether they have the prerequisites for learning what is expected of them in a program. If they do not, they are moved to a lower educational level and instructed in their identified areas of deficiency. Within the *progressive* stream, children's developmental levels are assessed and they are provided with experiences to create cognitive dissonance to help them move on to higher levels of development. In addition, the program may be reconstructed so that more appropriate activities are provided to help the children grasp the knowledge required of them.

Analyzing the Cultural Dimension

The cultural dimension relates to the knowledge we value not just for personal growth, but because it reflects society's view of what is true, what is right, and what is beautiful. Among the values that can be identified within any cultural context are those related to materialism and work, spiritualism and religion, individuality and freedom, community and power, family and sexuality, and equality and justice (Spodek, 1977). These values determine what the education of the young should include, since they reflect the basic values of society. The education we provide children is based on our judgment of what we want our children to be and to become (Biber, 1984).

Kessler (1991) has suggested that the content of early childhood programs be related to what it means to be an American and live in a democracy. This suggestion would carry over to method as well as content, for an antidemocratic method, no matter how consistent it might be with children's developmental levels—and how successful it might be in achieving its goals—would be inappropriate.

Analyzing the Knowledge Dimension

The knowledge dimension suggests that what and how one teaches young children should be consistent with the kind of knowledge that children need in their present circumstances and in the future. The written word—the Bible—was seen as the source of all cultural knowledge in colonial America. Because of this, literacy became the prime goal of education in these communities. What constitutes the necessary social knowledge in American society is considerably broader today. We require a more expanded set of educational goals, well beyond basic literacy, to enable children to access that knowledge.

How we teach the broad range of culturally defined knowledge is determined by our ideological view of children. If we view children as empty vessels to be filled with society's accumulated knowledge, then the cultural transmission ideology would be an acceptable basis for educating children. If, however, we view culture as expanding, and we value each individual's contribution to that expansion, we need to help children construct their own knowledge and validate that knowledge independent of authority. Approaches to education can differ considerably from one another even while each is considered to be developmentally appropriate. One approach might be considered more appropriate than the other, depending on one's view of appropriate content of early childhood education.

There is much we want children to know as they grow up in modern America and much they need to know to function both in our democratic society and within the global village we have become. Exploring what it takes for children to be participating members of that village and that society, as well as what they need to know to carry on the traditions of their culture, might help us identify what conceptions of knowledge we now value and what the early childhood curriculum should be.

Perhaps it is time to rethink the early childhood curriculum and to again seek out the basis for choosing the content of early childhood education programs. The knowledge base of our curriculum for young children should reflect the experience of both genders and of many cultures. It should include many conceptions of knowledge as well as many conceptions of development. There is a real possibility that no one curriculum will be acceptable to all and that no one true concept of development will be established.

A dialogue needs to be established among persons from varying points of view. Perhaps there can be no one proper curriculum for all children. Perhaps there should be many alternative approaches to early childhood curriculum competing with one another. These curricula may vary according to their basic ideologies, according to the children for whom they have been developed, according to the curriculum designer's views of what young children need to know, and according to the designer's conception of human development. But what will be the proper curriculum for all children?

In 1913, the Committee of Nineteen of the International Kindergarten Union issued a report on kindergarten curriculum. The committee was charged with reconciling differences between the traditional Froebelian approach to kindergarten education and the newer progressive approach. Since no one approach to curriculum could be accepted by all committee members, three reports were issued. The reports were introduced by a fable, as follows:

> A father had three sons whom he loved equally well. This father owned a precious ring—said to be endowed with the power to bring highest blessings to its owners. Each one of the sons asked the father to bestow the ring to him after the father's death. The father, in his great love for his sons, promised the ring to each one. In his old age, the father sent for a jeweler and asked him to make two rings exactly like the precious ring owned by him. The jeweler assented, and after a while he brought the three rings to the father, who could not distinguish the precious ring from the other two, so well were they made. When the time came that the father died, he called each of his sons separately, blessed him, and gave him a ring. After the father's burial, the three brothers met, and each one claimed the birthright and the ownership of the genuine ring. Finally, when they could not decide which was the original one, they went to a judge, who gave the decision in the form of advice, viz., "As the true ring is said to have the magic power of making the owner beloved and esteemed by God and man, and as each of you three brothers believes this ring to be the genuine or original one, so let each one, untouched by his prejudice, strive to reveal the power of the ring in his life by loving peaceableness, and by charity and sincere devotion to God; and when in later generations, the true ring reveals itself, I will call upon you again, before the 'seat of judgment.' A wiser man than I may be there and speak." (Laws, 1913, p. xv)

Perhaps there can be no one true, appropriate curriculum for young children. Although advocates of different positions related to early childhood curriculum believe that their approaches are genuine, all should compete, striving to demonstrate the worth of the approach they advocate while accepting the possibility that others might be equally or more valuable.

REFERENCES

Biber, B. (1984). *Early education and psychological development.* New Haven: Yale University Press.

Bloom, A. D. (1987). *The closing of the American mind*. New York: Simon and Schuster.

Boyd, W. (1914). *From Locke to Montessori*. London: Harrup and Co.

Bredekamp, S. (Ed.) (1987). *Developmentally appropriate practices in early childhood programs serving children from birth through age 8* (exp. ed.). Washington, DC: National Association for the Education of Young Children.

Burke, A. (1923). *A conduct curriculum for kindergarten and first grade*. New York: Scribner's.

Committee of Nineteen (1913). *The kindergarten: Reports of the Committee of Nineteen on the theory and practice of the kindergarten*. Boston: Houghton Mifflin.

Day, M. C., & Parker, R. K. (1977). *The preschool in action: Exploring early childhood programs* (2nd ed.). Boston: Allyn & Bacon.

Deasey, D. (1978). *Education under six*. New York: St. Martin's Press.

Dewey, J. (1938). *Experience and education*. New York: Macmillan.

Eisner, E. (1990). Who decides what schools teach? *Phi Delta Kappan, 71*, 523–526.

Evans, E. D. (1975). *Contemporary influences in early childhood education* (2nd ed.). New York: Holt, Rinehart & Winston.

Froebel, F. (1896). *The education of man*. New York: D. Appleton and Co.

Gesell, A. (1943). *Infant and child in the culture of today*. New York: Harper & Brothers.

Good, H., & Teller, J. (1973). *A history of American education*. New York: Macmillan.

Harrison, J. F. C. (1968). *Utopianism and education: Robert Owen and the Owenites*. New York: Teachers College Press.

Hohmann, M., Banet, B., & Weikart, D. P. (1979). *Young children in action: A manual for preschool educators*. Ypsilanti, MI: High/Scope Educational Research Foundation.

House, E. R., & Hutchins, E. J. (1979). Issues raised by the follow-through evaluation. In L. G. Katz (Ed.), *Current topics in early childhood education* (Vol. 2, pp. 1–12). Norwood, NJ: Ablex.

Hunt, J. M. (1961). *Intelligence and experience*. New York: Ronald Press.

Hymes, J. (1955). *The child development point of view*. Englewood Cliffs, NJ: Prentice Hall.

Jipson, J. (1990). *Developmentally appropriate practice: Limiting possibilities*. Paper presented at the annual meeting of the American Educational Research Association, Boston.

Kessler, S. A. (1991). Early childhood education as development. *Early Childhood Research Quarterly, 2*, 137–152.

Kilpatrick, W. H. (1916). *Froebel's kindergarten principles critically examined*. New York: Macmillan.

Kleibard, H. (1985). What happened to American schooling in the first part of the twentieth century? In E. Eisner (Ed.), *Learning and teaching the ways of knowing. Eighty-fourth yearbook of the National Society for the*

Study of Education, Part II (pp. 1–22). Chicago: The Society.

Kohlberg, L., & Mayer, R. (1972). Development as the aim of education. *Harvard Educational Review, 42,* 449–496.

Kramer, R. (1988). *Maria Montessori: A biography.* Reading, MA: Addison-Wesley.

Lane, H. (1976). *The wild boy of Aveyron.* Cambridge, MA: Harvard University Press.

Laws, A. (1913). Introduction. In Committee of Nineteen, International Kindergarten Union, *The kindergarten.* Boston: Houghton Mifflin.

May, D., & Vinovskis, M. A. (1977). A ray of millennial light: Early education and social reform in the infant school movement of Massachusetts, 1826–1840. In T. Haveran (Ed.), *Family and kin in urban communities, 1700–1930.* New York: New Viewpoints.

McMillan, M. (1919). *The nursery school.* London: J. M. Dent and Sons.

Montessori, M. (1964). *The Montessori method.* New York: Schocken. (Original work published 1912)

Montessori, M. (1965). *Spontaneous activity in education.* New York: Schocken. (Original work published 1917)

Owen, G. (1920). *Nursery school education.* New York: E. P. Dutton.

Owen, R. (1857). Essays on the formation of character. In R. Owen, *The life of Robert Owen* (Vol. I, pp. 287–307). London: Effingham Wilson.

Shapiro, M. S. (1983). *Child's garden: The kindergarten movement from Froebel to Dewey.* University Park, PA: Pennsylvania State University Press.

Spodek, B. (1973). *Early childhood education.* Englewood Cliffs, NJ: Prentice Hall.

Spodek, B. (1977). What constitutes worthwhile educational experiences for young children. In B. Spodek (Ed.), *Teaching practices: Reexamining assumptions* (pp. 5–20). Washington, DC: National Association for the Education of Young Children.

Spodek, B. (1985). *Goals and purposes of educational programs for 4- and 5-year-old children. Final report of the Commission on Appropriate Education.* Washington, DC: National Association for the Education of Young Children.

Spodek, B. (1986). Development, values and knowledge in the kindergarten curriculum. In B. Spodek (Ed.), *Today's kindergarten: Exploring the knowledge base, expanding the curriculum* (pp. 32–47). New York: Teachers College Press.

Strickland, C. E. (1982). Paths not taken: Seminal models of early childhood education in Jacksonian America. In B. Spodek (Ed.), *Handbook of research in early childhood education* (pp. 321–340). New York: Free Press.

Sylva, K. (1986). Developmental psychology and the preschool child. In J. Harris (Ed.), *Child psychology in action* (pp. 127–142). London: Croom Helm.

Talbot, M. E. (1964). *Edouard Seguin: A study of an educational approach to*

the treatment of mentally defective children. New York: Teachers College
      Press.
Thorndike, E. A. (1903). Notes on psychology for kindergartners. *Teachers
      College Record, 4,* 377–408.
Vandewalker, N. (1908). *The kindergarten in American education.* New
      York: Macmillan.

CHAPTER 2

Diversity and Change in Young Children

SOME EDUCATIONAL IMPLICATIONS

Herbert Zimiles

More now than in the past, teachers are being urged to be mindful of the differences among the children they teach and to render education that is responsive to those differences. This seemingly simple directive implicates a mass of quite different educational agendas. This chapter sorts out some of the issues that surround this admonition and examines its implications for the education of young children.

What must be confusing about this new focus is that educators, in the name of giving children their due, are being called upon to scan the horizon for instances of both sameness and difference. Combined with the determination to eliminate inequities in education (i.e., banish inequalities in the delivery of educational services and presumably in their outcomes) is a heightened interest in exploring the uniqueness that resides within each child as well as within different groups of children. Among the issues that are at stake with regard to educating for diversity are:

- The need to stamp out patterns of differential educational treatment that give rise to inequities in the distribution of educational achievement.
- The need to take into account variations in socioemotional experience and expectations among children that affect their receptivity to schooling and their ability to learn.
- The need to become aware of different modes of intellectual functioning that enable children to learn in a manner that is most effective for them.

- The need to be responsive to changes in children that stem from generational shifts in the nature of their psychological adaptation.
- The need to go beyond mere alteration of methods, to begin to frame educational objectives as well as methods in relation to the unique patterns of skill, ability, and interest shown by each child or each distinctive child group.
- The need to sensitize children to the diversity of humankind and the pluralistic character of our own society, thereby upholding "ethnic pride" and acknowledging distinctions that might otherwise go unrecognized.

Thus the concern with individual differences—one of the most long-standing and basic tenets of psychological measurement and educational practice—has developed some new wrinkles. It calls forth, on the one hand, a rigid preoccupation with equality, with sameness of educational opportunity that is aimed at ensuring equity and fairness, and, on the other hand, a renewal of interest in individuality. One is reminded of the oft-quoted observation made by Kluckhohn and Murray (1956) during their early exploration of the then-new concept of "personality," modified here to read: "Every child is like *all* other children, *some* other children, *no* other children." The task is one of sorting out similarities and differences to achieve equity, fairness, and greater educational effectiveness and psychological fulfillment.

One of the axioms of early childhood education that is almost self-evident is that teacher responsiveness must be individualized. Any group of young children, by virtue of the unevenness of their comparatively brief life/growth spans and the fact that their (inevitably) different home backgrounds have until now dominated their socialization experience, is bound to show a greater variability than that found among groups of older children. Young children (until recent times, at least) have spent the bulk of their lives at home where they have experienced distinctive patterns of stimulation. They have had relatively little opportunity to be socialized by agencies designed to provide a uniform mode of communication and interaction and a common thread of social values. There are also real limits on the degree to which young children can be socialized. They are less likely to take into account others' needs, nor can they be counted on to conform to general directives. Their behavior is predominantly driven by their own subjectively defined world.

Perhaps the greatest degree of sameness to be found among

young children is their continuing dependence on adults, their need for the presence of benign and nurturant adults to provide safety and help despite their persistent striving for autonomy and independence. A group of young children is an aggregate of distinct individuals with differing levels of maturation whose primary frame of reference is each child's own parents and family rather than some commonly experienced social framework. Young children not only require more individualized responses, they virtually demand them. Yet there is great variation in teachers' capacities to discern the layers of individuality in each child and to behave responsively.

ELIMINATING INEQUITIES IN EDUCATIONAL TREATMENT

Originally activated to enhance and equalize educational opportunities for the disenfranchised minorities who were receiving a second-class education in a racially segregated environment, the civil rights movement has given birth to what sometimes appears to be an unending series of demands for equal educational opportunity by heretofore excluded or neglected claimant groups. Following close on the heels of the civil rights legislation has been the mandate to "mainstream" handicapped children (Education for All Handicapped Children Act, 1975; Education of the Handicapped Act Amendments, 1986), who were largely excluded from regular public school classes. The largest constituency of all is that claimed by the feminist lobby, whose grievances are also directed at achieving a greater measure of educational equity. It is apparent that resentment over inequality of educational opportunity—defined differently for different groups—is widespread and will continue to provoke a concern for sameness as well as distinctiveness.

Educational Inequity Among Minorities and the Physically Handicapped

Most palpable among the charges of educational inequity are those pertaining to the inadequate physical facilities, materials, and personnel resources provided to communities that are economically underprivileged and politically impotent. Equally evident is the long-standing failure of buildings to provide access and accommodations for physically handicapped people. More difficult to document is the tentative and distant, often grudging and mistrustful, attitude that teachers often show toward children from ethnic minorities. Young children, especially, need to receive a warm and embracing greeting if they are to relax a vigilant stance that tends to close off the possibility of playful exploration and deep concentration. But children who are different, whether because of their minority background or their physical handicap, tend to elicit a wary, sometimes rejecting or anxious reaction from teachers that induces a reciprocal response from the children.

Among teachers who harbor more sympathetic attitudes toward children who are different, there is frequently a different form of maladaptive response, that of lowered expectations. This brings about a less challenging and less demanding school experience, which contributes to subpar academic achievement. Nor are the above disparate postures mutually exclusive. It is not uncommon for the same teacher to respond to children who arouse anxiety in them with rejecting hostility one moment and with overprotectiveness another. Given the subtle, largely unconscious character of modes of response to children who are disturbingly different, it is easy to see why the goal of achieving educational equity remains so elusive.

Gender Differences

A biased reaction that is more difficult to uncover is the tendency to treat girls and boys differently in school. Sex-typed behavioral expectations are introduced early in the lives of boys and girls as a means of socializing them to different roles. We have been slow to grasp some of the unforeseen implications of seemingly trivial adaptations to differences in gender.

A growing research literature has begun to document the process of systematic gender-distinct socialization that begins at birth. Parents of 24-hour-old infants spontaneously use different adjectives and concepts in describing their newborn sons and daughters (children they barely know), thereby setting in motion distinctive gender-determined patterns of lifelong development (Rubin, Provenzano & Luria, 1974). Observations of babies in their second year of life reveal consistent differences in their preferences for toys: Boys are more likely to play with trucks and cars, while girls prefer dolls and soft toys (Smith & Daglish, 1977). When asked to predict the toy preferences of other children, three- and four-year-olds are guided by differing ideas of what boys and girls would like (Eisenberg, Murray & Hite, 1982). Not surprisingly, six-year-olds have been observed to regard occupations according to adult sex-role stereotypes (Garrett, Ein & Tremaine, 1977).

Many studies have contributed to a description of how parent expectations and reward structures mediate the development of gender differences. Parents are more likely to reward their daughters' expressions of dependency and wishes to make contact with other people (Fagot, 1974). They are more tolerant of task deviations for the purpose of interpersonal interaction when the deviating child is a girl (Block, Block & Harrington, 1974). Young boys are more likely to be encouraged to engage in activities outside the home (Collard, 1964) and to receive more encouragement to be independent (Saegert & Hart, 1976).

These gender-specific patterns are subtly perpetuated and reinforced in school. Cuffaro (1975), among others, has noted that the sex-typical activity of girls playing "house" is less likely to enhance cognitive development than is the block building in which boys are encouraged to engage. Elementary school teachers are more likely to protectively dispense praise to girls when they are in danger of performing poorly, whereas boys receive more praise when they are expected to succeed (Parsons, Kaczala & Meece, 1982). Further, when boys succeed in school, teachers are more prone to attribute their success to ability, while hard work and perseverance are deemed responsible for the success of girls. Correspondingly, the low performance of girls is attributed to lack of ability, whereas the low performance of boys is more likely to be blamed on lack of effort (Dweck & Elliot, 1983). In many ways, then, girls and boys are being socialized differently into the realm of academic competence and striving.

Evaluation and the Politically Sensitive Role of Research

It has been noted that the discriminatory practices, both deliberate and unwitting, experienced in school by minority, handicapped, and female children are reinforced by evaluation procedures that are also damagingly inequitable. Minority children are not only treated differently in school, but their abilities and school performance are evaluated less fairly (Laosa, 1982). Gilligan (1982) has pointed to the male-centered character of evaluations of moral development. More insidious and more difficult to detect are the differential patterns of individual evaluative response accorded children almost daily because they are black or handicapped or of a particular gender (see Parsons, Kaczala & Meece, 1982). These serve to maintain images and expectations associated with particular types of children—without the teacher even being aware that he or she harbors such expectations or uses this form of evaluational control.

Evaluation studies are often less valid than they claim to be, and their data are subjected to both deliberate and unwitting misinterpretation. As a result, some forms of systematic study have been discouraged. For example, the widespread interest in uncovering and documenting discriminatory educational practices is seldom accompanied by a corresponding interest in investigating the effects of cumulative biased treatment. Yet it seems important to identify such realms of impairment. Slogans such as "difference not deficit" are invoked, and accusations of "blaming the victim" fill the air. A veil of censorship has been created in the belief that such assessments would do more harm than good by extending and buttressing negative stereotypes.

VARIATIONS IN SOCIOEMOTIONAL DEVELOPMENT THAT AFFECT RECEPTIVITY TO SCHOOLING

The teacher of any group of young children is destined to find wide variations in personality and social behavior. Children vary with respect to the degree of comfort they feel in being separated from home, a factor that affects their openness to the social and intellectual stimulation in the classroom (Ainsworth, 1973). There is also wide variation in such affective traits as impulse control, frustration tolerance, and emotional expressiveness. More recently, psychologists have focused on the role of temperament (Goldsmith et al., 1987), on seemingly enduring patterns of emotional reactivity that appear to be recognizable soon after birth, including such characteristics as emotionality and sociability. Whether or not such attributes are inborn and genetically transmitted matters little to the educator. But such distinguishable ways of dealing with inner feelings and of relating to others may affect the child's quality of learning—the degree of openness to new experiences and the ability to concentrate and persevere. These characteristics also have a bearing on how other children and the teacher respond to the child.

While the young child is struggling with the task of adapting to the school environment and dealing with the emotional loss and danger of separation from home, there is also an ongoing inner process of consolidation and integration. The child is engaged in the complex task of weaving together a consistent and distinctive mode of perceiving the world and responding to it that takes into account individual appetites, anxieties, wishes, temperamental traits, and modes of relating to others. These internal integrative processes will culminate in the formation of a coherent and functional personality structure. It matters a great deal whether teachers convey by their actions and policies that they honor the seriousness of children's purposes as they grope toward greater self-definition or choose, instead, to emphasize their own agendas and ignore these processes of inner resolution.

Cultural Variations in Emotional Readiness for Schooling

When entering the preschool environment for the first time, children with diverse family backgrounds may encounter differences in language and social behavior as well as differences in teacher expectations of independence. Separation from parents is likely to be more problematic for children who have been raised outside of the mainstream of American society, where early self-reliance is valued and cultivated. Children from ethnically diverse backgrounds may be expected to show distinctive patterns with respect to the experience of separation from family, ways of expressing dependency and their readiness to function autonomously, and habits of taste and preference in food and other sources of consolation and emotional support. They may also differ in their reaction to various classroom materials and activities and to styles of peer interaction, and in their communicative competence and readiness to engage in dramatic play.

In response to these issues, there is a growing research literature designed to investigate ethnic variations in early experience and child rearing that may begin to explain differential patterns of response to schooling and differing configurations of academic achievement. McLoyd (1990) has pointed to the patterns of strictness, power assertion, punitiveness, and arbitrariness that are more frequently found among parents who are struggling with poverty or who have experienced economic loss. Studies of contrasting parental beliefs that are to be found among ethnic minorities have been conducted by Durrett, O'Bryant, and Pennebaker (1975), Bartz and Levine (1978), Guttierrez and Sameroff (1990), and Stevenson, Chen, and Uttal (1990). Similarly, studies of ethnic variation in parenting behavior have been reported by Zeskind (1983), Chisholm (1983), Beckwith and Cohen (1984), Zepeda (1986), and Lin and Fu (1990). Descriptions of parents' teaching patterns that are distinctive to particular ethnic minorities have been provided by Steward and Steward (1973), Laosa (1980), and Fajardo and Freedman (1981). Canino and Canino (1980) and Delgado-Gaitan (1987) have described distinctive socialization goals of Puerto Rican and Mexican families. In a recent comparative study of the responses of black and Mexican-American eight- and eleven-year-olds to videotaped school scenes, Rotherman-Borus and Phinney (1990) found Mexican-American children to show a greater propensity for sharing and expecting authority figures to resolve social conflicts, while black children were more prone to initiate action and to be more expresssive of both anger and remorse. An overview of research findings that bear on family ecologies of ethnic minority children has been prepared by Harrison, Wilson, Pine, Chan, and Buriel (1990). Slaughter-Defoe, Nakagawa, Takanishi, and Johnson (1990) have reviewed research findings that examine the role of cultural/ecological factors that affect school performance among African-American and Asian-American children. Especially noteworthy in these explorations are Ogbu's (1988) contention that the caste-like history of African-Americans has led them to distrust extrafamilial institutions and Comer's (1980) emphasis on the importance of enhancing cooperation between home and school.

The research literature describing unique developmental experiences of minority children during the first three years of life has recently been reviewed by Coll (1990). In her exploration of factors that contribute to effective care of children under three years of age, Murphy (1969) emphasizes the need for caretakers to learn about the particular preferences of each child—specific information regarding how a child likes to be held, the preferred temperatures and textures of favorite foods, the intensity of stimulation that is most favored, as well as other appetites and habitual modes of receiving and responding to the world. This attentiveness to factors that make a difference to each child fosters a greater sense of personal comfort that allows for more effective adaptation. It also conveys a sense of environmental responsiveness that encourages the child to be more receptive to the expectations of the school.

DISTINCTIVE PATTERNS OF INTELLECTUAL FUNCTIONING

Although scientific analysis of the cognitive domain remains tentative and incomplete, there have been important advances in linking what is known about the intellectual life of children to the goals of education. Educational goals have been traditionally defined in terms of the acquisition of academic knowledge and skills. In the recent past, the study of intellectual functioning had been almost exclusively guided by a concern for promoting academic achievement. That situation has changed; cognitive development has become an object of study for its own sake. In addition, the ultimate usefulness of traditionally defined academic knowledge is being questioned in many quarters, and it is proposed that education be redirected toward the cultivation of thinking and problem-solving skills (Resnick, 1987; Perkins & Salomon, 1989). But irrespective of whether schools, in defining their goals, cling to academic subject matter or choose to emphasize generalized thinking skills, the realm of intellectual functioning remains central to education, a realm that has many dimensions of diversity. The tendency to regard thinking and the acquisition of knowledge, that is, learning, as separate entities seems misguided. In order to learn about something, one must think about it. Learning and thinking go hand and hand. The ability to think is the by-product of a life of learning; learning is a primary context for thinking behavior. A challenging and engaging educational program provides the best framework for supporting the ability to think.

The issue of diversity has surfaced in the rapidly growing research literature on children's cognitive functioning, but not always in a manner that is relevant to classroom teachers. Much of the study of children's cognitive functioning has been concerned with delineating the nature of cognitive development—that is, identifying how cognition changes with age during childhood—rather than with how children at the same developmental level differ in their intellectual lives. The work of Piaget (1970) has gained considerable support for the idea that cognitive development proceeds in stagelike advances that entail qualitatively different modes of organizing and apprehending the world. Those who favor an information-processing approach (e.g., Siegler, 1986) are guided, instead, by computer-derived ideas of how input is encoded and information is stored and retrieved. These theoretical speculations and empirical studies help educators examine whether their expectations of academic achievement are consonant with what is known about the nature of children's conceptual abilities. They are less useful, however, in shedding light on the nature of differences in intellectual functioning among children who are at the same developmental stage.

Psychometricians who have labored to test and analyze intelligence have long hoped that they would come up with an inventory of the basic ingredients of intellectual ability, the primary mental abilities, as Thurstone (1938) once described them. Within such a scheme it would be theoretically possible to arrive at an intellectual profile of each person, similar to a differentiated analysis of the functioning of the endocrine system or other physiological system. Such efforts foundered because there seemed to be no limit to the distinctions that could be made among the demands of various intellectual tasks; the list of abilities threatened to become endless. On the other hand, close inspection of scores on these diverse tasks indicated that they were so highly interrelated that it seemed unwarranted to emphasize their distinctiveness. Performance on a wide variety of different intellectual tasks to a great extent reflects some overall level of intellectual ability (Weinberg, 1989). Part of the problem was that such efforts were limited to what could be assessed by group-administered paper-and-pencil tests. This restriction limited the scope of such inquiries and called into question their value. One of the defects of research-derived knowledge is that it is often based on a view of reality constrained by practical problems associated with achieving efficient mass systematic assessment. Educators do not have to work within such limitations; as a result, they have access to the phenomena of children's intellectual functioning that are not available to existing methods of research (Zimiles, 1987b).

A notable exception to the above-described pattern is Gardner's (1983, 1989) recent effort to define the domain of intelligence in terms of strands of ability that go far beyond conventionally assessed distinctions in intellectual ability. In proposing that we consider intelligence as having seven different axes (logical-mathematical, linguistic, musical, spatial, bodily-kinesthetic, interpersonal, intrapersonal), Gardner has abandoned the arena of group paper-and-pencil testing as the primary framework for distinguishing among human abilities. On the one hand, Gardner's work frees students of the nature of intelligence from the tyranny of psychological testing. On the other, it demonstrates anew how virtually limitless are the ways of sorting the domains of intelligence.

Knowledge of the diversity of patterns of intellectual functioning is also being gained from clinical efforts to identify the nature of dysfunctioning observed among children with specific learning disabilities. In cases of dysfunctioning, it is somewhat easier to tease apart the nature (not the cause) of the specific pattern of dysfunctioning, thereby identifying some of the elements that contribute to the complex that is intellectual functioning (Silver, 1989).

One of the most useful tools for thinking about the diversity of the intellectual functioning of children comes from the work of the Russian psychologist Lev Vygotsky (1986), whose writings of a half-century ago have only recently become available in translation. Vygotsky insists that cognitive functioning be seen as interdigitated with the sociocultural setting in which it occurs. It makes no sense to think in terms of absolute and abstract descriptions of a child's ability; rather, one must consider a child's intellectual repertoire as a reflection of the sociocultural framework of thinking and perceiving in which it is embedded. The embeddedness of cognitive functioning in the milieu that calls it forth has led some researchers (Cole & Scribner, 1974; Rogoff & Mistry, 1985) to study patterns of cognitive functioning as a function of the unique cultural matrix of contrasting groups of children.

Bilingualism[1]

Among the differences in intellectual functioning that may be observed in young children, none is more fundamental than knowledge of the language that mediates communication. One need only spend an hour in a non-English-speaking environment to appreciate the feelings of disorientation and helplessness that are aroused when our accustomed tools of linguistic communication do not work. How much more stressful are such experiences for the young child who is already contending with feelings of separation anxiety? Yet large numbers of children who are enrolled in early childhood education programs have little or no knowledge of English.

Since second-language acquisition almost always requires extrafamilial stimulation, the classroom, with its group organizational structure and its rich linguistic environment, would appear to offer an ideal setting for mastering English as a second language. On the other hand, it presents a situation of extraordinary stress to the non-English-speaking child. It is challenging enough for young children to begin to understand what is expected of them in this new setting away from home without being handicapped by the lack of communicative skill. Children with incomplete mastery may have enough passive language to mask their linguistic disability, but they must bear the burden of maneuvering in a sea of confusion among others who may not even be aware of their limited understanding. In this regard, Snow (1987) has noted that the decontextualized language skills required in school develop independently of the contextual language skills of ordinary conversation.

Bilingual education programs allow children to learn conceptually challenging material in their first language while learning English as a second language. Since bilingual children engage in implicit thinking and problem solving in their first language (Saville-Troike, 1984), it would seem counterproductive to exclude the linguistic framework that enables them to think at their preferred and most advanced levels of conceptual functioning. Not surprisingly, it has been shown that school achievement is greater for children who attend bilingual programs (Willig, 1985). Diaz (1983) has further claimed that bilingualism helps to heighten metalinguistic awareness. If young bilingual children are asked to deal with the social demands and cognitive challenges of schooling in a second language, there is the danger that prolonged exposure to a confusing environment will lead them to question their own intellectual competence; such negative self-assessments, artifacts of bilingualism, may have enduring adverse impact.

Yet there are real limits to the degree to which bilingual education programs can be provided on a large scale. Given the rising immigration rates, it is probable that many different primary languages will be represented among the children in any given school. In such cases, it would not be practical to establish a comprehensive program of bilingual education. Moreover, the limited pool of eligible teachers might lead to other non-language-related hiring criteria being compromised, thereby adversely affecting the teacher selection process. Further, grouping bilingual students together encourages the very ghettoization of minority groups that the struggle for educational equity is attempting to overcome. Whether or not it is feasible or desirable to institute bilingual education in all early childhood education programs, it is important that aides be recruited who can serve as translators and communicative links for non-English-speaking children.

Being Heard and Being Spoken To

The issue of communication looms large for many children for whom English is not a second language. There are young children, usually from extremely deprived family backgrounds, who have comparatively few opportunities to communicate with adults because of their parents' unavailability or the austere character of their relationship to parents. Such children are unaccustomed to being spoken to (as opposed to being ordered about) and to being heard. As a result, there is a void in their development of fundamental processes of communication. For them, it is vital to have ample opportunity to be heard, to learn to expect to be heard, and to have extensive exposure to communicative adults. In such cases, conversing and exchanging become prime elements of the curriculum (P. Swartz, personal communication, March 1990).

Cognitive Style

One idea about cognitive functioning that has great appeal is that individual differences among children and among ethnic groups can be understood in terms of stylistic variations in their approaches to thinking and problem solving (Messick, 1984; Saracho & Spodek, 1986). The study of cognitive style has proceeded along two lines: (1) by laboratory investigations that have tentatively identified such stylistic variations in cognition as field dependence/independence, later referred to as psychological differentiation (Witkin, Moore, Goodenough & Cox, 1977), and reflectivity/impulsivity (Kagan, 1966); and (2) through inductive observation of differences among individuals and groups regarding distinctive cognitive characteristics of a particular ethnic group. For example, it has been suggested that native American children are more prone to learn from observation than from verbal explication and elucidation, and that they are less likely to use overt forms of trial-and-error learning (John, 1972).

Laboratory studies of cognitive style have yet to provide definitive evidence of the validity of their hypothesized distinctions. Part of the problem lies in the fact that such work is aimed at uncovering distinctions that are broadly applicable, that can serve as a basis for distinguishing among all children, rather than identifying what it is that is especially distinctive about a particular individual or group (Zimiles, 1986b). Teachers, on the other hand, have much more opportunity to engage in prolonged and repeated observation of children, an activity more likely to uncover idiographic patterns (i.e., ways of behaving that are unique to a particular individual or group) of cognitive style. Here again, the operational framework of the teacher opens up the possibility of apprehending levels of diversity that may not be discoverable by the methods of research.

It is not always clear, however, how such knowledge can be put to use. For example, in the course of observing native American children on the Oregon Warm Spring Reservation, Philips (1972) noted that they showed a great reluctance to talk in class, especially when the occasion for speaking was dictated by the teacher. This pattern seemed to be related to a lesser readiness to internalize prescribed rules of classroom interaction. When teachers began to acknowledge these preference patterns by calling on the native American children less often, these children received even less opportunity to communicate in the contexts that were most salient to performing well in school. In this instance, accommodating the distinctive styles of a particular group did not appear to be helpful.

Generally speaking, however, judicious use of information regarding cognitive and social predispositions and preferences that are distinct to a particular individual and/or group of children can bring about a more satisfying and productive school experience. It also conveys a level of teacher responsiveness that is reassuring to the child.

Background Knowledge

The overdue shift in focus from maximizing academic achievement to fostering cognitive competence—a trend to be applauded even though we are not yet able to define or assess the essence of the ability to think effectively—threatens to obscure a factor of fundamental importance in intellectual functioning: variation in background knowledge. To appreciate the impact of lack of relevant information, we need to recall how it feels when we converse with someone in authority who alludes to unfamiliar events and ideas. Not only does communication suffer, but the relationship with the speaker is also placed in jeopardy. Teachers of young children need to continually reassess their assumptions regarding the general availability of background knowledge that serves as an explanatory context for their statements. Studies of how children learn to read (e.g., Resnick & Weaver, 1979) demonstrate how background knowledge influences the degree to which the meaning of a narrative is grasped. Background knowledge remains one of the hidden determinants of academic achievement. It is probable that differences in academic achievement exhibited by different cultural groups are at least partially attributable to this factor. Inappropriate assumptions regarding children's background knowledge may undermine otherwise elegant teaching strategies. This can be an insidious source of bias.

Play Behavior

Especially salient to early childhood education is the readiness of a young child to engage in symbolic play. Two issues that have arisen with respect to this activity pertain to (1) whether there are cultural differences in children's capacity for and style of play, and (2) whether it is feasible or useful to stimulate and promote children's ability to play. The latter issue asks whether the very process of intervening for the sake of instruction does violence to the essential character of "free" play. If a child does not play, is it because the conditions for play have not been met for that child, or because the child literally does not know how to play?

Because of the inherent complexity and variety of play behavior and the degree to which it is influenced by the conditions under which it is being observed, these questions are not easily resolved by research. Comparative studies of play are difficult to carry out because play behavior cannot be obtained on demand, the idiosyncratic character of play does not lend itself to meaningful comparative study, and different settings are not likely to be equally supportive of play. The issue of the fruitfulness of play tutoring (Smilansky, 1968; Christie & Johnsen, 1985) is beclouded by differences in views of what constitutes play, what is psychologically significant in children's play, and the conditions under which play should be observed. The fluidity and wide-ranging content of dramatic play, characteristics that interfere with its researchability, nevertheless mark it as an arena that is especially revealing of the diversity of children's use of materials, their interests and imaginativeness, and their styles of self-expression and cognitive organization.

ADAPTING TO SOCIAL AND TECHNOLOGICAL CHANGE

A perennial challenge to teachers is that children are continuously undergoing change. The generation gap between teachers and their students, as Margaret Mead (1978) and others have noted, appears to be widening. Teachers cannot sanguinely look to their own childhoods to understand the children they now teach. Apart from the demographic shifts that are altering the distribution of children from various ethnic backgrounds and the commitment to meet the needs of a wider range of children, teachers must be prepared to encounter patterns of behavior in all children that are associated with the changing times, with the effects of the rapid pace of social and technological change (Zimiles, 1986c).

Elkind (1981) has called attention to the "hurried child" of today who lives in a faster-paced society in which children are both perceived and expected to attain landmarks of emotional maturity more rapidly. The child of today is encouraged to pretend to be advanced developmentally and is then left to face developmentally inappropriate expectations. Weiss (1979) called attention to the existence of a real acceleration of emotional development among children who have had to cope with parental divorce. In a similar vein, teachers report that most young children, when compared with those of the previous generation, have greater precocity, greater openness, and more freedom of expression (Zimiles, 1986a). Young children seem more polished and knowledgeable upon entering school. Many of them have had years of attending preschool education or day care prior to beginning public school. Thus, virtually all teachers of young children are encountering much more educationally experienced children and are being called upon to revise their expectations of young children.

However, children today seem less impelled to seek approval from teachers or to conform to their expectations; they are perceived as being more difficult to motivate. Their attention spans seem to be shorter and they appear to be generally less receptive to the rigors of education. As a result, they often fail to live up to the expectations aroused by their early manifestations of sophistication and worldliness.

Another factor that complicates the life of the child is the diminished presence of parents. The number of single-parent families is rising, and in two-parent families it is increasingly common for both parents to work full time. Expanded opportunities for education and recreation have made further inroads into parents' availability. Teachers report that children seem less cared for; they are more often sent to school when they are sick because there is no one at home to take care of them. The child in school feels less anchored at home and comes to school seeking a sense of stability and nurturance that was previously provided by the home. Teachers observe greater stress and irritability in children, which appear to be associated with tensions and dissatisfactions at home. Children are perceived to be more disgruntled and edgy, and at the same time, more needful.

Teachers encounter a range of extremes among parents. Along with indications of widespread parental neglect, they find increasing numbers of parents whose ambitions for their children are so intense as to be unrealistic and may even be potentially harmful. These parents have become aware of the importance of beginnings and the value of obtaining an early start in education. This heightened consciousness of development has produced a wave of parental demand for early academic training that is insensitive to the unevenness of development in young children and their fundamental need for open-ended exploration (Biber, 1984; Elkind, 1986).

In sum, educators encounter multiple signs of precocity in young children and the inevitable pressures and conflicts they arouse in parents. Teachers must update and reassess their grasp of the relation between children's outer signs of worldliness and social adaptability and their inner resources of intellectual understanding and emotional strength. These considerations point to the overriding importance of both intellectual and emotional groundedness in planning educational programs for young children and in communicating with their parents.

MATCHING EDUCATIONAL OBJECTIVES TO
UNIQUE DEVELOPMENTAL PATTERNS

Despite the pervasiveness of educational innovation and the mounting interest in student diversity, most forms of educational experimentation remain tied to achieving established educational objectives. New methods are usually viewed as alternative ways of achieving traditionally defined goals. Deviating from this conservative stance is the legacy of progressive education, including a range of "child-centered" programs. Rejecting traditional goals of academic achievement and the assessment of academic accomplishment by means of standardized achievement tests, these alternative programs tend to uphold more fluid forms of education that champion autonomy and individuality—for children and teachers. Their educational thrust is aimed at promoting psychological growth; their developmental perspective focuses on strengthening the coping capacities of children. While this alternative educational approach may subsume traditional goals of academic achievement within a more inclusive framework of human development and self-realization (Biber, 1984; Zimiles, 1986b), it represents a significant departure from traditional conceptions of what should be the main agenda of education. Issues of individuality and uniqueness play a much greater role in formulating educational objectives and implementing educational practice according to the tenets of child-centered education. This approach encompasses the most thoroughgoing adaptation of educational goals and methods to individuality to be found.

In light of the diversity and change to which the field of education is currently being exposed, it seems arbitrary and counterproductive to allow new awareness and knowledge to affect only the input side of education and remain tied to a fixed view of the goals of education. In fact, it is difficult to rigidly adhere to traditional goals amid this ferment. Experimenting with new methods tends to upset previously established equilibria as new forces are introduced that have the potential to cast a different light on the entire enterprise. It is not uncommon, then, for innovative and experimental educational programs to bring about an unintended revision of goals and a more individualized view of children's educational needs.

Promoting Pluralism and Tolerance in Young Children

The goal of sensitizing children to the diversity of humankind and the pluralistic character of our own society may seem distinct from that of fostering teacher responsiveness to individuality. They are, however, connected. When teachers engage in individualized teaching, they are expressing and modeling a respect for diversity. Conversely, when children learn about the range of variation that surrounds them, it is easier for them to find their niche and become attuned to their own distinctiveness.

Building an awareness of human variability and a sense of respect and appreciation for such differences begins by addressing the young child's concern for safety and stability with sameness and predictability. The school environment needs to be perceived as sufficiently safe and supportive for the child to be persuaded that the new opportunities to play and explore are worth separating from home and extending his or her perspective outward. The special lure of the classroom, and at the same time a primary source of misgivings, is the opportunity to interact with other children and the introduction of new dimensions of social interaction, play, and friendship.

There are two phases to the journey toward open and amiable relations with others: (1) achieving a feeling of safety and freedom, and (2) expanding one's orbit of play and interpersonal relationships in a manner that renders diversity of stimulation an asset. The less mature the child, the more important the first phase. Efforts to broaden a child's perspective, to extend the child's range of maneuverability outward and toward greater tolerance and generosity, are not likely to be successful unless they are built on a foundation of inner security.

The themes of intercultural acceptance and understanding fall under the purview of multicultural education. Rather than adding a module of multicultural education to early childhood education, it would seem more appropriate, as Ramsey (1987) has suggested, to introduce a multicultural perspective. One of the challenges posed to early childhood educators by the rising interest in multicultural education is to infuse the growing body of knowledge and awareness produced by this new field into ongoing programs without distorting the balance and rhythm of their prime mission.

The need to introduce ideas that are developmentally appropriate remains an overriding guidepost. There is a danger that zealous teachers may allude to abstract distinctions and classifications, or refer to far-off places and cultures that do not make sense to the young child. Preaching or expressions of disapproval may undermine the sense of freedom and positive regard that is fundamental to effective early education. Despite their importance, it is doubtful that issues of tolerance and justice can be targeted for very young children.

The strategies and program features that come into play in adopting a multicultural perspective in early childhood education are far-reaching (e.g., Derman-Sparks, 1987; Ramsey, 1987). As Ramsey has shown, they entail such diverse activities as preselecting materials to eliminate stereotypes and underrepresentation or misrepresentation of ethnic or gender groups; observing the spontaneous grouping and exclusionary patterns that occur in the classroom with an eye toward minimizing rejection and alienation; seizing opportunities to observe and experiment with linguistic diversity when a foreign language is encountered; planning field trips to observe ethnically diverse people interacting; choosing arts and crafts activities that call attention to the diversity of objects of beauty, and literature that portrays a wide range of human experience; and reducing the Eurocentric focus of themes and materials. While there are a great many facets to this particular strategy of intervention, it would be difficult to overestimate the influence of the teacher's own behavior—how generously, evenhandedly, and lovingly he or she treats all of the children, and the degree of openness, genuine interest, and delight the teacher spontaneously shows toward novelty and diversity.

SUMMARY

Today's teachers are besieged by heightened levels of diversity among children in school and revelations of difference and distinction. Our society has swung open the doors to the schools ever more widely. Major demographic shifts resulting from new immigration patterns and differential birth rates will combine to produce a student population whose ethnic composition and cultural heritage will be distributed dramatically differently. The ever-expanding and maturing fields of child development research are generating knowledge that offers new and more refined levels of differentiation of the phenomena of child development that give rise to alternative ways of conceptualizing school experience and framing educational objectives. The nation's children, growing up in a rapidly changing society, are themselves undergoing important changes.

This discussion of the mounting interest in diversity and change points to the multiplicity of forces that must be taken into account in addressing a changing student population. There are some paradoxical developments amid this complexity. After decades of deprivation and exclusion, large sectors of the population are claiming their fair share and full portion of the educational offering only to find that what they have been missing, and are now demanding, has been devalued. Now that a fair share of the pie has been won, it is being suggested that the pie is not so good after all. Thus, traditionally defined educational goals retain a stronger hold on the educational thinking of schools that work with ethnic minorities than they do on other sectors of the educational world. Also ironic is the fact that schools are being asked to do more while being respected less.

More visible than in the past, the rising volume of research is continually generating new categories, differentiations, and paradigms that call into question previous modes of thinking. These new ideas are not necessarily valid, and they may not be capable of being implemented in the classroom, but they create an atmosphere that challenges established ways of doing things and provide a steady flow of new ideas and propositions that are both provocative and distracting. The one-sided flow of information from research to educational practice has not been that rewarding; there is need for a more effective bidirectional exchange of knowledge and ideas between researchers and practitioners (Zimiles, 1987b).

This discussion of the role of diversity and change leads to the conclusion that the task of education is more effectively captured when it is viewed from the standpoint of child development, and that education is better implemented when it is delivered in individualized fashion. The pathway to achieving the increasingly complex goals that are being set for education appears to lie in strengthening the teacher's capacity to assimilate new knowledge, to respond with flexibility, and to arrive at a differentiated understanding of each child's developmental needs.

NOTE

1. Irene Serena made many helpful suggestions regarding the relevant research literature, but the treatment of this topic is solely the responsibility of the author.

REFERENCES

Ainsworth, M. (1973). The development of infant-mother attachment. In B. Caldwell and H. Ricciuti (Eds.), *Review of child development research, 3* (pp. 1–94). Chicago: University of Chicago Press.

Bartz, K., & Levine, E. (1978). Child rearing by black parents: A description and comparison to Anglo and Chicano parents. *Journal of Marriage and the Family, 40,* 709–719.

Beckwith, L., & Cohen, S. E. (1984). Home environment and cognitive competence in preterm children during the first five years. In A. Gottfried (Ed.), *Home environment and early cognitive development* (pp. 235–269). New York: Academic Press.

Biber, B. (1984). *Early education and psychological development.* New Haven, CT: Yale University Press

Block, J. H., Block, J., & Harrington, D. (1974). *Sex role typing and instrumental behavior: A developmental study.* Paper presented at the biennial meeting of the Society for Research in Child Development, Denver.

Canino, I. A., & Canino, G. (1980). Impact of stress on the Puerto Rican family: Treatment considerations. *American Journal of Orthopsychiatry, 50,* 535–541.

Chisholm, J. S. (1983). *Navajo infancy.* New York: Aldine.

Christie, J. F., & Johnsen, E. P. (1985). Questioning the results of play training research. *Educational Psychologist, 20*(1), 7–11.

Cole, M., & Scribner, S. (1974). *Culture and thought.* New York: Wiley.

Coll, C. T. G. (1990). Developmental outcome of minority infants: A process-oriented look into our beginnings. *Child Development, 61,* 270–289.

Collard, E. D. (1964). *Achievement motive in the four-year-old child and its relationship to achievement expectancies of the mother.* Unpublished doctoral dissertation, University of Michigan.

Comer, J. P. (1980). *School power: Implications of an intervention project.* New York: Free Press.

Cuffaro, H. K. (1975). Reevaluating basic premises: Curricula free of sexism. *Young Children, 30*(6), 469–479.

Delgado-Gaitan, C. (1987). Tradition and transitions in the learning process of Mexican children: An ethnographic view. In G. Spindler & L. Spindler (Eds.), *Interpretive ethnography of education: At home and abroad* (pp. 333–359). Hillsdale, NJ: Erlbaum.

Derman-Sparks, L., & the ABC Task Force. (1989). *Anti-bias curriculum: Tools for empowering young children.* Washington, DC: National Association for the Education of Young Children.

Diaz, R. (1983). Thought and two languages: The impact of bilingualism on cognitive development. In E. Gordon (Ed.), *Review of research in education, 10.* Washington, DC: American Educational Research Association.

Durrett, M., O'Bryant, S., & Pennebaker, J. (1975). Child rearing reports of white, black, and Mexican-American families. *Developmental Psychology, 11,* 871.

Dweck, C. S., & Elliott, E. S. (1983). Achievement motivation. In E. M. Hetherington (Ed.), *Handbook of child psychology, 4* (pp. 643–691). New York: Wiley.

Education for All Handicapped Children Act of 1975, PL 94-142.

Education of the Handicapped Act Amendments of 1986, PL 99-457.

Eisenberg, N., Murray, E., & Hite, T. (1982). Children's reasoning regarding sex-typed toy choices. *Child Development, 53,* 81–86.

Elkind, D. (1981). *The hurried child: Growing up too fast too soon.* Reading, MA: Addison Wesley.

Elkind, D. (1986). *The miseducation of child: Superkids at risk.* New York: Knopf.

Fagot, B. I. (1974). Sex differences in toddlers: Behavior and parental reaction. *Developmental Psychology, 10,* 554–558.

Fajardo, B. F., & Freedman, D. G. (1981). Maternal rhythmicity in three American cultures. In T. M. Field, A. M. Sostek & P. H. Leiderman (Eds.), *Culture and earlly interactions* (pp. 133–146). Hillsdale, NJ: Erlbaum.

Gardner, H. (1983). *Frames of mind.* New York: Basic Books.

Gardner, H., & Hatch, T. (1989). Multiple intelligences go to school: Educational implications of the theory of multiple intelligences. *Educational Researcher, 18*(8), 4–10.

Garrett, C. S., Ein, P. L., & Tremaine, L. (1977). The development of gender stereotyping of adult occupations in elementary school children. *Child Development, 48,* 507–512.

Gilligan, C. (1982). *In a different voice: Psychological theory and women's development.* Cambridge, MA: Harvard University Press.

Goldsmith, H. H., Buss, A. H., Plomin, R., Rothbart, M. K., Thomas, A., & Chess, S. (1987). Roundtable: What is temperament? *Child Development, 58,* 505–529.

Guttierrez, J., & Sameroff, A. (1990). Determinants of complexity in Mexican-American and Anglo-American mothers' conceptions of child development. *Child Development, 61,* 384–394.

Harrison, A. O., Wilson, M. N., Pine, C. J., Chan, S. Q., & Buriel, R. (1990). Family ecologies of ethnical minority children. *Child Development, 61,* 347–362.

John, V. P. (1972). Styles of learning—styles of teaching: Reflections on the education of Navajo children. In C. Cazden, V. P. John & D. Hymes (Eds.), *Functions of language in the classroom* (pp. 331–343). New York: Teachers College Press.

Kagan, J. (1966). Reflection-impulsivity: The generality and dynamics of conceptual tempo. *Journal of Abnormal Psychology, 71,* 17–24.

Kluckhohn, C., & Murray, H. A. (1956). Personality formation: The determinants. In C. Kluckhohn, H. A. Murray & D. M. Schneider (Eds.), *Personality in nature, society, and culture* (2nd ed.) (pp. 53–70). New York: Knopf.

Laosa, L. M. (1980). Maternal teaching strategies in Chicano and Anglo American families: The influence of culture and education on maternal behavior. *Child Development, 51,* 759–765.

Laosa, L. M. (1982). The sociocultural context of evaluation. In B. Spodek (Ed.), *Handbook of research in early childhood education* (pp. 501–520). New York: Free Press.

Lin, C. L., & Fu, V. R. (1990). A comparison of child-rearing practices among Chinese, immigrant Chinese, and caucasian-American parents. *Child Development, 61,* 429–433.

McLoyd, V. C. (1990). The impact of economic hardship on black families and children: Psychological distress, parenting, and socioemotional development. *Child Development, 61,* 311–346.

Mead, M. (1978). *Culture and commitment: The new relations between generations in the 1970s.* New York: Columbia University Press.

Messick, S. (1984). The nature of cognitive styles. *Educational Psychologist, 19*(2), 59–74.

Murphy, L. B. (1969). Children under three—Finding ways to stimulate development. *Children, 16*(2), 46–52.

Ogbu, J. (1988). Cultural diversity and human development. In D. Slaughter (Ed.), *Black children and poverty: A developmental perspective* (pp. 11–28). San Francisco: Jossey-Bass.

Parsons, J. E., Kaczala, C., & Meece, J. (1982). Socialization of achievement attitudes and beliefs: Classroom influences. *Child Development, 53,* 322–339.

Perkins, D. N., & Salomon, G. (1989). Are cognitive skills context-bound? *Educational Researcher, 18*(1), 16–25.

Philips, S. U. (1972). Participant structures and communicative competence: Warm Springs children in community and classroom. In C. Cazden, V. P. John & D. Hymes (Eds.), *Functions of language in the classroom* (pp. 370–394). New York: Teachers College Press.

Piaget, J. (1970). Piaget's theory. In P. Mussen (Ed.), *Carmichael's manual of child psychology* (pp. 703–732). New York: Wiley.

Ramsey, P. G. (1987). *Teaching and learning in a diverse world: Multicultural education for young children.* New York: Teachers College Press.

Resnick, L. B. (1987). *Education and learning to think.* Washington, DC: National Academy Press.

Resnick, L. B., & Weaver, P. A. (1979). *Theory and practice of early reading.* Hillsdale, NJ: Erlbaum.

Rogoff, B., & Mistry, J. J. (1985). Memory development in cultural context. In M. Pressley & C. Brainerd (Eds.), *Progress in cognitive development* (pp. 117–142). New York: Springer Verlag.

Rotherman-Borus, M. J., & Phinney, J. S. (1990). Patterns of social expectations among black Mexican-American children. *Child Development, 61,* 542–556.

Rubin, J. Z., Provenzano, F. J., & Luria, Z. (1974). The eye of the beholder: Parents' view on sex of newborns. *American Journal of Orthopsychiatry, 44,* 512–519.

Saegart, S., & Hart, R. (1976). The development of environmental competence in girls and boys. In P. Burent (Ed.), *Women and society.* Chicago: Maaroufa Press.

Saracho, O. N., & Spodek, B. (1986). Cognitive style and children's learning: Individual variation in cognitive processes. In L. G. Katz (Ed.), *Current topics in early childhood education* (Vol. 6, pp. 177–194). Norwood, NJ: Ablex.

Saville-Troike, M. (1984). What really matters in second language learning for academic achievement? *TESOL Quarterly, 18*(2), 199–219.

Siegler, R. S. (1986). *Children's thinking.* Englewood Cliffs, NJ: Prentice Hall.

Silver, L. B. (1989). Learning disabilities. *Journal of the American Academy of Child and Adolescent Psychiatry, 28,* 309–313.

Slaughter-Defoe, D. T., Nakagawa, K., Takanishi, R., & Johnson, D. J. (1990). Toward cultural/ecological perspectives on schooling and achievement in African- and Asian-American children. *Child Development, 61,*563–583.

Smilansky, S. (1968). *The effects of sociodramatic play on disadvantaged preschool children.* New York: Wiley.

Smith, P. K., & Daglish, L. (1977). Sex differences in parent and infant behavior in the home. *Child Development, 48,* 1250–1254.

Snow, C. (1987). Beyond conversation: Second language learners' acquisition of description and explanation. In J. P. Lantolf & A. Labarca (Eds.), *Research in second language learning: Focus on the classroom* (pp. 3–16). Norwood, NJ: Ablex.

Stevenson, H. W., Chen, C., & Uttal, D. H. (1990). Beliefs and achievement: A study of black, white and hispanic children. *Child Development, 61,* 508–523.

Steward, M. S., & Steward, D. S. (1973). The observation of Anglo-Mexican and Chinese-American mothers teaching their young sons. *Child Development, 44,* 329–337.

Thurstone, L. L. (1938). Primary mental abilities. *Psychometric Monographs, 1.*

Vygotsky, L. S. (1986). *Mind in society: The development of higher psychological processes* (M. Cole, V. John-Steiner, S. Scribner & E. Souberman, Eds. & Trans.). New York: Plenum Press.

Weinberg, R. A. (1989). Intelligence and IQ: Landmark issues and great debates. *American Psychologist, 44*(2), 98–104.

Weiss, R. (1979). Growing up a little faster: The experience of growing up in a single-parent household. *Journal of Social Issues, 35,* 97–111.

Willig, A. (1985). A meta-analysis of selected studies on the effectiveness of bilingual education. *Review of Educational Research, 55*(3), 269–317.

Witkin, H. A., Moore, C. A., Goodenough, D. R., & Cox, P. W. (1977). Field-dependent and field-independent cognitive styles and their educational implications. *Review of Educational Research, 47,* 1–64.

Zepeda, M. (1986). *Early caregiving in a Mexican origin population.* Paper presented at the International Conference on Infant Studies, Los Angeles.

Zeskind, P. S. (1983). Cross-cultural differences in maternal perception of cries of low- and high-risk infants. *Child Development, 54,* 1119–1128.

Zimiles, H. (1986a). The changing American child: The perspective of educators. In T. M. Tomlinson & H. J. Walberg (Eds.), *Academic work and educational excellence* (pp. 61–84). Berkeley, CA: McCutchan.

Zimiles, H. (1986b). Guiding the study of cognition to a framework of greater complexity. In D. J. Bearsion & H. Zimiles (Eds.), *Thought and emotion: Developmental perspectives* (pp. 75–92). Hillsdale, NJ: Erlbaum.

Zimiles, H. (1986c). The social context of early childhood in an era of expanding preschool education. In B. Spodek (Ed.), *Today's kindergarten: Exploring the knowledge base, expanding the curriculum* (pp. 1–14). New York: Teachers College Press.

Zimiles, H. (1987a). The Bank Street approach. In J. L. Roopnarine & J. E. Johnson (Eds.), *Approaches to early childhood education* (pp. 164–176). Columbus, OH: Merrill.

Zimiles, H. (1987b). Quandaries in the trend toward earlier education: The role of research. In R. B. Woolner (Ed.), *The Lipman papers* (pp. 43–53). Memphis: Memphis State University.

CHAPTER 3

The Concept of Development in the Early Childhood Curriculum

Anthony D. Pellegrini

Janna Dresden

This chapter discusses the concept of development and applies it to early childhood education curriculum. The question addressed is, to what extent and in what ways can the principles of development inform our practice as early childhood researchers and educators?

The term *development* is used in many different ways by those of us interested in children. For example, some states, such as Georgia, have developmental first grades; *developmental* in such cases refers to special programs for children who have not been promoted directly to first grade from kindergarten. In the phrase *developmentally appropriate,* development connotes certain kinds of curricula and evaluation procedures (National Association for the Education of Young Children, 1988) that should be congruent with the children's levels of competence and other age-related character- istics. For example, in the area of evaluation, because preschool and kindergarten children's test-taking motivation is highly variable (e.g., affected by their familiarity with the tester and the testing environment), more naturalistic approaches to evaluation (e.g., ob- servation of behavior) are developmentally appropriate for this age group.

In this chapter we examine the definition of development by considering some "outmoded" concepts of development. Then some of the basic concepts of development as currently conceptualized by developmental psychologists and ethologists are presented. The ways in which developmental child study can be executed are also specified. Finally, these concepts are applied to the areas of literacy and numeracy.

OUTMODED CONCEPTS OF DEVELOPMENT

In order to understand what development is, we must first consider what it is not. Further, it is important to examine and correct these outmoded concepts that are still used to design curriculum, since such inadequate theoretical bases are bound to result in inadequate curriculum. We begin with a description of a set of outmoded concepts of development as specified by Gottlieb (1983). These outmoded concepts have not been empirically supported and, because they are inaccurate, confound our understanding of children and educational programs. In short, these outmoded concepts, because they provide inaccurate descriptions of children, have no place in the design of curriculum for young children.

Ontogeny Recapitulates Phylogeny.   The concept that ontogeny (individual development) recapitulates phylogeny (across-species development), popularized by G. S. Hall (1916), suggests that the development of individual human beings repeats the evolutionary path of the species *Homo sapiens.* For example, Hall considered the presence of gills in human embryos evidence of a repetition of that part of our phylogenetic history when animals lived in water. Similarly, the tree climbing and war play of preschool children were said to be a recapitulation of our primate and hunter/gatherer histories, respectively. This is an outmoded concept because different species have different ontogenetic histories that suit them to their environments.

Despite its flaws, there is some value in this outmoded theory. It points out the fact that humans do seem to develop through a series of stages in a specific order (a topic addressed later in this chapter) and that stages are qualitatively different from one another. The logic of Hall, and his intellectual forebear Haeckel (1891), needs to be inverted, however. That is, phylogeny seems to be affected by ontogeny to the extent that individual changes may affect evolution (de Beers, 1958, cited in Gottlieb, 1983). More specifically, the adaptive changes (i.e., changes that result in increased survival rates) experienced during ontogeny will be incorporated into the phylogenetic histories of the species.

Nature and Nurture.   Nature (our genetic endowment) and nurture (the environment in which we live) have independent effects on behavior and learning. For example, common knowledge may hold that height is determined by nature (genetically) while social skills are determined by environment. In truth, nature and nurture are inextricably linked. Height is affected by environmental factors, such as the mother's diet during pregnancy, in addition to genetic factors. And social skills can have a biological component, such as temperament, in addition to the perhaps more obvious contributions of the environment.

Although a dichotomy between nature and nurture is simplistic, it is useful to recognize that children's behaviors can be placed on a continuum from those that are relatively stable (implying a strong genetic component), such as infants crying when in pain, to those that are more labile (implying an environmental effect), such as ability to read (Hinde, 1983). As such, we should recognize that all behavior has environmental and genetic components. Genetic endowment seems to set limits on development, but the realization of the endowment is determined by the environment.

The Maturation vs. Experience Dichotomy. Maturation is typically used to describe processes that are minimally affected by environmental, or experiential, factors and are stable across time (Hinde, 1983). For example, a child's temperament may be stable throughout the early school years. However, this stability, rather than being attributable to either internal maturation or environmental experience, is probably due to both. For example, a child's temperament may be due to maturation, self-regulatory processes, and a specific consistent mother-child interaction environment. In short, maturation and experience, like nature and nurture, should be considered complementary.

CURRENT CONCEPTS OF DEVELOPMENT

Now that we know what development is not, it is time to consider what it is. The following principles of development are drawn from current research in developmental psychology (Gottlieb, 1983) and ethology (Hinde, 1983). The theme that should become evident in this section is the idea that human beings progress through qualitatively different periods in their development. The following concepts provide evidence for and elaborate on this premise.

Forward Reference of Newborns. Under the concept of the forward reference, or preadapted quality, of newborns (Gottlieb, 1983), some behaviors, such as the sucking and grasping reflexes, are present prenatally so as to maximize the probability of early survival.

This principle further states that early neural and behavioral development affects later development. An excellent example of this principle is the extent to which the grasping and sucking reflexes are incorporated into later cognitive development in Piaget's (1970) theory. These "ready-made schema" of grasping and sucking are used, in later infancy, to explore the attributes of objects. Knowledge of object attributes is, in turn, used during early childhood for fantasy play.

Differentiation and Hierarchical Organization. Organs and organisms undergo differentiation and move from a homogeneous (relatively undifferentiated) to a heterogeneous (differentiated) state. The concept can be and has been applied to development at both the organ (e.g., reproductive organs) and organism levels. At the latter level, children's motor skills become more differentiated with age. For example, a child's ability to eat with a spoon develops from repetitive actions with the spoon, to a spoon-to-dish-to-mouth action sequence, to putting food on the spoon, to using the whole routine to eat (Connolly & Dalgleish, 1989).

Optimum Stage or Critical/Sensitive Periods. There are certain periods in development that are critical to the development of specific behaviors. For example, there seems to be an optimal period to learn language (see Brown, 1973). An equally familiar example of the critical-period hypothesis is infant attachment. Early theory held that if infants did not securely attach to their mothers they would suffer from subsequent personality anomalies (see Bowlby, 1969, for a thorough review). The critical-period hypothesis was based on Lorenz's (1935, cited in Hinde, 1983) imprinting experiments with birds, wherein within the first hours of life birds would respond to a moving object as if it were a parent. This process was thought to be irreversible; thus, the notion of critical stage. Current research, however, does not support the idea of a critical period to the extent that adverse conditions encountered during those critical periods cannot be remedied; thus, we advance the notion of sensitive, rather than critical, periods. For example, the effects of maternal deprivation during a critical period can be remedied in later life through systematic exposure to younger peers (Suomi & Harlow, 1972).

Individual Differences. This concept suggests that individual variations exist within a species. For example, some boys may be physically active while others may be more sedentary. Individual differences are often thought to have biological origins but, as noted above, nature/nurture and maturation/learning are interdependent processes. A child's level of activity may be affected by prenatal environmental factors, such as the mother's level of tobacco and alcohol consumption. Further, that boys are more active than girls may be a result of different hormonal and social learning histories (Maccoby, 1986).

Sequence of Behavior Stages: Regularity Despite Individual Differences. Regularity refers to the specific sequence, or order, in which behaviors appear. This well-known concept is best illustrated in Piaget's (1970) theory of cognitive development wherein children progress from sensorimotor, to preoperational, to operational levels of intelligence. Though the ages may vary for each stage, they appear in the specified order. This stage-sequence concept further incorporates the idea that stages are qualitatively different from one another. That is, the world is viewed differently, and concepts at stage 1 are qualitatively different from those at stage 2. For example, a preoperational child's concept of the number five is different from that of a formal operational child to the extent that for the former, this array (1 1 1 1 1) may be greater than this array (11111); they would be equal for the older child.

Functional Considerations. Specific behaviors may serve different functions during development. By the function of a behavior, biologists often mean the reproductive value of that behavior. Social scientists more typically use function to mean the beneficial consequences of a behavior (Hinde, 1983). The important point to stress here, which is related to the stage-sequence concept, is that a specific behavior may serve different functions at different periods of development. For example, crying serves very different functions in infancy and middle childhood. It would be a developmentally appropriate behavior for an infant's request for food; it would not be an appropriate way for an older child to request food. Another example involves imposing the behavior of older children (e.g., the importance of letter/sound correspondence for reading during the primary grades) on younger children (e.g., teaching letter/sound correspondence to preschoolers). The lesson here is that we should not consider the function of a specific behavior in childhood in relation to another developmental period. Different behaviors serve different functions at different periods of development.

Discontinuity/Continuity in Development.   Behaviors, traits, or skills can be continuous (stable) or discontinuous (unstable) across the life span; for example, are intelligence and temperament stable from infancy through childhood? This concept, in conjunction with the earlier concepts, is particularly important from an applied perspective because it tells us the relative importance of specific behaviors/skills at specific periods. For example, is behavior A stable from time 1 to time 2, and does it serve similar or different functions at each time? The remainder of this section addresses this important concept in detail, based on Kagan's (1971) discussion of the issue.

Aspects of development can be continuous or discontinuous. Continuity or stability in behavior may be due to endogenous (internal) or exogenous (external) processes. For example, the stability of a child's verbal ability across the preschool and primary school periods may be due primarily to an inherited trait, or it may be due primarily to a particular home environment. Of course, we should keep in mind that such dichotomies between internal/external and nature/nurture are outmoded. The point to be made here, however, is that stability in development is affected by internal and external forces, probably working in conjunction.

In some cases, continuity of similar behaviors is observed across time; for example, a child may be very active during the infant and preschool years. In this case of *homotypic* continuity, we have similar response modes across time, that is, locomotion. *Heterotypic* continuity, in contrast, involves the interrelation of different response modes across time and is consequently more difficult to gauge. Though in different modes, heterotypic continuity can be established when the behaviors are theoretically related. For example, the ability to engage in make-believe play at three years of age is related to word writing at five years of age (Galda, Pellegrini & Cox, 1989). In this case, make-believe play and word writing involve different response modes but are theoretically related to the extent that both involve the production of symbolic representations.

Heterotypic continuity has rightfully been labeled cryptic by Kagan (1971). It is cryptic to the extent that discovering relations between dissimilar phenomena is akin to solving a puzzle or mystery. This is, however, the essence of "being developmental" in that there are qualitative changes, via transformations, across the life span. Our job is to try to chart them. Our map in this journey must be good developmental theory. Only through such theory can we explain the relation between seemingly different sets of behaviors.

There are situations that provide clues to the solution of this mystery. Kagan (1971) lists principles that can be applied to detecting continuity/discontinuity. First, homotypic continuity is less common during the first ten years of life than later. Specifically, there are two critical junctures during this period in which heterotypic continuity is most likely to occur: from 18 to 24 months of age and from five to seven years of age. At the first juncture, children move from concern with the sensorimotor coordination of objects to their symbolic representation. For example, children prior to this shift may spend their time learning how to handle blocks and the properties of the blocks that enable them to build with them. After the shift, children may be concerned with using the blocks to create make-believe themes.

The second period, five to seven years of age, is marked by a qualitative change in children's cognitive functioning whereby they become more able to inhibit irrelevant acts and select appropriate ones, maintain a problem-solving set, and appreciate the requirements of a problem. For example, children before this shift may have more difficulty maintaining attention and motivation on a test than older children. In short, children become more reflective and more able to maintain a problem-solving, or school behavior, set.

A developmental approach involves conceptualizing children as qualitatively different at different periods. They are certainly different from adults. This translates into discovering those behaviors/skills that are typical for a particular stage or period. In identifying such behaviors and skills we should be aware that the criterion for selection is relevance for that period, not adulthood. The next step in our applied endeavor involves making the theoretical connection of behaviors/skills from one stage or period to another.

DEVELOPMENTAL CHILD STUDY

A developmental approach to studying children is necessary before we can design curriculum: Curriculum should be matched with children's developmental status. Developmental study, generally, takes one of two directions. First, there is the normative/descriptive type of work in which we describe children's behaviors/skills at various stages of development. Part of such a description, of course, involves addressing issues of continuity/discontinuity—that is, to what extent is behavior A at time 1 related to behavior A (continuous development) or behavior B (discontinuous development) at time 2?

Further, these studies often take place in children's natural environments—schools, homes, and hospitals—and are longitudinal (studying the same children across time) not cross-sectional (studying different children at different ages).

The second type of developmental study is experimental, not naturalistic. The motivation behind experimental studies of development is a search for "causality." For example, to address the critical/sensitive period issue discussed above, experimental studies have been used to determine the extent to which monkeys isolated from their mothers during infancy could later be rehabilitated (Suomi & Harlow, 1972). Although such experimental manipulation allows us to begin to make causal inferences about specific relations, serious concerns have been raised about the experimental approach from the areas of "basic" and "applied" studies of child development. One of the most influential indictments of the experimental approach comes from Bronfenbrenner (1979), who has characterized the current state of experimental child development studies as descriptions of strange environmental factors on one behavior of a child in an artificial situation. In other words, experiments study isolated factors (such as specific toys) affecting individual behaviors (such as sharing behaviors) of children in a laboratory playroom. The results of such experimental manipulations indicate that children's behaviors can or cannot be changed in the predicted direction. The more interesting question is to what extent these factors actually affect behavior (McCall, 1977). The experimental results may tell us that by exposing children to specific toys their play can be changed in predictable directions. However, in the "real world" these children may not play with these toys; therefore their play behavior in the experiments is different from their play in the real world. In short, the experimental results may not provide insight into the ways in which children develop naturally.

We should not throw out the baby with the bathwater, however. Experiments are important in child development to identify possible causes and can be ecologically valid (Bronfenbrenner, 1979). Such experiments should be analogues to children's real-world environments. Further, we should compare such experimental results with naturalistic results, such as the same or similar children playing with the same toys in their preschool classroom. Following these guidelines, we can test the ecological validity of an experiment (see Pellegrini & Perlmutter, 1989, for an example of such an experiment). For example, in designing an ecologically valid experiment to study the effects of specific toys on children's play, we should use toys actually found in the children's environment (e.g., dolls and dress-up clothes) and have our experimental social groups be similar to those found in that environment (e.g., same-gender dyads). Further, the demands placed on children in the experiments should be similar to those at school; if children are assigned to specific learning centers in school, the experiment could also manipulate their exposure to centers.

Developmental studies should also be longitudinal. If we are interested in understanding development, or changes within individuals across time, we should study them across time. Although cross-sectional studies can be used initially, they are not the final word in developmental study. An example should make the point: If we are interested in the developmental relations between mothers reading books to toddlers and children's subsequent kindergarten literacy, we could begin by examining the relations between mother-child behaviors and measures of reading with two separate age groups of children. Results from such an investigation would give us insight into age differences in mothers' reading styles and relations between these styles and children's reading. Longitudinal research is needed to determine the ways in which mothers' and children's behaviors change from the toddler to the kindergarten period. Further, to determine the extent to which book-reading behaviors predict reading, the antecedent-subsequent dimensions of a longitudinal design are necessary.

DEVELOPMENTALLY APPROPRIATE CURRICULUM

A developmentally appropriate curriculum is based on what we know about the developing abilities of young children. Our understanding of the process of development helps us to see the connections between behaviors that might otherwise appear discontinuous. For example, the motor development of young children generally proceeds from crawling to standing to walking. Parents are likely to give their children many opportunities to crawl before they begin to expect them to walk. Early childhood educators should also base their plans and expectations on established developmental pathways.

There are several caveats, however. We must bear in mind that all curriculum choices are inevitably based on ethical and moral beliefs as well as developmental processes (Bruner, 1985). In addition, we must be aware that the process of development is uneven and proceeds differently in each child (Almy & associates, 1970). Finally, we should view a developmental curriculum as dynamic and ever-changing rather than as a static set of rules etched in stone. As research provides us with more insight into the process of development and as our experience as educators provides us with greater understanding of individual children, the curriculum will undoubtedly change a great deal. In the light of these caveats, we will examine a developmentally appropriate curriculum in the areas of literacy and numeracy, making specific reference to the ways in which current concepts of development are operating.

Literacy

By literacy we mean children's ability to read and write traditional school-based text. An excellent discussion of the definition of literacy is presented by Heath (1989). School-based writing and reading involves the ability to convey meaning through conventional orthography and comprehend the meaning of written words, respectively (Sulzby, 1988). Young children can best be prepared for these skills through specific forms of symbolic play and verbal interaction with adults and peers. These suggestions are based on research we have conducted with children in various preschool classrooms (Galda, Pellegrini & Cox, 1989) and with children and their mothers (Pellegrini, Perlmutter, Galda & Brody, 1990). The relation between play and literacy is an excellent example of discontinuous development to the extent that one set of behaviors (i.e., make-believe transformations) predicts a seemingly very different set of behaviors (i.e., early writing).

Children's writing status is defined as the ability to write individual words using conventional orthography. This ability, as Vygotsky (1978) suggested, is based on children's ability to represent meaning with abstract signifiers. The word *car* is a signifier for that expensive thing we drive around, as a broomstick represents a horse in children's make-believe play. Children's ability to engage in symbolic representation begins in make-believe, using concrete and functionally explicit props to represent meaning, such as a doll to represent a baby. As children progress through the preschool period (usually by three to four years of age), they are not dependent on props for their make-believe representations; for example, a boy's imitation of a man's deep voice can be used to signify his role as an adult male (McLoyd, 1980; Pellegrini, 1987).

This ability to move from object-dependent to object-independent play illustrates the concept of stage. Children must engage in object-dependent play before they can engage in make-believe without objects. It also illustrates the concept of differentiation to the extent that children's signifiers become more varied and elaborate; the components of a "Mommy" role become more varied and elaborate. It illustrates the concept of forward reference as well. Children's early experiences with objects in play are incorporated in their later play; the relation between exploration and play illustrates this point nicely (see Pellegrini & Boyd, in press).

The ability to use representational media to convey meaning in play is applied to the ability to have written words represent meaning. In our research we have found that 3½-year-olds' levels of symbolic play predict their ability to use conventional orthography one year later (Galda et al., 1989).

The ways in which educators can stimulate children's use of such forms of symbolic play are relatively simple. If children are given props that are functionally ambiguous, such as pipe cleaners and styrofoam shapes used in packing stereos, they will use these abstract forms of symbolization. Of course, children will initially have to explore these novel props before they play with them symbolically. But after this exploration period, the props will elicit the desired forms of play.

Regarding children's reading, we have found two types of developmental precursors. The first involves ways in which mothers read with their children; the second involves ways in which children interact with their peers. We have found that a specific class of words (linguistic words) used by mothers during these sessions seems to predict children's participation in this important literacy event (Pellegrini et al., 1990). When mothers use linguistic terms such as *read, word, write, sentence,* and *talk,* they are exposing children to a class of words that makes linguistic processes explicit (Olson, 1983). This ability to reflect upon linguistic and reading processes, or metalinguistic awareness, is an important dimension in learning to read. Preschoolers' use of these terms is a significant predictor of their reading status (Galda et al., 1989). Exposure to these words is only the first step in the child's developing metalinguistic awareness.

Children practice using this class of words in their peer interaction. At 3½ years of age, children use linguistic words during their make-believe play. Our favorite example of this is: "Doctors don't *say* poo poo." In this case the child is encoding a linguistic verb and reflecting, or going "meta," on it. It seems that children practice using this new class of words in play, a place where newly acquired skills are often practiced. At 4½ years of age, children's use of linguistic terms increases in frequency, but such use occurs more often in realistic peer discourse than in make-believe discourse. In short, children are exposed to these verbs during book reading with their mothers, practice using them in fantasy, and later generalize their use to realistic peer discourse and reading.

In applying the final two concepts of development (i.e., sensitive period and individual differences) to symbolic play and literacy, we find that the use of symbolic play in the curriculum during the preschool period is most appropriate. This is the time when children spontaneously spend the most time engaging in this activity. Thus, the preschool period may be a sensitive period for the use of symbolic play to the extent that it might be maximally affective at that point. Regarding individual differences, some young preschool children, labeled dramatists by Howard Gardner and colleagues (Shotwell, Wolf & Gardner, 1979), are more likely to engage in dramatic play than others; these "others" have been labeled patterners by Gardner. It seems that each group of children chooses a different route to similar developmental outcomes. There is no one best road to development!

Numeracy

Unlike the area of literacy, the development of numeracy has suffered from a lack of longitudinal research. The vast majority of work in this area has utilized a cross-sectional methodology (Wagner & Walters, 1982). Although the results from these cross-sectional studies do provide some information and insight, they do not provide the fundamental information needed regarding the behavioral and experiential precursors of numeracy. Because of the paucity of longitudinal research in this area, we will pose some questions that might lead to fruitful investigation and important contributions in this area.

Extant research has apparently focused on those preschool activities that are thought to be related to later mathematical understanding (e.g., block building) or on the increasing sophistication of numerical skills, rather than on the relationship between prenumber activities and later competence. The former relationship is an example of discontinuous development, and the latter is an example of continuous development.

With regard to prenumber activities, it has often been proposed that children's play with blocks enables them to actively manipulate concepts of length, volume, and number and thus begin to construct their own understanding of mathematics (Leeb-Lundberg, 1974). In fact, evidence suggests that play with blocks follows a developmental, stagelike sequence that is indicative of the increasing complexity and sophistication of logico-mathematical abilities (Forman, 1982; Reifel & Greenfield, 1982). But exactly how these activities and abilities relate to concurrent or later arithmetic competence has not been shown.

Regarding the increasing sophistication of numerical skills (an illustration of the concept of differentiation in development), much research has focused directly on traditional school-related arithmetic activities without regard to the antecedents of these behaviors. Nonetheless, it is possible to extract some relevant information from this body of work, and so it is worthwhile to briefly examine some of these results.

One significant advancement in numerical competence that occurs during the preschool years is the internalization of counting. Children begin by touching objects and saying the numerals out loud when they count. Later they are able to look at a series of items and produce the numerals silently (Cobb, 1987; Fuson, 1988; Steffe, in press; Vygotsky, 1962). Consistent with this process of internalization is the fact that the concept of number becomes increasingly abstract during this period of development. Children begin by viewing number as a property of a set (Gelman & Gallistel, 1986) and later are able to perceive number as an independent entity that can be acted upon (Fuson, 1988). An interesting developmental question thus relates to the origin of these verbal strategies. Do they, as Vygotsky (1962) noted, originate in adult-child dialogue?

Beginning arithmetic abilities also show a similar forward reference, progression from concrete to abstract. In order to perform the operations of addition and subtraction, children are initially dependent on concrete props or aids; they then develop a variety of mental strategies (such as counting on from the larger number), and later come to rely primarily on memorized facts (Baroody & Ginsburg, 1986; Carpenter & Moser, 1983; Resnick, 1983). The question we pose here is: Might this representational competence, like early writing, originate in early symbolic play?

It is also known that both computational skill and conceptual understanding develop during the beginning school years. What are the functional implications here? The development of meaning or conceptual understanding is thought to be especially important because skills are easily forgotten if they are not connected to a network of semantic meaning (Lampert, 1986a; Larkin, 1983; Resnick,

1989) and because skills are of little value if one does not know when to use them (Lampert, 1986a; Resnick, 1989). Conceptual or meaningful understanding derives from the process of making connections between different pieces of information or ways of knowing (Lampert, 1986b; Larkin, 1983). This process of making connections is also referred to as the process of constructing relationships (Davis, 1986) and is facilitated in two ways. First, learners must be active rather than passive (Cobb, 1987; Kamii, 1985; Larkin, 1983; Resnick, 1989), and group activity is especially productive (Cobb, 1987; Kamii, 1985; Brown, Collins & Duguid, 1989). By active we mean that children choose (within a finite set) activities and also choose the ways in which they will interact with the materials or problems they have chosen. Group activity with peers is especially important because it often results in advanced conceptual understanding. In addition, to promote the development of meaningful understanding, new information should be situated or embedded within a network of understanding (Collins, Brown & Newman, 1989; Resnick, 1989; Saxe, 1988).

A significant exception to the lack of truly developmental research on children's mathematical ability can be found in the work of Wagner and Walters (1982). Their intensive study of nine children for a period of five years seems to indicate that the concept of number is constructed over time rather than learned through imitation or drill, and that the concept of number is not a unitary construct but a collection of different developmental strands.

Despite the variety of ways in which the development of numerical and arithmetic competence has been studied and the paucity of studies that connect preschool activities with later school-type arithmetic activities, the recommendations for practice that follow from these results are remarkably similar. They are as follows:

1. Children should be provided with extensive opportunities for "hands-on" concrete activities before the introduction of symbolic (mental or pencil and paper) activities.
2. Because the "network of understanding" available to most young children is that of their daily experience, numerical and arithmetic activities should be embedded within that context.
3. Children should be given extensive opportunities for group interaction and individual activity.

These recommendations for practice will hardly seem new to

anyone at all familiar with traditional early childhood curricula. We hope, however, we have added theoretical and empirical support to early childhood teachers' intuitions by highlighting the importance of the concepts of continuous and discontinuous development in the education of young children. In teaching children to be literate and numerate by the end of the preschool period, teachers should encourage children to engage in abstract symbolic play, use linguistic terms, and be involved in a wide variety of concrete and active numerical experiences. The best way to teach something to children in a period of developmental flux, it seems, is not always to break a mature skill, such as reading, writing, or computing, into simpler parts for the child to digest. Our task is to find continuity in discontinuity.

SUMMARY

We have attempted to establish a developmental basis for early childhood education curriculum. Current concepts of development were outlined and illustrated with examples from the literacy and numeracy literature. The challenge to the early childhood educator is to document how specific activities at different points in the lives of young children are meaningful to their current and later developmental status. This venture becomes especially challenging when we chart the discontinuous and individualized routes that children often follow through childhood. The current developmental concepts outlined above can act as a useful heuristic for this venture.

REFERENCES

Almy, M., & associates (1970). *Logical thinking in second grade.* New York: Teachers College Press.

Baroody, A. J., & Ginsburg, H. P. (1986). The relationship between initial meaningful and mechanical knowledge of arithmetic. In J. Hiebert (Ed.), *Conceptual and procedural knowledge: The case of mathematics* (pp. 75–112). Hillsdale, NJ: Erlbaum.

Bowlby, J. (1969). *Attachment and loss: Vol. 1. Attachment.* New York: Basic Books.

Bronfenbrenner, U. (1979). *The ecology of human development.* Cambridge, MA: Harvard University Press.

Brown, J. S., Collins, A., & Duguid, P. (1989). Situated cognition and the culture of learning. *Educational Researcher, 18*(4), 32–41.

Brown, R. (1973). *A first language.* Cambridge, MA: Harvard University Press.

Bruner, J. (1985). Models of the learner. *Educational Researcher, 14*(6), 5–8.

Carpenter, T. P., & Moser, J. M. (1983). The acquisition of addition and subtraction concepts. In R. Lesh & M. Landau (Eds.), *Acquisition of mathematics concepts and processes* (pp. 7–44). New York: Academic Press.

Cobb, P. (1987). An analysis of three models of early number development. *Journal for Research in Mathematics Education, 18,* 163–179.

Collins, A., Brown, J. S., & Newman, S. E. (1989). Cognitive apprenticeship: Teaching the crafts of reading, writing, and mathematics. In L. B. Resnick (Ed.), *Knowing,learning, and instruction: Essays in honor of Robert Glaser* (pp. 453–494). Hillsdale, NJ: Erlbaum.

Connolly, K., & Dalgleish, M. (1989). The emergence of a tool-using skill in infancy. *Developmental Psychology, 23,* 894–912.

Davis, R. B. (1986). Conceptual and procedural knowledge in mathematics: A summary analysis. In J. Hiebert (Ed.), *Conceptual and procedural knowledge: The case of mathematics* (pp. 265–300). Hillsdale, NJ: Erlbaum.

de Beers, G. (1958). *Embryos and ancestors.* London: Oxford.

Forman, G. E. (1982). A search for the origins of equivalence concepts through a microanalysis of block play. In G. E. Forman (Ed.), *Action and thought: From sensorimotor schemes to symbolic operations* (pp. 97–135). New York: Academic Press.

Fuson, D. C. (1988). *Children's counting and concepts of number.* New York: Springer-Verlag.

Galda, L., Pellegrini, A. D., & Cox, S. (1989). A short-term longitudinal study of preschoolers' emergent literacy. *Research in the Teaching of English, 23,* 292–309.

Gelman, R., & Gallistel, C. R. (1986). *The child's understanding of number.* Cambridge, MA: Harvard University Press.

Gottlieb, G. (1983). The psychobiological approach to developmental issues. In J. J. Campos & M. Haith (Eds.), *Handbook of child psychology: Infancy and developmental psychobiology* (Vol. II, pp. 1–26). New York: Wiley.

Haeckel, E. (1891). *Anthropogenie odev Entwick Lungsgeschichte des Mensches.* Leipzig: W. Engelman.

Hall, G. S. (1916). *Adolescence.* New York: Appleton.

Heath, S. B. (1989). Oral and literate traditions among black Americans living in poverty. *American Psychology, 44,* 367–373.

Hinde, R. (1983). Ethology and child development. In J. J. Campos & M. H. Haith (Eds.), *Handbook of child psychology: Infancy and developmental psychobiology* (Vol. II, pp. 27–94). New York: Wiley.

Kagan, J. (1971). *Change and continuity in infancy.* New York: Wiley.

Kamii, C. K. (1985). *Young children reinvent arithmetic.* New York: Teachers College Press.

Larkin, J. (1983). An information processing approach to teaching about slopes. *Instructional Science, 12,* 232–236.

Lampert, M. (1986a). Teaching multiplication. *Journal of Mathematical Behavior, 5,* 241–280.

Lampert, M. (1986b). Knowing, doing, and teaching multiplication. *Cognition and Instruction, 3,* 305–342.

Leeb-Lundberg, K. (1974). The block builder mathematician. In E. S. Hirsch (Ed.), *The block book.* Washington, DC: National Association for the Education of Young Children.

Maccoby, E. (1986). Social groupings in childhood. Their relationship to prosocial and antisocial behavior in boys and girls. In D. Olweus, J. Block & M. Radke-Yarrow (Eds.), *Development of antisocial and prosocial behavior* (pp. 263–280). New York: Academic Press.

McCall, R. B. (1977). Challenges to a science of developmental psychology. *Child Development, 48,* 333–394.

McLoyd, V. (1980). Verbally expressed modes of transformation in the fantasy of black preschool children. *Child Development, 51,* 113–1139.

National Association for the Education of Young Children (1988). NAEYC position statement on developmentally appropriate practice in the primary grades, serving 5- through 8-year-olds. *Young Children, 43*(2), 64–84.

Olson, D. (1983). "See, Jumping!" Some oral language antecedents of literacy. In H. Goelman, A. Oberg & F. Smith (Eds.), *Awakening to literacy* (pp. 185–192). Exeter, NH: Heinnemann.

Pellegrini, A. D. (1987). The effects of play context on children's verbalized fantasy. *Semiotica, 65,* 285–293.

Pellegrini, A. D., & Boyd, B. (in press). The educational and developmental roles of play in early education. In B. Spodek (Ed.), *Handbook of research on the education of young children.* New York: Macmillan.

Pellegrini, A. D., & Perlmutter, J. (1989). Classroom contextual effects on children's play. *Developmental Psychology, 25,* 289–296.

Pellegrini, A. D., Perlmutter, J., Galda, L., & Brody, G. (1990). Joint book reading between black Head Start children and their mothers. *Child Development, 61,* 443–453.

Piaget, J. (1970). Piaget's theory. In P. Mussen (Ed.), *Carmichael's manual of child psychology* (Vol. 1, pp. 703–732). New York: Wiley.

Reifel, S., & Greenfield, P. M. (1982). Structural development in a symbolic medium: The representational use of block constructions. In G. E. Forman (Ed.), *Action and thought: From sensorimotor schemes to symbolic operations* (pp. 203–205). New York: Academic Press.

Resnick, L. B. (1983). A developmental theory of number understanding. In H. P. Ginsburg (Ed.), *The development of mathematical thinking* (pp. 109–152). Orlando, FL: Academic Press.

Resnick, L. B. (1989). Introduction. In L. B. Resnick (Ed.), *Knowing, learning, and instruction: Essays in honor of Robert Glaser* (pp. 1–24). Hillsdale, NJ: Erlbaum.

Saxe, G. (1988). The mathematics of child street vendors. *Child Development, 59,* 1415–1425.

Shotwell, J., Wolf, D., & Gardner, H. (1979). Exploring early symbolization: Styles of achievement. In B. Sutton-Smith (Ed.), *Play and learning* (pp.127–155). New York: Wiley.

Steffe, L. P. (in press). Children's construction of meaning for arithmetical words: A curriculum problem. In D. Tirosh (Ed.), *Implicit and explicit knowledge: An educational approach.* Norwood, NJ: Ablex.

Sulzby, E. (1988). A study of children's early reading development. In A. D. Pellegrini (Ed.), *Psychological bases of early education* (pp. 39–75). Chichester, England: Wiley.

Suomi, S. J., & Harlow, H. F. (1972). Social verbalization of isolate-reared monkeys. *Developmental Psychobiology, 6,* 487–496.

Vygotsky, L. (1962). *Thought and language.* Cambridge, MA: MIT Press.

Vygotsky, L. (1978). *Mind in society.* Cambridge, MA: Harvard University Press.

Wagner, S. H., & Walters, J. (1982). A longitudinal analysis of early number concepts: From numbers to number. In G. E. Forman (Ed.), *Action and thought: From sensorimotor schemes to symbolic operations* (pp. 137–161). New York: Academic Press.

CHAPTER 4

A View of Materials as the Texts of the Early Childhood Curriculum

Harriet K. Cuffaro

The recurring question raised in discussions on professionalism and teacher preparation is: What shall or should be the knowledge base of teachers? Implicit within this question is a series of further questions that also must be asked. What is it that we want young children to learn? What knowledge do we choose? Which principles guide us as we select both the content and the materials and activities of early childhood curriculum?

A basic premise exists in the perspective of this chapter and in the examination of early childhood curriculum that follows. From my research on the development of certain materials used in early education, I have come to regard materials as the textbooks of early childhood classrooms. Unlike the texts of elementary school, books filled with facts and printed words, early childhood materials/texts are more like outlines. They offer openings or pathways by and through which children may enter the ordered knowledge of the adult world. Materials become tools with which children give form to and express their understanding of the world and the meanings they have constructed. Bringing their experiences and imagination to the potential of the material, children use the outlines they are offered—the solidity of wood, the malleability of clay, the fluidity of paint—and with these author their own texts, create meanings, and make sense of the world. The degree to which children are permitted or invited to contribute to the selection and authorship of knowledge has been and continues to be a recurring theme in early education. From the Froebelian kindergartens to the present, it is in the choices teachers make concerning materials and their use that the nature of the relationship between children and teachers is revealed. Reviewing these curricular choices also allows us to examine the kinds of knowledge early childhood educators have promoted, and a vantage point is offered from which to examine the theoretical and philosophical grounding of practice.

The first part of this chapter deals with the specific, the changes and development of one material, blocks, to illustrate the relationship between materials and the introductory questions concerning aims and knowledge. This is followed by a general examination of psychological theories and societal concerns that have affected the development of curriculum in early education, which in turn then influenced the choices of educators concerning knowledge, materials, and activities.

THE FROEBELIAN BLOCKS

In the English infant schools created by Samuel Wilderspin in the early decades of the nineteenth century, wooden blocks or "bricks" were used with the youngest children in the periods of activity that alternated with time spent in learning the alphabet. Children "were encouraged to build walls and houses and to construct bridges, using the principle of the arch" with wooden blocks that were $4\frac{1}{2}$ inches long, $1\frac{1}{2}$ inches thick, and $2\frac{1}{2}$ inches wide (McCann & Young, 1982, p. 24). These wooden blocks were provided as toys for the pleasurable activity of construction and as a respite from periods of direct instruction.

It is in the kindergarten created by Froebel in Germany during the same period that we find the origin of many of the materials and activities of early childhood curriculum and in which blocks—Froebel's *gifts*—became a central means and text for learning. The gifts consisted of a series of manipulative materials. The first gift, a set of six colored worsted balls, used by mothers with infants and toddlers, was followed by a set of wooden shapes—a sphere, a cube, and a cylinder.

The shapes of many of today's unit blocks may be traced to the two- and three-inch wooden cubes that comprise Froebel's third through sixth gifts. Each of these wooden cubes was divided with varying and increasing complexity to produce smaller cubes, rectangles, oblongs, and triangles. The geometric shapes that resulted were used in a variety of activities on child-sized tables with one-inch grid tops. In their division and in their wholeness, the gifts symbolized Froebel's encompassing vision of the unity and diversity of an ordered universe, a universe that was the living work and manifestation of God (Isaacs, 1969). In Froebel's spiritual view, the aim of each life was to bring forth the divine essence present in each person and to express this essence through creative activity. At the same time, each person was to bring within self the experienced outer world and discover in the diversity and plurality of that world its universal laws, its divinity, and the connectedness of all life (Isaacs, 1969). This philosophical foundation determined the curriculum of the Froebelian kindergarten.

In the hands of young children, the gifts were the unworded texts that were to stir and guide the "hearts and minds" of children to Froebel's vision. In his insightful understanding of the connection between play and learning, he used the natural activities of children as the means by which these texts would be opened and their meanings intuited by the child.

Though highly abstract and symbolic, what Froebel wanted children to know and understand, to be and become, was present in a curriculum explicitly intended to unfold and guide the child's spiritual, mental, physical, and social development through the materials and activities he created. The lawful order, the unity and connectedness, that Froebel sought in the universe, he found in mathematics. His compelling attraction to and love of mathematics led him to create a wealth of activities with the gifts that would lead young children to intuit mathematical principles. He named the work in mathematics "forms of knowledge," knowledge that was important in understanding nature and life.

There were also activities with the blocks in which the child represented and named the world by building objects such as the houses, bridges, beds, and tables found in the child's environment. These representations in which children gave form to their experiences in the world were called "forms of life." The last category of activities in which children formed increasingly intricate, symmetrical patterns with the blocks was named "forms of beauty." These activities were planned to awaken a sense of beauty in children and to offer them opportunities to express their inner essence.

The knowledge to which children were led resided in the mathematical, representational, and aesthetic activities with the gifts. With guidance from the teacher in the form of questions, comments, songs, and modeling, the child participated in a program that also included games, stories, gardening, and activities called "occupations" such as sewing, paper folding, drawing, weaving, and working with clay. In the balance of gift work and occupations, the child's essential nature would unfold in stages. Over time, this curriculum with its specific materials and spiritual goals was changed and amended as it was used to serve a variety of educational aims and causes.

CHANGING TEXTS AND MEANINGS

The kindergarten was introduced in the United States in the period from 1855 to 1876 (Vandewalker, 1971). Froebel's philosophy found a ready response in the idealism of the growing new nation. The sociopolitical conditions and the economic consequences of national growth and expansion gave rise to the proliferation of kindergartens by the last quarter of the nineteenth century. They became an instrument of response to the poverty and illness, the crowded tenements, and the exploited existence of immigrants in cities. Teacher reports from these philanthropic kindergartens reveal that more than one curriculum existed. Eliciting the divine essence of children became secondary to shaping their characters to conform to American standards and values. In the Thirteenth Annual Report of the New York Kindergarten Association (1902–03), the president noted:

> They are children of foreign parentage, born in an atmosphere entirely different from that which the American child breathes. . . . If this army of children, born of foreign parents, saturated with foreign traditions, inheriting foreign prejudices, is to be made an army of American citizens, it must be because the American spirit, in the form of American education, seeks them in the homes in which they live at the earliest moment, and drops the first seeds in their minds. This is precisely what the kindergarten does. (p. 8)

While the Froebelian metaphor of seeds and growth remained, a shift occurred. Now the gardener-educator's task focused on pruning existing growth in order to create the genus *Americanus*.

As the need for kindergartens increased, the training of many teachers became cursory, fragmented, and hurried. Froebel's spirit of experimentation and his honoring of children's play were often supplanted by dull, repetitive routines. Math activities with the gifts resembled drills of military precision. Individual play with the gifts often became group work with teacher demonstrations. Didactic, mindless teaching—a facade of activity disconnected from its philosophical grounding—characterized the life of many kindergartens. These changes did not go unnoticed, particularly among those educators who found in Froebel the philosophical and theoretical principles to guide their work rather than prescriptions to be followed blindly.

Anna Bryan, in a speech to the kindergarten department of the National Education Association in 1890, severely criticized rigid and mindless adherence to a system and warned of the "great danger and temptation of mistaking the schemes of work and the mathematical sequence in gift work as a prescribed, formal line of teaching, instead of as tools to be skillfully and discriminatingly used" (Forest, 1927, p. 174). In the innovative kindergartens she directed in Louisville, in which Patty Smith Hill worked, Anna Bryan moved beyond words to action. She removed many of the occupations, and "children were allowed to play imaginatively with the gifts, making paper dolls to fit the beds made with the third and fourth gifts, and generally considering the gift blocks as toys rather than a sacrosanct collection of symbols" (Forest, 1935, p. 7).

Though it is difficult to establish with certainty, there are many indications that it was Anna Bryan who took the bold step of enlarging the gifts. While Froebel had experimented with and used different sized blocks, a standard form had evolved (Liebschner, 1975). Enlarging the blocks liberated children and teachers from the prescriptive, lockstep sequence of activities that had come to characterize the American kindergarten. Enlarging the blocks expanded their use and increased the opportunities for children to contribute their own themes and meanings to play. Further, the almost sacred aura that had come to characterize the Froebelian materials was challenged. Teachers could see the gifts as materials rather than as a "sacrosanct collection of symbols" with predetermined texts. The enlargement of the blocks altered the scale in which children worked; their activities moved from tabletops to open floor space; and the content and purpose of early childhood curriculum changed fundamentally.

THE PROGRESSIVE'S VIEW OF CHILDREN AND KNOWLEDGE

Innovative approaches to materials and curriculum content were sparked by the imaginative experimentation and independent thinking of Anna Bryan, Patty Hill, Alice Temple, and other kindergartners. Their efforts were supported by the intellectual ferment of the period. The theory of evolution challenged long-established truths and beliefs, and the scientific method of objective investigation provided a new lens for viewing children's development. The kindergarten in particular was affected directly by the work of G. S. Hall and the child study movement, and a new image of the child emerged based on scientific knowledge derived from the new psychology. In the last years of the nineteenth century, another experiment began that would influence greatly the content and activities of early education—John Dewey's Laboratory School at the University of Chicago.

The turn of the century found the field of early education immersed in conflict and debate concerning the aims and practices of education. The proceedings of the International Kindergarten Union during these years record the thinking and questions of teachers concerning children and education. While they were all Froebelians, the more significant labels at this time were whether they were identified as traditional-conservative or liberal-progressive. The debates between these groups reflected the upheaval caused by the newly emerging view of the child and the shift from a spiritual perspective with reliance on symbols and abstractions to a secular view that prized knowledge of the real world. Was growth to be defined as the unfolding and awakening of the essential nature of the child, or was growth the realization of potential and capacity resulting from interaction with the environment? Was play to be free or directed? Was it sparked by a search for universal principles or the interests and curiosity of the child? And in twentieth century America, not Germany in the mid-1800s, what knowledge was worthy of knowing? Often these concerns surfaced in a basic question: How shall the gifts be used? Questions about the *why* of teaching, of necessity, included consideration of the *how* and *what* of learning.

The Dewey Laboratory School

In an outline of the year's curriculum for the four- and five-year-olds at the Dewey Laboratory School, the choices concerning knowledge were clearly evident (Scates, 1900; DePencier, 1967). The curriculum for the youngest group began with discussions about the different members of the family. Reflecting the attitudes and roles of the time, this meant discussing the occupation of the father and the household duties of the mother. From there the children went on to study the interests of their siblings and, in particular, the care of babies.

The attention given to the care, dressing, and feeding of babies gave prominence to dolls and "housekeeping" play. The care of babies is the dramatic play described frequently both at the Laboratory School and in other early childhood settings of this period. The significance of dolls is underscored in notes for a speech presented by Patty Hill (1911) at Teachers College:

> The doll is the hero, the heroine, the centre of dramatic play. . . . In the main the child himself and the doll play the same role. They are Hamlet in the play—the other toys are the setting to further the dramatization of his own life, or through his representative—in toy land—the doll. The doll, thus represents humanity. It is a symbol of humanity—in the best sense of symbol.

Learning about family members led to examining household tasks such as washing, ironing, baking, and cleaning, and these tasks led to occupations outside the home. For example, washing and ironing led to investigating the use of coal, which in turn led to learning about coal yards and wagons. At the center of the curriculum was the family, and from this essential hub spokes led outward into the larger community. Much time was devoted to learning about the interior and exterior construction of homes and the work of the carpenter. Knowledge and skills gained were then used at the workbench. Mathematics grew out of measuring wood to make a doll's bed or the cups of milk and cereal measured to make the daily lunch. Children's knowledge of the social and physical world of family, and of work and interdependencies, was expressed in the models of homes and neighborhoods they constructed with wood, blocks, and cardboard. The materials used tended to be dolls, construction materials, and tools of the real world.

It would be inaccurate to read into this curriculum from 1900 that its only or primary source was the interests of the children, a myth that eventually came to haunt progressive education. Children's interests were shaped and directed by the units of study planned by the teachers, with themes such as family and occupations in the fall and winter, and gardening and outdoor work in the spring. The early progressives were as certain of the knowledge and values they wanted children to acquire as were the traditional Froebelians. They directed children toward knowledge of the workings of society both past and present, focusing the children's attention on social purpose and the interdependent nature of community life. Innovation existed in the fact that once ideas and themes were presented, the initiative and experiences of the children, rather than consistent teacher dictation and modeling, sustained children's work and at times took it in unplanned directions. The materials that were provided were not texts containing predetermined lessons; they were tools with which children could sort, organize, and make sense of the information they were gathering. In the process of constructing their understanding of the social and physical world with open-ended materials, with understanding rooted in their own experience, children would discover connections and relationships. Their purposeful activity was what Dewey said of learning from experience: "an experiment with the world to find out what it is like." And in their "discovery of the connection of things," new questions and problems emerged (Dewey, 1966, p. 140).

Patty Smith Hill and Caroline Pratt

Blocks continued to be a primary material in early education in the first decades of the twentieth century. From private and public school records of teachers and in listings of equipment, reference is made to increasing variety in block sizes and shapes (Scates, 1900; Hunt, 1918). More important than the variety of blocks or their measurement were the leadership that teachers assumed and the initiative they displayed as they accepted the challenge of creating new curricula, curricula more fitting to their social aims and their understanding of children. Two educators who exemplified such leadership and imagination were Patty Smith Hill of Teachers College and Caroline Pratt, who founded the City and Country School in New York City. Each made a fundamental contribution to the content of early education and to the design and development of blocks. The choices they made concerning knowledge and play differed as much as the appearance of the blocks each created.

The first Hill floor blocks in all probability were derived from the original enlargement of the gifts by Bryan in Louisville. The set consisted of seven shapes based on a six-inch unit with the longest block, an oblong, measuring 24 inches in length. During the period when Hill directed the Kindergarten Department at Teachers College, this set was altered in design and dimension. Grooved corner blocks were added in heights of 15 inches to 27 inches into which blocks varying in length from 6 inches to 36 inches would fit. The large structures constructed with these blocks were stabilized by using pegs, copper wire rods, and girders and became houses, post offices, stores, and restaurants into which children entered and in which they dramatized directly their understanding of families and occupations. The size of blocks communicates to children the scale in which they are to work. The size and design of the Hill blocks stated clearly that children were to work directly in the structures they had created together, jointly elaborating a common theme. The group work encouraged by the Hill blocks made them a popular choice for teacher-initiated projects related to community workers, families, and transportation. For example, a trip to the post office provided information on the workings of the system. Books and discussion added further detail. The information gathered formed the basis for constructing a classroom post office in which children then enacted the roles of postal workers and customers.

It is interesting to note the change in Hill's focus on materials in her time at Teachers College, and the opposing pulls, as it shifted gradually from the materials themselves to the children's behaviors when using the materials. Seeking a scientific base for early education and influenced by the work of Thorndike, Hill found in the activities of children with materials—drawing, painting, building— an arena in which to observe and measure behavior. Children's skill in handling blocks, their ability to work cooperatively, and the understandings they demonstrated as they enacted family and occupational roles were now behaviors to be observed, measured, and shaped with scientific accuracy. In the Conduct Curriculum developed by Hill (1923) and her colleagues at Teachers College, "the specifics of desirable behavior became the goals of early childhood education in this curriculum" (Weber, 1984, p. 71). The knowledge children gained was in the realm of socially desired skills and behaviors.

A different view of children's play, knowledge, and materials is offered in the blocks designed by Caroline Pratt. Her unit blocks have remained as the standard blocks used in early childhood settings. In contrast to the Hill blocks, the stability of a structure built with the Pratt blocks is achieved through the skill and architectural understanding of the builder rather than through the placement of pegs and girders. This fact, in combination with the smaller dimensions of the Pratt blocks, communicated to children that the buildings they created would not accommodate their direct participation for prolonged periods of play. While similar themes of home, stores, and occupations also emerged in play with the unit blocks, their smaller size elicited a different type of dramatic play, a form that was intentionally encouraged and supported by Pratt. She created scaled wooden people and animals with which children populated their buildings. With these symbolic representations of self the children revealed their thoughts and feelings in play, telling and acting stories about themselves and the world in which they lived (Pratt, 1971).

In creating these figures, Caroline Pratt offered children a supplementary material to the blocks that increased their freedom to create their own texts and interactions. Rather than one structure in which all children organized and enacted a common theme, now a variety of structures created a common setting, a landscape in which interactions multiplied and various dramas unfolded. In their imaginative play—with the hospitals, garages, homes, jails, castles, and post offices they built—children were at once writers, directors, producers, set designers, and actors on a communal stage (Cuffaro, 1974). The trips Pratt planned became catalysts to awaken questions and thinking that would then be given form in dramatic play.

> We sat for an hour at a time . . . watching the boats coming and going. . . . But the mere accumulation of information was not our purpose . . . to know something and to be able to relate and use that knowledge is the beginning of learning to think . . . after we had discovered some new facts . . . we hurried back to school to put them to use. . . . Here we performed our exercises in thinking, on the floor, with the blocks and toys. Here the children put to use the facts they had acquired, some by asking questions, but most through their own eyes and ears. (Pratt, 1971, pp. 46–47)

In the collaboration between the City and Country School and the Bureau of Educational Experiments, later known as Bank Street College of Education, Pratt worked with Harriet Johnson (1933), who documented the stages of block building, and Lucy Sprague Mitchell (1934), who articulated in great detail the knowledge to which work with blocks could lead. Trips, mapping, stories, and building became a key to enter the interconnected knowledge of social studies.

Blocks as texts have been used to intuit knowledge of universal principles, and they have been used as a means to construct knowledge of the social and physical world. While knowledge of the workings of the real world was the goal of both Hill and Pratt, the outlines they offered children differed. In addition to the size of her blocks, the wooden animals and people created by Pratt made a profound difference. With them the child moved from enactment and imitation of roles to creating situations, contexts in which new texts could be authored and one's view of the world, with its unique questions, could be articulated, shared, and transformed. Over time, blocks serving as texts have been revised by educators to accommodate their particular visions and social purposes.

THE INFLUENCE OF PSYCHOLOGICAL THEORY

From the 1920s on, early education expanded in size, in the variety of settings and sponsorship of programs, and in the ages of the children served. The direction of the field was steered by societal needs, psychological theories, and an increasing desire to attain professional status (Bloch, 1987; Weber, 1984). There was the growing nursery school movement, which included the university laboratory schools doing longitudinal studies of children; programs for young children during the Depression era; and the centers created during World War II. The work of teachers was informed by the maturationist perspective of Gesell and by psychoanalytic theory. Healthy growth could be viewed in terms of norms, the essence of four- or five-year-oldness, and in terms of personality, the conflicts and impulses of the individual. The increased use of testing standardized children and reinforced grouping by chronological age. By examining some of the curriculum books of the next decades, one can see the impact of these influences on early education.

The *Curriculum Guides for Teachers of Children From Two to Six Years* (Andrus & associates, 1937) exemplifies a continuation of the progressive's view of children and education. In contrast to curriculum books that would follow in the coming decades, there is no special section devoted to developmental theory. Rather, knowledge of the child is incorporated, assumed, and made evident in the descriptions of the children and what are noted as their "needs." Children are seen as active, experimenting, curious, social individuals. Dewey's (1963) criteria for learning from experience, his utilization of children's interests, and his focus on the social nature of education are internalized within the authors' perspective. The family, work, and the community continue to be the content of curriculum. The major part of the book, developed by a group of teachers and supervisors in New York State, consists of anecdotal records that are analyzed using certain categories: identification of the interest that initiated the activity and the ages of the children involved; evidence and duration of the children's interest; the teacher's guidance or participation; the activities and learnings that resulted from the initial situation; and notes on possible experiences that may extend the initial interest.

The criteria for selecting materials in the Andrus book unfolds further the educational aims of the authors. Blocks, paints, clay, crayons, sand—the "raw materials," which in the future would be called unstructured materials—are favored because they allow for "creative and challenging use"; provide satisfaction to the child, which is a "foundation for mental health"; and make for "inquiring and experimenting minds." A passage that follows the selection of raw materials offers an interesting contrast to views expressed by earlier progressives about domestic play.

> The housekeeping material provides in a somewhat more limited fashion, for a similar rehearsal of experiences, although, because of its set nature, it invites largely to dramatizations of domestic life. We have definitely avoided too elaborate housekeeping set-up, because we have felt such elaboration is a limitation rather than a challenge to the child's thinking and activity. (Andrus, 1937, p. 286)

By the 1940s and 1950s, the growing psychological orientation of early childhood curriculum became more influential in how curriculum and materials were viewed and used. Katherine Read's *The Nursery School: A Human Relationships Laboratory* (1950), a standard textbook, reflected this influence. Through many editions, a developmental orientation remained constant, with special attention given to the emotional life of the child. The curriculum was guided by the conditions and opportunities that would best promote healthy, balanced emotional growth. The influence of psychoanalytic theory is apparent in the language of the text and the topics chosen for elaboration. Case histories appear throughout the book with titles such as, "Jean, who needed to be messy at the table"; "Sam, who felt big by being hostile." Essentially, the curriculum was to provide the setting, understanding, and opportunities for individual children to resolve conflicts and to support emotional growth. Little space is devoted to materials, to a discussion of their use, other than to state the presence of art, music, science, literature, and trips for social studies. Dramatic play, in which children may reveal their feelings, receives most attention.

In *Understanding Children's Play* (Hartley, Frank & Goldenson, 1952), a psychoanalytic orientation permeates all aspects of curriculum. Children's dramatic play and the materials they use are viewed as being in the service of emotional needs and social development. The benefit of dramatic play was that it offered children opportunities to express feelings, to relieve anxieties, to deal with conflicting impulses, and help in setting the boundaries between reality and unreality. Materials play a key role, for it is through the child's use of materials that the teacher may observe and understand the child's inner conflicts and difficulties. At the same time, it is the materials provided by the teacher that offer the child the means to reduce tension and achieve healthy resolution of conflict. Here materials become the texts with which the teacher may understand children. For children, materials are the tools with which to express complex emotions and needs and relieve anxieties. Understanding the world of work and interdependencies appears secondary to achieving understanding of self.

With time, many early childhood settings became standardized and predictable. There were blocks, paints, crayons, clay, manipulatives, sand, water, and domestic settings for dramatic play. Activity and direct experience were accepted as the ways in which young children learn. Depending on the lens provided by different theories, curriculum and the use of materials were shaped to address particular aspects of development. The child's development became in many instances the rationale for, if not the philosophy of, education. In psychologizing education, in making development a primary aim, the gains obtained were in acquiring a scientific base and the legitimacy of professionalism (Bloch, 1987). What was diminished was the context for educating and a narrowing of the why of teaching and learning. As Popkewitz (1987) has observed, "Questions about school knowledge cannot be derived from questions of psychology or the social sciences. The choice of curriculum involves philosophical, political, and ethical questions" (p. 16).

Another book from this period, but with a much broader perspective, *Teaching Young Children* (Gans, Stendler & Almy, 1952) foreshadows in its organization and focus on content areas the curriculum books that would appear in the coming decades. The range of early education extends from nursery through the primary years in this volume. There is an introductory section on developmental theory and the organization and evaluation of learning experiences; the remainder of the book is devoted to the content of curriculum. The chapters are titled "The child as reader," "The child as speaker, writer, and listener," and "The child as social scientist," "mathematician," "scientist," "artist," and "musician." The last listing is "The child at play." By introducing knowledge domains, with the child personifying the content, from the start, the authors present the child as competent, capable, and in the world. The teacher's task was to create a stimulating environment in which knowledge would be pursued, deepened, and extended. Materials are included in each chapter and their use enriched when the same material, for example, blocks, is discussed as serving the work of the social scientist, the artist, and the mathematician. Materials are seen as means by which children may clarify and reinforce their understanding of the world. For teachers, what children reveal in their use of materials is their information and misinformation and ideas not easily expressed in words. What the teacher is offered is an entry point for clarifying and ordering children's ideas and a view of children's thinking. The development of curriculum was seen as a partnership between teacher planning and guidance and the interests presented by children.

SOCIETAL ISSUES AND MODELS OF EARLY EDUCATION

The events influencing early education in the 1960s and 1970s have been amply documented. In the education models of Head Start and Follow Through, sponsors articulated both their aims in education and the means with which to realize them. The programs served the entire range of early education, from infants and toddlers to the primary grades. Once again, psychology played a dominant role in this massive educational undertaking, since the majority of program sponsors were psychologists. It was the particular theory and emphasis of the sponsors of each model that determined the direction of the curriculum created to meet the needs of children of poverty.

Initially there were 14 models, and by 1970–71, 22 models were operational (Evans, 1975). Not only were there different views of the child as learner, there were also differences in relation to which aspect of development would be emphasized. The intervention and compensatory nature of the programs tended to give primacy to language and cognitive development. Some programs had a behavioral orientation; others facilitated cognitive development; and others stressed "the interrelationships between intellectual processes and social-emotional growth" (Maccoby & Zellner, 1970, p. 30).

Follow Through created the opportunity to influence the curriculum of the primary grades. In the history of early education there is a recurring theme: to bring to the primary years the same activity, experimentation, and the use of materials that existed in the nursery and kindergarten. This long-standing effort became a reality in programs such as the Education Development Center Approach, the Bank Street Program, the Tucson Education Model, and the Cognitively Oriented Approach (Maccoby & Zellner, 1970). The reverse was true in two other models in which an academic skills approach reached down into the kindergarten. The Engelman-Becker Program focused primarily on academic skills, while the

Behavior Analysis Program of the University of Kansas used systematic reinforcement procedures to teach academic skills and the social skills deemed necessary to school success.

How early childhood materials were used and for what purpose were determined by the particular focus and theory of each model. Materials served as tools, as open-ended outlines, as reinforcements. For example, the same material—blocks—was used in the Behavior Analysis kindergarten as a play activity and to be bought with tokens earned during skill work periods. Blocks were present also in the Bank Street Program as one of the means available to children to construct and give form to their understanding of the world. No innovative uses were found for existing materials; no new materials were developed. Rather, what was offered was a panoramic view of how the same materials could be used to serve a variety of aims.

Piagetian theory had an enormous impact during this period and became the rationale for many early education programs. Egocentricity, assimilation, accommodation, and "the construction of knowledge" became the vocabulary of the day. Many of the experiments of Piaget's clinical method were used as classroom activities. Science and mathematics became major curriculum areas. A packaged Piagetian curriculum consisting of materials and a large range of activities and lessons was developed by Lavatelli (1970).

For many teachers the materials found typically in early childhood classrooms were revitalized when viewed from a Piagetian perspective. For example, painting was not only an expressive medium, it also offered physical knowledge; in its representational stage it was an important step on the road to formal operations. Specific activities and games were created to stimulate children's actions on materials and to foster situations of dissonance to generate further questions and experimentation. An important consequence of Piagetian theory was that the early childhood educator's long-standing view of children learning through activity and the use of materials was detailed and substantiated. Early education benefited greatly from Piagetian theory in terms of enlarging its knowledge base and increasing its sense of professionalism. There was also a debit side. While educators expanded their knowledge of children's cognitive development, the focus of the theory narrowed their view of the whole of development and, to some extent, the knowledge to be sought.

Beyond the models, the expanded understanding of cognitive development, and the research findings and reports, what was also learned in this period was our failure as a nation to meet the basic needs of a vast number of children in this country.

THE 1980s: ACADEMICS AND PROJECTS

Though Montessori materials have been in use since the early decades of this century, they are mentioned briefly at this point because of their increasing popularity and the recent appearance of Montessori programs in public kindergartens and primary grades. The Montessori materials offer children varied and contrasting opportunities to discover knowledge of the physical world, its order and dimensionality, through their senses. Knowledge gained through sensorial experience is refined through the repetition and mastery of tasks. A sensorial approach is also applied to teaching reading, arithmetic, and writing through the use of sandpaper letters, beaded rods, and the tracing of letters in rock salt. Using these sensorial materials as texts offers children the freedom to make discoveries through their own manipulation; the materials teach. At the same time, what is to be learned is defined by both the construction of the material and the specific task that is presented.

Throughout the history of American education there are periods marked by educational experimentation and innovation and periods of narrow academic focus. Early education has not been exempt from these recurring cycles. The 1980s were a decade marked by the encroaching presence in the kindergarten of a narrow definition of an academic-skills approach and a major increase in the testing of young children. It was a time of "kindergarten failure" and transitional classes. The idea of "readiness" was replaced by working directly on the acquisition of reading and math skills and the increased use of workbooks. Time for play and the use of materials became increasingly limited and devalued as a time for learning.

The appearance of the computer also may have influenced the resurgence of an academic approach in the 1980s. While many programs allow young children to "draw" or "paint" on the screen, much of the software tends to center on letter recognition, concept formation, and number work. Viewed as a material, the computer appears to offer choice and open possibilities to children as they manipulate keys and objects on the screen. In actuality, choice is determined by the program, a fact not available to the child's examination or manipulation (Cuffaro, 1984). As a new material or tool for early childhood classrooms, the potential of the computer is perhaps best realized in special education, where computers allow young children access to activities previously denied them.

In response to the push for academics and testing in the 1980s, the National Association for the Education of Young Children developed guidelines for developmentally appropriate practice in early childhood programs (Bredekamp, 1987). Basically the aim of the guidelines is to create congruence between our accumulated knowledge of the whole of children's development and the curriculum created for children throughout the continuum of early education, from birth through age eight. Widely publicized, the guidelines serve as a standard for early childhood educators and, further, have influenced policy for early education programs in many states. What is offered is the detailing of the how and when of educating young children, the match between development and classroom activities. The what and why questions of teaching remain open to the choice of individual teachers, whose choices are affected by school requirements as well as their own aims and values.

Another response to academic pressure has been the increasing popularity of a project or theme approach in early education. The project approach presented by Katz and Chard (1989) is also interesting as a bridge between past and present. Their work combines a focus on intellectual functioning—the engaging of children's minds—with methods and practices rooted in the progressive era, in particular the project method of W. H. Kilpatrick. The project approach of the 1980s is similar also to the unit or theme approach described earlier in connection with the Hill floor blocks. Topics with which children are familiar, such as "going to the hospital," "the bus that brings us to school," become the in-depth studies undertaken by children and are based on extensive advance teacher planning. As the authors note, project work refers to a way of teaching and learning as well as to the content of what is taught and learned. Trips, discussion, activity, and materials are essential to the method. In the project approach, materials are tools with which to construct, record, and express one's understanding of a presented theme or topic. Materials are means with which to solidify, connect, and consolidate information gained. What is underlined by the authors is that neither a formal academic program nor the spontaneous play of children is sufficient to engage the minds of children. While a play modality characterizes the many activities of the project approach, a noteworthy distinction is made. "Although informal, project work differs from spontaneous play because the activities are more purposeful, and the teacher has an important role in guiding and facilitating the work undertaken" (Katz & Chard, 1989, p. 45).

PRESENT QUESTIONS AND ISSUES

In addressing what constitutes the knowledge base of teachers, we are also shaping what shall be the curriculum of early education. It seems evident from present discussions that while psychology and developmental theory are necessary to early education, they are insufficient to serve as the foundation on which to base curricular decisions (Silin, 1988; Spodek & Saracho, 1988). What we want children to learn speaks to more than simply development because education strives invariably to promote certain kinds of development. Education is intentional; it has aims. In stating this, it is essential to remember that "education as such has no aims. Only persons, parents and teachers, etc. have aims, not an abstract idea like education" (Dewey, 1966, p. 107).

Throughout the history of early education, connections have been made between education and society. Education has been used as a means to answer the problems of society, and it has also been viewed as a means to change society. In either case, results invariably fall short of expectations because education alone cannot do either. Fundamental change in either society or education depends greatly on what we choose to confront.

Some of the questions and issues raised by the societal upheaval of the 1960s and 1970s are visible in efforts to introduce content into the early childhood curriculum that confronts the racism, sexism, classism, and other "isms" that permeate American society. With heightened consciousness, curriculum content and materials have been examined. When this work began, books, puzzles, games, blocks, and housekeeping accessories were found to reflect a view of the world as white, middle class, able-bodied, and in which men did the important work. This scrutiny led to the development of new puzzles, games, block accessories, and books, many created by teachers, that were nonstereotypic and included, rather than excluded, the diversity of people. The potential of materials, of the tools and outlines offered to children, was enlarged.

In many instances multicultural education has become the larger heading under which a variety of such issues has been included in early education. An excellent analysis of multicultural education by Sleeter and Grant (1987) reveals great variety in aims, methods, theory, and focus among programs. Multiculturalism in early education exists in many forms. Generally, the goals appear to be a celebration of diversity, the acceptance and valuing of differences among people and of definitions of family. These are essential goals in a pluralistic society. At the same time, fundamental questions surface for the teacher. Are issues to be discussed when raised by children's interests and comments or introduced purposely by teachers? As part of the curriculum are issues to be introduced as units or as a perspective permeating all aspects of classroom life? These questions are not new. The history of early education records many situations in which teachers of young children worked as advocates for social change. Such questions are asked whenever situations arise in which a dialogue is created between the values and purposes of teachers and their conceptions of childhood. This balancing of the psychological and the social also is present in current curricular discussions concerning people with AIDS, people who are homeless, people who are poor, and the drugs and violence of our society. What shall, or should, teachers do?

Anti-Bias Curriculum: Tools for Empowering Young Children (Derman-Sparks, 1989), published by the National Association for the Education of Young Children, is one example of the balancing of the social and psychological aspects of curriculum. An understanding of the capacities and abilities of children is combined with a social perspective that permeates the life and activities of the classroom. In this curriculum children are seen as members of and participants in the society in which they live. Finding out about the world also includes knowing about its human problems and dilemmas and learning that one's attitudes and actions in the world have consequences. "Anti-bias teaching requires critical thinking and problem solving by both teachers and children. . . . At heart anti-bias curriculum is about social change" (p. x).

The classroom materials discussed throughout this chapter as the texts and tools of early education appear in the present to be taken for granted, accepted as *the* equipment for early education classrooms, and as such seem to be given little detailed attention. Materials are there because they are supposed to be there, and the *why* of their presence is often a global, generalized response. While this description may appear extreme, its truth is evident when teachers assume that clay, plasticene, and playdough all offer the same learning opportunity and aesthetic experience for children because they are all malleable; or when unit blocks are seen as interchangeable with Lego because both are construction materials; or when teachers talk of painting, experimentation, and creativity and at the same time offer children premixed jars of orange and green paint. Each instance reveals a lack of understanding of the potential and limitation of individual materials and of the opportunities each offers the child. In their taken-for-grantedness, materials become the background against which other activities are introduced. In some instances this describes classrooms in which the foreground is teacher-directed activities, and when these are finished children move into the unhighlighted background of play and materials.

The potential and the power of materials—the opportunities they offer children and the purposes they are to fulfill—lie in the understanding of teachers, because it is they who arrange the space and time in which the materials are to be used. It is teachers who decide whether materials will be used as tools, as open or limited outlines, as "time out" from learning. Children do not make these decisions. What teachers do—the settings they create, the materials they offer, the questions they choose to ask, the time and space they offer children to form their own questions and vision—influences how children view the world and perceive themselves in that world. To understand this is to accept the responsibility that comes with teaching.

> The rhetoric of the professionalization of teaching is grounded primarily in the knowledge base of teaching, not the moral base. . . . Without the specification of the moral principles and purposes of teaching, the concept amounts to little more than a technical performance to no particular point . . . a teacher without moral purpose is aimless. (Fenstermacher, 1990, pp. 132–133)

REFERENCES

Andrus, R., & associates. (1937). *Curriculum guides for teachers of children from two to six.* New York: John Day.

Bloch, M. N. (1987). Becoming scientific and professional: An historical perspective on the aims and effects of early education. In T. S. Popkewitz (Ed.), *The formation of the school subjects: The struggle for creating an American institution* (pp. 25–62). New York: Falmer Press.

Bredekamp, S. (Ed.) (1987). *Developmentally appropriate practice in early childhood programs serving children from birth through age 8* (exp. ed.). Washington, DC: National Association for the Education of Young Children.

Cuffaro, H. K. (1974). Dramatic play: The experience of block building. In E.

S. Hirsch (Ed.), *The block book* (pp. 69–78). Washington, DC: National Association for the Education of Young Children.

Cuffaro, H. K. (1984). Microcomputers in education: Why is earlier better? *Teachers College Record, 85* (4), 559–568.

DePencier, I. B. (1967). *The history of the laboratory schools: The University of Chicago 1896–1965.* Chicago: Quadrangle Books.

Derman-Sparks, L., & the ABC Task Force. (1989). *Anti-bias curriculum: Tools for empowering young children.* Washington, DC: National Association for the Education of Young Children.

Dewey, J. (1963). *Experience and education.* New York: Collier Books.

Dewey, J. (1966). *Democracy and education.* New York: Free Press.

Evans, E. D. (1975). *Contemporary influences in early childhood education* (2nd ed.). New York: Holt, Rinehart & Winston.

Fenstermacher, G. D. (1990). Some moral considerations on teaching as a profession. In J. I. Goodlad, R. Soder & K. A. Sirotnik (Eds.), *The moral dimensions of teaching* (pp. 130–151). San Francisco: Jossey-Bass.

Forest, I. (1927). *Preschool education: An historical and critical study.* New York: Macmillan.

Forest, I. (1935). *The school for the child from two to six.* Boston: Ginn.

Gans, R., Stendler, C. B., & Almy, M. (1952). *Teaching young children.* Yonkers-on-Hudson, NY: World Books.

Hartley, R. E., Frank, L. K., & Goldenson, R. M. (1952). *Understanding children's play.* New York: Columbia University Press. Hill, P. S. (1911). *Toys and books.* Handwritten notes for a speech at Toy Exhibit, Teachers College. From the Patty Smith Hill Collection, Manuscript Department, The Filson Club, Louisville, KY.

Hill, P. S. (1923). *A conduct curriculum for kindergarten and first grades.* New York: Charles Scribner's Sons.

Hunt, J. L. (1918). *A catalogue of play equipment.* New York: Bureau of Educational Experiments.

Isaacs, N. (1969). Froebel's educational philosophy in 1952. In E. Lawrence (Ed.), *Froebel and English education* (pp. 179–233). New York: Schocken.

Johnson, H. (1933). *The art of block building.* New York: Bank Street College of Education Publications.

Katz, L. G., & Chard, S. (1989). *Engaging children's minds: The project approach.* Norwood, NJ: Ablex.

Lavatelli, C. (1970). *Piaget's theory applied to an early childhood curriculum.* Boston: American Science & Engineering.

Liebschner, H. P. J. (1975). *Freedom and play in Froebel's theory and practice.* Unpublished master's thesis, University of Leicester, England.

Maccoby, E. E., & Zellner, M. (1970). *Experiments in primary education: Aspects of project Follow Through.* New York: Harcourt Brace Jovanovich.

McCann, P., & Young, F. A. (1982). *Samuel Wilderspin and the infant school movement.* London: Croom Helm.

Mitchell, L. S. (1934). *Young geographers.* New York: Bank Street College of Education.

Popkewitz, T. S. (1987). The formation of school subjects and the political context of schooling. In T. S. Popkewitz (Ed.), *The formation of the school subjects: The struggle for creating an American institution* (pp. 1–24). New York: Falmer Press.

Pratt, C. (1971). *I learn from children.* New York: Cornerstone Library.

Read, K. H. (1950). *The nursery school: A human relationship laboratory.* Philadelphia: W. B. Saunders.

Scates, G. P. (1900). School reports. The subprimary (kindergarten) department. *The Elementary School Journal, 1*(5), 129–142.

Silin, J. G. (1988). On becoming knowledgeable professionals. In B. Spodek, O. N. Saracho & D. L. Peters (Eds.), *Professionalism and the early childhood practitioner* (pp. 117–134). New York: Teachers College Press.

Sleeter, C. E., & Grant, C. A. (1987). An analysis of multicultural education in the United States. *Harvard Educational Review, 57*(4), 421–444.

Spodek, B., & Saracho, O. N. (1988). Professionalism in early childhood education. In B. Spodek, O. N. Saracho & D. L. Peters (Eds.), *Professionalism and the early childhood practitioner* (pp. 59–74). New York: Teachers College Press.

Thirteenth Annual Report of the New York Kindergarten Association. (1902–03). New York: Scheuter Printing.

Vandewalker, N. C. (1971). *The kindergarten in American education.* New York: Arno Press.

Weber, E. (1984). *Ideas influencing early childhood education.* New York: Teachers College Press.

CHAPTER 5

The Role of Play in the Early Childhood Curriculum

Olivia N. Saracho

The role of play in early childhood education curriculum has shifted over the years. Friedrich Froebel (1782–1852), who originated the kindergarten over 150 years ago, valued play as an important component in children's development and used play in the program he developed (Ransbury, 1982). His curriculum included using manipulative materials (gifts) and craft activities (occupations). The gifts were sets of objects including balls, wooden blocks, and other materials. The occupations included activities such as paper weaving, paper folding and cutting, sewing, and other arts-and-crafts activities. These items symbolized Froebel's fundamental concepts about the unity of the individual, God, and nature.

Froebel (1887) used the word *freedom* in his writing, a term that would suggest a modern conception of play. However, his kindergarten activities were prescriptive, with children following specific instructions in using the materials. Without spontaneity, Froebel's activities would not be considered play today.

At the beginning of the twentieth century, Maria Montessori developed a very different early childhood curriculum—the Montessori Method (Montessori, 1965, 1973). Children in this program also manipulated materials in prescribed ways. These manipulative activities were considered work rather than play.

Both of these approaches to early childhood education used observations of children's play as the source of program ideas. However, each curriculum developer interpreted the observations and abstracted prescribed activities for their curricula. Although the source of activities was children's play, the activities themselves were far from playful.

John Dewey's (1916) view of children's learning was the basis for the contemporary perspective on the educational use of children's play. Dewey broke from earlier views of children's play activities that were rooted in colonial times, when adults admonished children "to avoid the frivolity of play" in order to become more work-oriented as they matured (Hartley & Goldenson, 1963, p. 1). Dewey advocated an education for young children that was embedded in their experience and in the world surrounding them. Play was used to help children reconstruct their experience in order to function at higher levels of consciousness and action (Dewey, 1900). Play was not to be a totally free activity, however. Rather, teachers were to create an environment to nurture children's play that would support desirable mental and moral growth (Dewey, 1916). The modern concept of play as a medium for early childhood education, and especially the valuing of dramatic play, is rooted in progressive education. It made the distinction between play as reflecting the free and natural impulses of children and play as all children's activities. Play was considered an activity done for its own sake, as opposed to work, which is an activity done for external reward or requirement. This does not necessarily mean that play is a frivolous activity. Children's play is a serious activity and an important part of early childhood education (Spodek & Saracho, 1987).

DEFINING PLAY

The word *play* is used in many ways. *Webster's New World Dictionary* (1972) has 59 definitions of play, including: (1) a dramatic performance; (2) an individual playing a musical instrument (a performance); (3) kidding around; and (4) a play on words (a pun). Play, because it can be characterized in so many ways, is actually difficult to define accurately. For many decades educators, psychologists, philosophers, and others have been intrigued with the phenomenon of play. They have attempted to define it, explain it, understand it, create criteria for it, and relate it to other human activities. Because it appears in many forms, the concept of play is difficult to understand. In addition, while play is an activity of young children, adults, and nonhuman animals, it is not necessarily the same for all players.

Researchers have tried to arrive at a consensus on a definition of children's play. However, in spite of all the study, these definitional problems continue (Matthews & Matthews, 1982). Definitions of play include structural definitions (e.g., delineation of typical gestures or movements) as well as functional and causal definitions (e.g., delineation of enjoyable activities without considering the purposes of the activities). Play affects almost every human achievement and is the basis for human culture (Huizinga, 1950).

Smith and Vollstedt (1985) recommended analyzing many characteristics of a play activity rather than focusing on one single feature to identify play behavior in defining play. Many scholars (e.g., Krasnor & Pepler, 1980; Rubin, Fein & Vandenberg, 1983; Spodek, Saracho & Davis, 1991) have suggested sets of criteria to determine children's play behaviors.

Rubin and his associates (1983), for example, define play according to the following criteria:

1. Play is personally motivated by the satisfaction embedded in the activity and not governed either by basic needs and drives or by social demands.
2. Players are concerned with activities more than with goals. Goals are self-imposed, and the behavior of the players is spontaneous.
3. Play occurs with familiar objects, or following the exploration of unfamiliar objects. Children supply their own meanings to play activities and control the activities themselves.
4. Play activities can be nonliteral.
5. Play is free from rules imposed from the outside, and the rules that do exist can be modified by the players.
6. Play requires the active engagement of the players.

There is limited empirical support for characteristics to be used in identifying a play episode. Smith and Vollstedt (1985) tested one set of criteria (intrinsic motivation, nonliterality, positive affect, flexibility, and means/ends of distinctions) to identify a play activity. Their results showed that only three of these criteria were used to determine a play activity. Most observers used a combination of nonliterality, positive affect, and flexibility to rate more than half of the play episodes presented. Intrinsic motivation, interestingly, was disregarded. Apparently, observers viewed play as enjoyable, flexible, and, most typically, as "pretend." These researchers recommended that these criteria become the basis for an acceptable definition of play, even though there are other criteria available. Perhaps the widest set of criteria available should be used to classify children's activity as play.

UNDERSTANDING PLAY

Several theories have been developed to help understand play. Gilmore (1971) categorized the various theories into classical and dynamic theories of play. Classical theories, the older theories, strive to justify the reasons individuals play, while dynamic theories acknowledge the fact that individuals, in effect, play. The classical theories of play include the surplus energy theory, the relaxation theory, the recapitulation theory, and the pre-exercise theory, which are summarized below.

1. *Surplus energy theory.* Organisms constantly accumulate energy, which must be worked out. Play uses up excess retained energy that the body does not need.
2. *Relaxation theory.* Play re-creates the energy that has been used up through work. Therefore, after rigorous work, a relaxing play activity allows the individual to restore energy, which can be used in more work.
3. *Recapitulation theory.* Individuals personally evolve through phases of development that resemble phases in the development of the human race. In an intuitive way, play eliminates those primitive skills and drives conserved by heredity through generations of civilization. Through play, individuals transcend these primitive phases of life and engage in modern life activities.
4. *Pre-exercise theory.* Play is an intuitive mode of preparing children for their roles in adult life. Young children's play activities are comparable to adult experiences, enabling young children to rehearse skills they will need as adults.

These four classical theories justify the basis for play in human activities, but they constitute conflicting pairs. The surplus energy theory and relaxation theory conflict; one theory suggests that play consumes energy, while the other suggests it creates new energy. Similarly, the pre-exercise theory describes play as a way to anticipate the future, while the recapitulation theory reflects the past history of civilization, again a contradiction. Indeed, none of the classical theories provides a satisfactory justification for play in the early childhood curriculum.

Gilmore also identifies two dynamic theories of play, one evolved from psychoanalytic theory, the other from Piagetian theory. In psychoanalytic theory, play serves a cathartic function, allowing children to communicate and thus rid themselves of any distressing feelings. In skillfully playing out distressful situations in pretend play, children overcome emotional pain. This psychodynamic theory of play is based on the work of Sigmund Freud. Freud believed that children could communicate and vanquish their fears and anxieties, without raising them to a level of consciousness, by expressing them in play. Pretend play allows children to cope with those parts of their lives they are having trouble managing directly. Difficult incidents, which are not manageable on their own scale, can be dealt with in a small and uncomplicated play scale. In helping children to communicate adversities and difficulties, play becomes a form of therapy. The language of play parallels the verbal language adults use in psychoanalysis.

Constructivist theory, based on Jean Piaget's work, conceives of two complementary processes allowing children to construct knowledge. In assimilation, individuals acquire information through experiences. This information is assimilated or integrated into the individual's structure of understanding, a scheme in the individual's mind. Information that cannot be integrated into a scheme of understanding or that contradicts the individual's present knowledge leads to the modification of the existing point of view, or an accommodation. The new balance is referred to as equilibrium. Play is a mode of processing information about the outside world and integrating it in the individual's scheme of understanding, which has already been developed through prior experiences.

Play, according to Piaget (1962), allows children to abstract aspects from the outside world and manipulate them in a way that can be adapted into their personal organizational schemes. Therefore, play contributes to the children's emerging intellect and perseveres to a degree in adult intellectual behavior. Theory development denotes a play construct. The theorist suspends reality and deals with hypothetical predicaments, assimilating and accommodating in the process.

Piaget (1962) delineated three discrete levels in play. The first, the sensorimotor stage of infancy, is supported by reflexive patterns of physical behaviors. The second level, symbolic, dramatic, or pretend play, characterizes most preschool and kindergarten children. The third stage, games with rules, is the typical play of older children. As children move through early childhood to the primary grades, they engage more in games but less in dramatic play.

Dramatic or symbolic play is a form of representation. Children represent the outside world and manipulate the elements within it by using the processes of assimilation and accommodation. When children's play reaches the representational level, it becomes an intellectual activity.

In the first stage, sensorimotor play, accommodation is more pronounced. At the beginning of the second stage, symbolic play, assimilation predominates over accommodation, permitting children to personally modify reality by disregarding objective reality (Saracho, 1986). Children's ability to manipulate and change meanings provides them with pleasure in symbolic play (Piaget, 1962). They use different patterns of action without a specific purpose. They enjoy play, adjust to distressing incidents, and master new concepts, skills, and feelings. Thus in play, children challenge themselves and develop opportunities to meet the challenge (Saracho, 1986).

Ellis (1973) suggests another play theory. He uses competence motivation and arousal-seeking to understand play. White's (1959) competence motivation theory suggests that people receive satisfaction from developing competency, disregarding any external rewards in the process. Play develops competency when children effectively control their surroundings.

According to arousal-seeking theory, human beings engage in continuous information-processing activities. Lack of stimuli in an individual's environment creates discomfort, directing him or her to increase any available perceptual information either by seeking it externally or by developing it internally. An overabundance of stimulation can influence individuals to "turn off" their surroundings by attending less to them. Through play, children mediate any available stimulation to fulfill an optimal arousal level.

Within the last few decades, other theories—not all of them new—have surfaced to clarify various aspects of children's play, to simplify the understanding and justify the significance of children's play. Vygotsky (1967) believes that play promotes language and thought development. Children play with meanings and objects. When children use signs and tools during play, they construct mental patterns. Through pretend play children gain higher-order thought processes. In addition, pretend play liberates children from the boundaries of the real world that surround them. Thus, children can manage a difficult situation more effectively through pretend play than they could in reality.

These theories collectively justify children's play as an educational activity. Children participate in a play activity in a natural way. Play helps them to cognitively and affectively understand and express their thoughts and feelings about the world. Through play children gain a feeling of control and command over features of their environment. Children employ symbols, actions, or objects to represent reality. Pretend play allows children to take imaginative journeys that develop their understanding of the world as well as their creativity.

EDUCATIONAL PLAY

Although play is a natural activity of children, occurring in a variety of settings without any adult stimulation, it can have educational consequences. This was intuitively understood by the pioneers in early childhood education. But not all children's play is equally educational. Spodek and Saracho (1987) make the distinction between educational and noneducational play. The difference is not in the activity but in the purposes ascribed to the activity: Educational play is designed to further children's learning. Educational play may be used to help children explore and gain information from their world as well as to process that information to create meaning. It can further physical, social, and intellectual goals and help children better understand and cope with their feelings. Play becomes educational when the teacher, or another adult in a similar role, modifies the spontaneous play of children so that it has educational value.

Educational play begins in infancy when infants in their cribs experience sensorimotor and social experiences; it advances to adulthood with games containing sophisticated rule structures. During their first six years, children's play experiences serve a major function in their knowledge development. Corrigan (1987) describes the sequence of pretend play in children between 14 and 26 months of age. Ito (1989) found that the four-month-old infant enjoys peek-a-boo not for the pleasure of waiting, but because of the mutual empathy with the adult's smile and voice. Being able to understand object permanence and maintain the representation of a person, the six- to eight-month-old infant waits for the reappearance of the hidden adult with the expectation of an empathetic reaction. Cohen (1987) describes the evolution of children's play in early childhood from undifferentiated indiscriminate object manipulation, to functionally appropriate uses of toys, to the emergence of symbolic play and the child's capacity to ascribe idiosyncratic properties to objects and events in order to act out an internalized scenario. Howes and Farver (1987) found that two-year-olds engaged in social pretend play and asymmetrical interaction. In play, children use the knowledge they acquire to construct new ideas. They compare and contrast new information with their old knowledge to reject, confirm, expand, or modify their ideas.

Early childhood programs engage young children in active learning through play experiences that allow them to construct, test, and apply their developing knowledge. There are various kinds of educational play. Spodek (1985) identifies dramatic play, physical play, manipulative play, and games. Dramatic play has cognitive, creative, language, and social dimensions to it (Saracho, 1986).

Dramatic Play

In dramatic play, sometimes called sociodramatic play, children assume adult roles and play out scenarios that they create spontaneously. Dramatic play is symbolic play, since children use objects to stand for things other than themselves and engage in roles in imaginary and realistic ways. Children continuously shuttle back and forth from imaginary to realistic play.

The relationship of dramatic play situations to real-life situations varies. Children's play situations extend from those that symbolize immediate day-to-day situations, such as playing house or games, to situations that are remote from real-life situations, such as playing pirates, cops and robbers, cowboys, or cartoon characters. The context of play can be used to examine a broad range of issues.

Play situations can help children develop intellectual skills. Golomb, Growing, and Friedman (1982) found significance in the combination of pretend play and training to induce successful conserving responses in four-year-old children. The teacher trained the students in conservation and provided a learning environment for pretend play such as developing knowledge, concepts, and skills and knowledge of instructional materials.

The social nature of play also nurtures intellectual development. Children's interactions with their peers in dramatic play require them to process information that differs from their existing knowledge. These differences are often found when two or more children assume roles in re-creating a real-life situation, for example, assuming the roles of family members at the dinner meal or of firefighters putting out a make-believe fire (Christie, 1980, 1982).

Language is one of the symbolic elements of dramatic play. Young children express themselves using symbolic objects (e.g., a doll for a baby or a piece of paper for a blanket) and words (e.g., representing objects with sounds). Both language and objects represent reality and convey meaning in pretend play (Saracho, 1986). Children first manipulate objects to convey thoughts, then they assume a variety of roles to isolate meaning from actual objects (Vygotsky, 1962). During play episodes, young children generally engage in speech play to explore and manipulate the numerous principles in their language, maneuvering their actions with verbal descriptions. Speech play promotes the formation of metalinguistic awareness, which initiates literacy as young children become conscious of the rules in their language. In pretend play, young children verbally encode play role transformations and object transformations (Pellegrini, 1982).

Schrader (1989) found that children write and read what they write during their participation in sociodramatic play. She also found that the purposes of children's writing were instrumental, regulatory, interactional, personal, and informational. However, they did not write for imaginative or heuristic purposes. In a longitudinal study, Ogura (1988) found positive correlations between the number of different words and the percentage of occurrence in pretend self-play, pretend other play, and the total of symbolic play. The emergence of the first word corresponded to the onset of functional-relational manipulation and container-relational manipulation.

Garvey and Kramer (1989), reviewing the literature on the language of social pretend play, identified differences that exist in the linguistic forms and expressions children use in pretend play as opposed to nonpretend activities. They also identified age-related differences in preschool children's language in their social pretend play.

Block play sometimes has the attributes of dramatic play. In the early stages of block play, children simply manipulate the blocks, piling them up, creating enclosures, and the like. In these stages the blocks themselves become the focus of children's play. After a while, however, blocks take on a more symbolic function. Children then use block structures to represent something else: a house or an airplane, for example. Functionally, this type of play takes on many of the attributes of dramatic play, with the exception that in working with unit blocks, the children do not become the players. Instead they manipulate dolls, play figures, and other small pieces of apparatus just as children manipulate puppets in a puppet show, staying outside the play, but engaging in it.

Physical Play

In addition to representational or pretend play, children engage in many forms of nonrepresentational play. Chafel (1987) provided an overview of the research on young children's achievement of knowledge about self and others through the use of physical objects and social fantasy play. Her review describes how young children make social comparisons during two types of play activity (i.e., physical object and social fantasy play).

Physical play takes place both out-of-doors and in the classroom. Local climate may place limits on, as well as create opportunities for, outdoor play. In addition, particular play settings encourage certain types of play. Outdoor play areas have apparatus that allow digging, running, riding wheel toys, and climbing, for example. These are activities not generally supported indoors. Thus, more physical play, including rough-and-tumble play and super-hero play—forms of physical play that may have dramatic content—often occurs in the outdoor area (Scales, 1987).

Manipulative Play

Play with manipulative materials allows children to learn from their sensorimotor experiences. Many of the Montessori materials, for example, are designed to allow children to manipulate them in order to learn to seriate, compare, and contrast sensorimotor experiences. They are also used to teach children practical skills, such as fastening clothing, preparing food, and washing apparatus.

Nursery school educators picked up on the use of manipulative materials to enhance children's learning. In addition to the Montessori-type materials, one also finds parquetry puzzles, nesting and stacking toys, a variety of construction sets, and materials designed to teach mathematical concepts of quantity and shape to children. There is a general sense that these materials are educationally useful and are seen as the backbone of math and science programs for young children.

Games

Games represent the third of Piaget's stages of play. Games for young children should have simple, uncomplicated rules. They can be physical games, which require children to follow specific directions and sequences of action, such as games of tag or hiding games. They could also be board games or card games, which are more sedentary. Such games require specific play materials. Kamii and DeVries (1980) suggest that educationally useful games (1) provide a challenge for children, (2) allow children to judge their own success, and (3) permit all children to participate actively throughout the game.

SUPPORTING THE PLAY CURRICULUM

In order for teachers to use educational play to support their curricula, they must be aware not only of their goals, but also of how they can use play resources to further these goals. Teachers need to become aware of the various elements of play and sensitive to the uses they can make of each of these elements. Guidance of play always needs to be responsive to the play activities themselves, for if the activity is distorted or the control is taken away from the children, the activity ceases to be play. The elements of play include the children (players), the materials with which they play (toys), and the play setting (space inside and outside the classroom). The teacher, as guide, is also an important element.

Children as Players

The play of children is not all alike. Gender and age differences have been found in children's play. Although Pinkett and Quay (1987) found no differences in the cognitive play types and no racial differences for people and object orientation, they did find that boys were involved more often than girls in the highest level of social interaction. Black (1989) found sex and age differences in preschool children's social and symbolic play. Girls spent more time discussing issues concerning taking turns and having conversational dialogues. Girls and younger boys favored topics related to daily incidents, while older boys favored fanciful topics. Younger children depended more than older ones upon props and themes of daily incidents. Boys preferred to participate more in solitary pretend play. Howes and Farver (1987) found that two-year-olds participated more in social pretend play with older partners than with same-age partners. During mixed play sessions, two- and five-year-olds participated in asymmetrical interaction. In addition, five-year-olds utilized comparable social behaviors with same-age and younger partners. Howes (1988) also found that preference for same-sex playmates was strongest with the oldest girls. Boys either ignored or refused girls' initiations if the initiations assumed the form of specific requests to play a game in contrast to a more general approach. Holloway and Reichart-Erickson (1988) examined child care quality related to children's free-play behavior and social problem-solving skills. Relationships were found between the quality of interaction with teachers, arrangement of the physical space, and spaciousness of the environment and children's involvement in solitary play and the use of their knowledge to solve social problems.

Teachers need to observe children's play behaviors carefully. Information about gender or age can provide the teacher with indicators to look for, but our knowledge of children tells us that there is great variability among groups of children, even when there are strong indicators of central tendencies. In addition, the quality of the early childhood environment will influence children's play.

Play Materials

Toys are the tools children use in play. Young children utilize play materials differently according to their age (Westby, 1980). Consequently, age should be a criterion for selecting toys. The preschool setting, for example, usually includes an assortment of toys that are suitable for young children, such as miniature toys representing objects (e.g., dolls, doll furniture, wagons, engines) and symbolizing the children's lives. Such toys (1) assist the children in assuming various roles or in dramatizing adult experiences, (2) supply young children with information and meaning, and (3) help children understand the social life surrounding them by allowing them to assume a variety of roles and access others' thoughts and feelings.

Research evidence suggests that the quality and quantity of play materials influence the types of play children engage in (Rubin, Fein & Vandenberg, 1983). Children engage in solitary play, for example, when using playdough, clay, and sand and water, while the use of art construction material leads to constructive, nonsocial play. The ratio of realistic to nonrealistic play materials also affects dramatic play. Younger children are encouraged by realistic materials, and older children are encouraged by nonrealistic materials (McLoyd, 1986). Carefully stocking the classroom with particular types of play materials will help teachers influence children's play and help to achieve desired educational goals.

Play Settings

Research data, as noted above, confirm that high-quality play environments are conducive to academic learning and support young children's development. Teachers need to design indoor and outdoor play settings that provide adequate space for desired children's play. Many early childhood educators (e.g., Spodek, Saracho & Davis, 1991) recommend that early childhood classrooms be organized into activity centers. Each center would provide adequate space and include appropriate materials and equipment to support one kind of educational play. While such an arrangement is generally desirable, care must be taken that the centers do not lead to a fragmentation of the curriculum and that maintenance of the centers does not become an end in itself.

Similarly, Frost and Klein (1983) suggest that outdoor play space be organized into zones to support different kinds of play. Frost and Wortham (1988) additionally suggest that outdoor play space allow for activities similar to those found in indoor curriculum areas.

However the classroom and outdoor area are organized, careful attention must be given to safety factors and the need to supervise all play areas.

Teachers' Roles

When teachers promote children's play, they sometimes serve as facilitators and sometimes as participants. As a facilitator, the teacher selects, organizes, and presents objects, materials, and props and conceives experiences regarding designated concepts or themes. Teachers intervene to supplement any critical elements of play that are scant. The intervention should revitalize, clarify, and expand the play, but it should not manage the activities. Before intervening, teachers must systematically observe the children's play to identify the critical elements the children may be lacking and assess how the children assume roles and manipulate pertinent props and language.

A variety of play training studies have been conducted over the past few years that demonstrate that teacher intervention in play significantly affects the children's learning. In spite of the many studies conducted, it is difficult to assess what in the intervention has contributed the most to children's learning. The influence of peer contact, adult contact, and the play activities themselves might all be contributing factors, but it is uncertain which is the most important (Christie & Johnson, 1983). In spite of this, there is ample evidence to suggest that play interventions can extend children's play and enhance their learning.

Smilansky (1968) identified two sorts of interventions that teachers can use to extend children's play: (1) providing suggestions and questions from outside the play, and (2) participating in play, assuming a role, and modeling correct play behaviors. She also found that a combination of adult play-tutoring and excursions was effective. Smilansky's interventions have been adopted by other researchers whose studies have yielded positive results (e.g., Freyberg, 1973; Smith & Syddall, 1978; Dansky, 1980).

While all teachers intervene in children's play activities, not all do so consciously and deliberately. Some teachers value child-initiated activities more than adult-initiated activities. They may see their primary role as setting the stage for play, a form of intervention. But once the child begins to play, the child's curriculum takes precedence over the teacher's. Rothlein and Brett (1987) found that teachers perceived play both as fun and as an opportunity for cognitive and social development. Sylva, Roy, and Painter (1980) found that teachers view play as the children's business; teacher intervention would disturb the play situation, altering the progression of play and impeding children's ability to distinguish reality from fantasy. Smilansky (1968) found that teachers were reluctant to intervene in children's play, disregarding research that justifies such teacher intervention.

Two types of interaction styles have been identified among teachers: an extending style and a redirecting style (Tamburrini, 1986). In the extending style the teacher first determines the purpose of children's play and then interacts with the children within a play progression. For example, if children encounter a problem, by extending their play, teachers will help children solve it. Teachers may also help children use their imaginations in their play, believing that there is a relationship between play and imaginativeness. In this case, teachers may select strategies to help children be more inventive or less repetitive, or to elaborate a theme. Their assessment of play may include (1) diagnosing the children's purposes, which is a crucial requirement of this style, and (2) measuring the quality of the children's imaginativeness in their play, to promote their imaginativeness.

In the redirecting style, teachers use their own preconceptions and curriculum priorities to focus the children's concentration on some element in their play. For example, in a play episode, if children build a structure with blocks, the teacher might intervene by asking the children to measure the height of the structure they built. In redirecting, teachers usually resist play activities and direct the children into other kinds of nonplay activities (e.g., exploration or demanding that children log the consequences of their activities). Teachers use redirecting to exploit what they regard as incidental learning, because they believe this supports intellectual development. They assume that children are learning even though they are not conscious of their actions.

Initiating Children's Play.   In initiating children's play, teachers create settings and stimulate children to engage in a particular type of play. The teacher may initiate play activities by providing children with attractive play materials and reasonable play opportunities and by offering some novelty. A short planning period before playtime can help children know what is available and what is expected of them in their play areas. In addition, the planning session provides an opportunity to familiarize children with new pieces of equipment or new toys and their purposes, uses, and limitations.

Children's interest can be aroused by presenting variety and novelty in play activities. This can be accomplished by offering children new play materials or by presenting existing materials in new forms. Teachers can reorganize or relocate the block area, create new signs in the dramatic play area, or add a few new materials to reconstruct an old activity into a splendid new activity. A new play activity should arouse children's interest and imagination. Activities that contribute to children's knowledge such as taking them for a walk through the neighborhood, reading a book to them on a specific play topic, or showing them a film will also arouse interest in a play theme.

Extending Children's Play. Teachers can extend children's play in a variety of ways. Sometimes teachers may join in the children's play, although teachers must be careful to continually foster children's independence and minimize intervention. They should not become the focus of attention or the major source of play ideas, because this can limit the children's play initiatives. Teachers must calculate the consequences of their actions; they must be sensitive to the children's play.

A number of studies have shown how teachers intervene in children's play. Spidell (1986) noted that teachers generally intervene under four conditions:

1. When there is a breech of discipline and children harm themselves or others, misuse materials, or violate rules.
2. When a teacher judges a child to be isolated and at social risk.
3. When a child requests that a teacher intervene.
4. When a teacher, after some observation, acts to enrich play.

Spidell also found that teachers use eight different intervention strategies: instruction (telling a child how to engage in play), demonstration (showing a child how to engage in play), praise (showing a child approval), conversation (talking with a child), maintenance (doing something to keep the play going), environmental modification (changing the play setting), participation (joining in the play), and redirection (moving a child into a different activity). In general, these interventions change children's play, with redirection—the most extreme—removing a child from one play setting into another.

Shin (1991) adopted Spidell's (1986) categories with two additions, coaching and command, to study the relationship between types of interventions and children's play patterns. She found that teachers used different patterns of play interventions in different play settings. This suggests that teachers may be aware of the consequences of different interventions and use them selectively. Preferences for play interventions may depend on teachers' educational philosophies or their personal teaching styles. While we know that different intervention strategies are used by teachers, there is still no information regarding the specific consequences of each of the strategies on children's play.

Young children's play behavior is transformed as they grow. Teachers need to observe children's play behaviors to know the level at which children are playing. Once teachers have made this assessment, they can generate play interventions, adjust the setting, include new materials, or moderately engage in the children's play to clarify concepts. Teachers must be careful that their interventions do not constrain children to become more conscious of reality or of the teacher's authority. Teachers can support young children's play by accepting children's existing play patterns. Children who have decided not to participate in play activities must be released from this pressure and provided with alternative activities.

CONCLUSION

In the American culture, where the work ethic persists, play is regarded as a frivolous activity, without any serious consequences. Although this view is not supported by research, it does influence the early childhood curriculum. In some early childhood classes, the cultural belief that learning results from work leads teachers to establish a work curriculum. In early childhood classrooms, play is justified by characterizing it as "child's work." In fact, play—even though it is fun and fanciful—can have important educational consequences for young children. Play helps young children learn about their world.

The teacher's role is critical in the play curriculum. Appropriate arrangement, interpretation, and intervention strategies can encourage and expand the children's involvement in play, which ultimately promotes their learning. Teachers need to observe children play, acquire insight about the children's perceptions of their world, and develop strategies to facilitate children's learning. Teachers must assume the role of *facilitators* of learning through play rather than *directors*. Children must learn complex concepts to live successfully in modern society. Teachers can provide young children with the kinds of play experiences that help them to assimilate and accommodate knowledge. In designing a curriculum for young children, teachers must utilize play as a learning medium (Spodek & Saracho, 1987).

An effective play curriculum requires teachers to (1) provide a supportive environment with enough play areas, materials, and equipment; (2) nourish positive social interactions; and (3) complement children's play to make it more productive. Teachers must understand the consequences of the different forms of play that are relevant to young children.

REFERENCES

Black, B. (1989). Interactive pretense: Social and symbolic skills in preschool play groups. *Merrill-Palmer Quarterly, 35,* 370–397.

Chafel, J. A. (1987). Achieving knowledge about self and others through physical object and social fantasy play. *Early Childhood Research Quarterly, 2,* 27–43.

Christie, J. F. (1980). The cognitive significance of children's play: A review of selected research. *Journal of Education, 62*(4), 23–33.

Christie, J. F. (1982). Sociodramatic play training. *Young Children, 37*(4), 25–32.

Christie, J. F., & Johnson, E. P. (1983). The role of play in social-intellectual development. *Review of Educational Research, 53*(1), 93–115.

Cohen, D. (1987). *The development of play.* New York: New York University Press.

Corrigan, R. (1987). A developmental sequence of actor-object pretend play in young children. *Merrill-Palmer Quarterly, 33,* 87–106.

Dansky, J. L. (1980). Cognitive consequences of sociodramatic play and exploration training for economically disadvantaged preschoolers. *Journal of Child Psychology and Psychiatry and Allied Disciplines, 21*(1), 47–58.

Dewey, J. (1900). Froebel's educational principles. *Elementary School Record, 1,* 143–145.

Dewey, J. (1916). *Democracy and education.* Carbondale, IL: Southern Illinois University Press.

Ellis, M. (1973). *Why people play.* Englewood Cliffs, NJ: Prentice Hall.

Froebel, F. (1887). *The education of man.* New York: Appleton-Century.

Freyberg, J. T. (1973). Increasing the imaginative play of urban disadvantaged kindergarten children through systematic training. In J. L. Singer (Ed.), *The child's world of make-believe: Experimental studies of imaginative play* (pp. 129–154). New York: Academic Press.

Frost, J. L., & Klein, B. L. (1983). *Children's play and playgrounds.* Austin, TX: Playgrounds International.

Frost, J. L., & Wortham, S. C. (1988). The evolution of American playgrounds. *Young Children, 43*(5), 19–28.

Garvey, C., & Kramer, T. L. (1989). The language of social pretend play. *Developmental Review, 9,* 364–382.

Gilmore, J. B. (1971). Play: A special behavior. In R. E. Herron & B. Sutton-Smith (Eds.), *Child's play* (pp. 343–355). New York: Wiley.

Golomb, C., Growing, E. D. G., & Friedman, L. (1982). Play and cognition: Studies of pretense play and conservation of quantity. *Journal of Experimental Child Psychology, 33,* 257–279.

Hartley, R., & Goldenson, R. (1963). *The complete book of children's play.* New York: Crowell.

Holloway, S. D., & Reichart-Erickson, M. (1988). The relationship of day care quality to children's free-play behavior and social problem-solving skills. *Early Childhood Research Quarterly, 3,* 39–53.

Howes, C. (1988). Same- and cross-sex friends: Implications for interaction and social skills. *Early Childhood Research Quarterly, 3,* 21–37.

Howes, C., & Farver, J. (1987). Social pretend play in 2-year-olds: Effects of age of partner. *Early Childhood Research Quarterly, 2,* 305–314.

Huizinga, J. (1950). *Homo Ludens: A study of the play-element in culture.* London: Routledge & Kegan Paul.

Ito, R. (1989). Why an infant enjoys the peek-a-boo game. *The Research Institute for the Education of Exceptional Children Report, 38,* 99–103.

Kamii, C., & DeVries, R. (1980). *Group games in early education: Implications of Piaget's theory.* Washington, DC: National Association for the Education of Young Children.

Krasnor, L. R., & Pepler, D. J. (1980). The study of children's play: Some suggested future directions. In K. H. Rubin (Ed.), *New directions in child development: Children's play* (No. 3, pp. 85–96). San Francisco: Jossey-Bass.

Matthews, W. S., & Matthews, R. J. (1982). Eliminating operational definitions. In D. J. Pepler & K. H. Rubin (Eds.), *The play of children: Current theory and research* (pp. 21–30). Basel, Switzerland: Karger AG.

McLoyd, V. (1986). Scaffolds or shackles? The role of toys in preschool children's pretend play. In G. G. Fein & M. S. Rivkin (Eds.), *The young child at play: Reviews of research* (Vol. 4, pp. 63–77). Washington, DC: National Association for the Education of Young Children.

Montessori, M. (1965). *Dr. Montessori's own handbook.* New York: Schocken. (Original work published 1914)

Montessori, M. (1973). *The Montessori method.* Cambridge, MA: Bently.

Ogura, T. (1988). A longitudinal study of relationship between early language development and manipulation of objects and play development. *Japanese Journal of Educational Psychology, 36,* 19–28.

Pellegrini, A. (1982). Preschoolers' generation of cohesive text in two play contexts. *Discourse Processes, 5,* 101–107.

Piaget, J. (1962). *Play, dreams and imitation in childhood.* New York: Norton.

Pinkett, K. E. L., & Quay, L. C. (1987). Race versus social class: Social orientation and cognitive play in black and white middle SES preschool children. *Journal of Applied Developmental Psychology, 8,* 343–350.

Ransbury, M. K. (1982). Friedrich Froebel 1782–1852: A reexamination of Froebel's principles of children's learning. *Childhood Education, 59,* 104–106.

Rothlein, L., & Brett, A. (1987). Children's, teachers', and parents' perceptions of play. *Early Childhood Research Quarterly, 2,* 45–53.

Rubin, K. H., Fein, G. G., & Vandenberg B. (1983). Play. In E. M. Hetherington (Ed.), *Handbook of child psychology: Vol 4. Socialization, personality, and social development* (pp. 698–774). New York: Wiley.

Saracho, O. N. (1986). Play and young children's learning. In B. Spodek (Ed.), *Today's kindergarten: Exploring the knowledge base, expanding the curriculum* (pp. 91–109). New York: Teachers College Press.

Scales, B. (1987). Play the child's unseen curriculum. In P. Monighan-Nourot, B. Scales, J. Van Horn & M. Almy, *Looking at children's play: A bridge between theory and practice* (pp. 89–115). New York: Teachers College Press.

Schrader, C. T. (1989). Written language and use within the context of young children's symbolic play. *Early Childhood Research Quarterly, 4,* 225–244.

Shin, E. (1991). *The relationship between types of teacher intervention and preschool children's play.* Paper presented at the annual meeting of the American Educational Research Association, Chicago.

Smilansky, S. (1968). *The effects of sociodramatic play on disadvantaged preschool children.* New York: Wiley.

Smith, P. K., & Syddall S. (1978). Play and non-play tutoring in preschool children: Is it play or tutoring which matters? *British Journal of Educational Psychology, 48*(3), 315–325.

Smith, P. K., & Vollstedt, R. (1985). On defining play: An empirical study of the relationship between play and various play criteria. *Child Development, 56,* 1042–1050.

Spidell, R. A. (1986). *Preschool teachers' interventions in children's play.* Unpublished doctoral dissertation, University of Illinois.

Spodek, B. (1985). *Teaching in the early years* (3rd ed.). Englewood Cliffs, NJ: Prentice Hall.

Spodek, B., & Saracho, O. N. (1987). The challenge of educational play. In D. Bergen (Ed.), *Play as a learning medium for learning and development: A handbook of theory and practice* (pp. 1–22). Portsmouth, NH: Heinemann.

Spodek, B., Saracho, O. N., & Davis, M. D. (1991). *Foundations of early childhood education* (2nd ed.). Englewood Cliffs, NJ: Prentice Hall.

Sylva, K., Roy, C., & Painter, M. (1980). Adults at play. In D. J. Wood (Ed.), *Working with under fives* (pp. 127–161). London: Grant McIntyre.

Tamburrini, J. (1986). Play and the role of the teacher. In S. Burroughs & R. Evans (Eds.), *Play, language and socialization: Perspectives on adult roles* (pp. 39–47). New York: Gordon and Breach.

Vygotsky, L. S. (1962). *Thought and language.* Cambridge, MA: MIT Press.
Vygotsky, L. S. (1967). Play and its role in the mental development of the child. *Soviet Psychology, 12,* 62–76.
Webster's New World Dictionary: Second College Edition. (1972). New York: World.
Westby, C. E. (1980). Assessment of cognitive and language abilities through play. *Language, Speech, and Hearing Services in Schools, 11,* 154–168.
White, R. F. (1959). Motivation reconsidered: The concept of competence. *Psychological Review, 66,* 297–333.

CHAPTER 6

Current Technology and the Early Childhood Curriculum

Douglas H. Clements

More than a decade ago, the microcomputer entered the school arena. We have since seen phases of curiosity, enthusiasm, fear, and apathy come and go. Present-day emotions may lack the intensity of past debates, but the issues are real and important. Despite a decline of popular attention, computers are increasingly being integrated into the homes and classrooms of young children (Goodwin, Goodwin & Garel, 1986; Lieberman, 1985). Fortunately, our knowledge regarding the use of computers is surprisingly rich, given their short existence.

UNDERSTANDING COMPUTER TECHNOLOGY FOR YOUNG CHILDREN

Research shows that children approach computers with comfort and confidence and appear to enjoy exploring this new medium (Clements & Nastasi, in press). While a computer with a keyboard and monitor (screen) is familiar to many children and teachers, there are now many other devices that attach to computers, such as a joystick or a mouse (a box-shaped input device rolled to move the screen pointer and clicked to select or move screen objects). Which are most appropriate for young children?

An early concern was that the standard keyboard would be too small and disorganized. However, research and practice indicate that using the standard keyboard is not problematic for young children. In fact, typing appears to be a source of motivation and competence for many—they like to emulate adults (Borgh & Dickson, 1986b; Hungate & Heller, 1984; Lipinski, Nida, Shade & Watson, 1986; Muller & Perlmutter, 1985). The alphabetization of the keyboard is not usually helpful. Most young students do not have a high-level mastery of alphabetization. More important, they tend not to use alphabetical order when locating keys, often preferring spatial search strategies.

One then might ask whether young children can or should learn touch typing. Research appears to indicate that instruction can improve keyboarding skills of children in kindergarten through second grade (Britten, 1988). Touch typing, however, does not appear to increase benefits from language arts computer activities (Clements & Nastasi, in press). The recommendation is not to directly teach keyboarding skills to young children. If one does, emphasis should be on familiarization and on the typing of ideas rather than on speed. For the best effect, the optimal ratio is one keyboard to every one or two children.

Certain other input devices are worthwhile additions to the basic keyboard. For instance, young children find using a mouse intuitive and easy. Ideal for tasks such as painting, it is also excellent for selecting items on the screen. Other devices, such as touch screens and joysticks, are adequate for certain kinds of tasks.

Even preschool children can handle more than these input devices. They can learn to turn the computer on and off, remove and replace diskettes properly, follow instructions from a picture menu, use situational and visual cues in the aid of reading, and talk meaningfully about their computer activities (Hess & McGarvey, 1987; Watson, Chadwick & Brinkley, 1986).

Using Computer Software

More important than children's use of hardware is their ability to interact meaningfully with computer programs. Research indicates that preschool children can use software requiring only one or two character keystrokes. Although three-year-olds take longer to acclimate to the keyboard than five-year-olds (Sivin, Lee & Vollmer, 1985), there are no major differences between the way younger and older preschoolers use computers (Essa, 1987; Lewis, 1981). Some researchers recommend that three years of age is an appropriate time to introduce a child to discovery-oriented software. Others suggest that even two-year-olds might be introduced to simple single-key-stroke software, mainly for developing positive attitudes (Shade & Watson, 1987). Whether benefits from very early use are substantive or lasting, however, is an open question.

Older boys have more access to computers, own more computers, and use computers more frequently and with more control than do girls (Lieberman, 1985). Some studies have reported similar trends for the early years (Beeson & Williams, 1985; Klinzing & Hall, 1985). Most researchers, however, report that young girls and boys do not differ in the amount or type of computer use (Hess & McGarvey, 1987; Hoover & Austin, 1986; Lipinski et al., 1986; Muller & Perlmutter, 1985; Shade, Nida, Lipinski & Watson, 1986; Swigger, Campbell & Swigger, 1983). On this basis, many have recommended that children be introduced to computers during the early years.

Once the decision is made to use computers, appropriate software should be considered. Software can be classified into four basic types, not all of which are equally appropriate for young children.

Drill Software.   Drill software provides knowledge and practice on skills to help students remember and use what they have been taught. Drill programs should be designed to increase automaticity in essential skills. They should emphasize accuracy and speed, present only a few items at once, keep sessions short and spaced, and dynamically adapt instruction to the child. Preschool children do not learn best from drill (Haugland & Shade, 1990; Clements & Nastasi, 1985). Even older primary grade children should receive as much practice as possible in the context of higher-level experiences such as real reading, writing, and mathematical problem solving (Clements, 1985).

Tutorial Software.   Tutorial software teaches new subject-matter content. It attempts to interact with a student in the way a teacher would in a one-to-one situation. Few presently available tutorials adequately interact with young children, and most suffer from the same weaknesses as drill software.

Simulations.   Simulations are models of some part of the world. Games such as Life and Monopoly are simulations. Simulations should not replace hands-on activities. Some simulations, however, allow greater control of a situation (e.g., a pendulum swinging) than do real objects. In such a case, careful comparison of a simulation and a real-world event may benefit elementary school children (Clements, 1989). Similarly, simulations of events such as running a store or making ethical decisions when faced with a simulated classroom social problem may lead to conjectures and discussions. Used carefully and critically, simulations can help children explore and develop intuition about events and situations that are too dangerous, expensive, complex, or time-consuming to experience directly. If the teacher facilitates transfer, they may promote decision-making, problem-posing, and problem-solving abilities. These first three types of software are often called computer-assisted instruction (CAI).

Instructional Games and Exploratory Software. "Games" here do not mean drills transplanted to an outer-space setting. In true instructional games, the concepts to be learned are intrinsic to the structure and content of the game. For example, in one program children learn about coordinates by selecting points on a grid to create a picture. Such computer games can be intrinsically motivating. Three features are especially important in engendering this motivation: challenge, fantasy, and curiosity (Malone, 1980). These are consistent with sound early childhood practice. In other exploratory programs, children might paint, construct robot pictures out of given shapes, or move animated pictures and type text to tell a story. Such activities encourage problem solving and planning.

Selecting Appropriate Software

Software, like hardware, should be selected according to sound educational principles. Preschool children respond correctly more often using software that incorporates such principles. Research suggests the following:

• Actions and graphics should provide a meaningful context for children. Programs should make sense by reflecting the young child's world.

• Reading level, assumed attention span, and way of responding should be appropriate for the age level. Instructions should be clear, such as simple choices in the form of a picture menu. Using speech synthesis to provide voice assistance is often helpful for the youngest children. After initial adult support, children should be able to use the software independently. There should be multiple opportunities for success.

• Feedback can also help extend children's attention span. Young children stay on task longer when they receive feedback concerning their progress in a computer lesson; for example, a graphic display indicating how far they have progressed (Hungate & Heller, 1984). Global feedback, in the form of a long-range, visible goal, enhances children's involvement.

• Children should be in control. They should be able to modify, move, and rearrange any and all parts of what they are creating. They should have an "undo" function that shows the "undoing" action, thus embodying the important Piagetian concept of reversibility (Kuschner, 1985). They need to use and see continuous transformations. In addition, children prefer programs that give them a feeling of control over the computer through animation, problem solving, and interactivity (Lewis, 1981; Shade et al., 1986; Sivin et al., 1985).

• Children should be able to see the results of their efforts. Favorite software often provides a print option or at least the chance to save work on a computer disk.

• Software should allow children to create, program, or invent new activities. It should have the potential for independent use but should also challenge. It should be flexible and allow more than one correct response. As with all instructional activities, the nature of computer activities should change with age and with individual needs (Haugland & Shade, 1990).

• Finally, the computer should be a means, not an end. Do not waste time merely exposing children to the computer. Use technology when it makes a special contribution to children's learning and development (Clements, 1985).

SELECTING HIGH-TECHNOLOGY CURRICULUM COMPONENTS

Computers can be useful tools in many areas of the early childhood education curriculum.

Special Education

As educational tools and as prosthetic devices, computers can make a special contribution to special populations. They can help shore up handicapped senses. They can enhance mobility and communication. They can help develop cognitive, language, and perceptual abilities (Clements, 1985; Clements & Nastasi, in press). The mildly handicapped are usually able to use existing hardware and software, merely using lower levels and slower pacing (Watson et al., 1986). Modifications in hardware, such as switches for input devices, allow the physically impaired to use computers. The developmental abilities of the child should be considered in choosing software (Clements, 1985). Like the nonhandicapped, these children choose computers frequently and prefer software that has color, graphics, and animation and is under their control. Need for teacher support is high initially but declines over time as students become more independent or learn to rely on peers. Very low-functioning students (e.g., IQ below 65), however, may require constant teacher assistance.

With teacher support, CAI may be particularly effective in providing basic skills instruction to special education students (Clements & Nastasi, in press). Students perceive CAI as less threatening than traditional classroom instruction (Swan, Guerrero, Mitrani & Schoener, 1989). In addition, CAI can offer systematic presentation of information in small increments, immediate feedback and positive reinforcement, consistent correction procedures, well-sequenced instruction, high frequency of student response, and the opportunity for extended remediation through branching (Watson et al., 1986). For these reasons, CAI can successfully provide basic skills instruction to educationally disadvantaged school-aged children (Swan et al., 1989) and teach reading and writing skills to preschool and elementary-aged hearing-impaired children. For example, three- to six-year-old deaf children make significant gains after using a program in which they indicate a word such as *flower* and see a picture of a flower, the word, and a graphic representation of a manual sign (Prinz, Nelson & Stedt, 1982).

CAI's success may have had one unfortunate consequence: Special education teachers use computers predominantly for drill and practice and for rewarding desired behaviors (Christensen & Cosden, 1986). This may limit students' use of software such as the Logo programming language. This is lamentable because special students can gain both knowledge and self-confidence through the use of such discovery-oriented software (Watson et al., 1986; Weir, Russell & Valente, 1982).

The Language Arts and Reading

Computers can be a significant part of an environment that cultivates young children's language development. For example, preschoolers' language activity is almost twice as high at the computer than at other activities such as playdough, blocks, art, or games (Muhlstein & Croft, 1986). Computer activity is slightly more effective than toy play in stimulating disabled preschoolers' vocalizations (McCormick, 1987).

Certain programs are more likely to generate language than others. Those in which children create pictures are especially potent. For example, preschoolers tell longer and more structured stories following a computer graphics presentation than following a static presentation (Riding & Tite, 1985). They dictate significantly more about their Logo computer pictures than about their hand-drawn pictures (Clements & Nastasi, in press). Drawing with Logo's screen "turtle" engenders interaction and language rich with emotion, humor, and imagination (Genishi, McCollum & Strand, 1985). Embedded in a narrative context, work with Logo enhances language-impaired preschool children's perceptual-language skills (Lehrer & deBernard, 1987) and first graders' visual-motor development, vocabulary, and listening comprehension (Robinson & Uhlig, 1988).

Prereading and Reading Skills. Several research projects have evaluated the effect of CAI on primary children's reading skills. Just ten minutes' work with such software significantly increases achievement (Ragosta, Holland & Jamison, 1981), especially for low achievers (Clements & Mcloughlin, 1986; Lavin & Sanders, 1983). There are reports of preschoolers making gains in reading-readiness skills such as visual discrimination, letter naming, and beginning word recognition (Swigger & Campbell, 1981), although other short-term studies have found no such effects (Goodwin, Goodwin, Nansel & Helm, 1986). Placing computers and software in classrooms for several months significantly facilitates kindergartners' acquisition of school-readiness and reading-readiness skills. Placing a computer in each child's home leads to even greater gains (Hess & McGarvey, 1987). In addition, just adding speech feedback to CAI practice leads to increased reading efficiency (Clements & Nastasi, in press).

In most software, reading is a linear, hierarchically ordered process that begins with the features of letters or words. In contrast, whole-language approaches view reading as a problem-solving process that begins with ideas about the nature of print and concepts about the world. There is evidence that this holistic approach is as effective as—possibly even more effective than—the subskills approach. Several researchers have engaged children in either skills-oriented or problem-solving-oriented CAI. Children who worked with problem-solving CAI made the greatest gains (Clements, 1987a; Norton & Resta, 1986). Similar results have been obtained for children as young as five, where problem-solving computer activities were especially helpful for children who had initially low reading attainment (Riding & Powell, 1987). As a final example, Logo programming in first grade can increase reading vocabulary and comprehension in later grades (Clements, 1987b). We need more studies that employ holistically oriented language software.

Computers for Writing. The main advantage of composing and editing on a computer screen is that it provides scaffolding (Clements, 1987a). Educational scaffolding serves as a support for children, helping them achieve personal communicative goals that otherwise would not have been possible. From the beginning, children can experiment with letters and words without being distracted by the fine motor aspects of handwriting. Children using word processors write more, have fewer fine motor control problems, worry less about making mistakes, and make fewer mechanical errors (Clements, 1987a; Hawisher, 1989; Roblyer, Castine & King, 1988). Findings regarding holistic ratings of quality are mixed, but generally positive (Bangert-Drowns, 1989; Hawisher, 1989).

Children who have the most difficulty writing may benefit the most (Bangert-Drowns, 1989). Even those not yet capable of writing by hand are able to learn to write with a keyboard. Those reluctant to write with a pencil seem to enjoy writing with a word processor (Cochran-Smith, Kahn & Paris, 1988).

Primary grade students with learning difficulties also show a strikingly positive change of attitude toward writing, especially in accepting editing as an important part of the writing process (Riel, 1985). All young children derive satisfaction from being able to edit easily and produce clean printed copies of their work. So, students develop positive attitudes toward writing and word processing by working with computers (Bangert-Drowns, 1989; Hawisher, 1989; Lehrer, Levin, DeHart & Comeaux, 1987).

Word processors can support a process approach to composition. Children in the K–4 classrooms of one study began invented spelling at the computer, producing only random letters with paper and pencil (Cochran-Smith et al., 1988). Word processing helped preschool and kindergarten children learn about elements of text, such as words, and elements of the writing process, such as thinking about the topic before writing about it. This awareness may have resulted from their willingness to "play" with units of writing (Lehrer et al., 1987). First and second grade children collaborating on paper-and-pencil compositions talked little about their writing and wrote less than when working alone. But on the computer, these children planned, revised, and discussed spelling, punctuation, spacing, and text meaning and style (Dickinson, 1986).

Many word processors include speech synthesis, permitting the computer to pronounce what children type. Such speech provides an extra level of scaffolding for young writers (Borgh & Dickson, 1986a; Rosegrant, 1985). It helps children build links between conversation and composition. Such talking word processors more effectively help preschool children learn about symbol-sound relationships, the importance of vowels, the need for spaces between words, and the purposes and processes of writing (Lehrer et al., 1987). Reading along with the computer, children add intonations that complete the meaning. Ultimately, children develop an inner voice—they "hear" whether or not the text "sounds right" (Lehrer et al., 1987; Rosegrant, 1988). They then take more risks and revise more frequently. Hearing their composition read encourages them to take the perspective of their audience (Rosegrant, 1985, 1988).

Time spent writing on computers also improves basic skills such as spelling, punctuation, and grammar (Bangert-Drowns, 1989). Children using talking word processors improve significantly in their ability to name letters and sound out words (Rosegrant, 1985, 1988).

Talking word processors can play a critical role in supporting the writing, reading, and even verbalizations of handicapped students, including nonvocal, severely physically impaired children. Deaf children as young as three to five years old have improved their writing, reading, and general communication skills by composing with a special keyboard that includes animation of color pictures and representations of signs from American Sign Language (Prinz, Pemberton & Nelson, 1985).

Computer programs may also provide specialized scaffolding for particular phases of the writing process. For example, there are prewriting programs designed to help young writers in the planning stage of their writing. They facilitate "brainstorming" or ask key questions about purpose, audience, and tentative ideas. Computers may lend even greater assistance at the editing phase by checking spelling and grammar (e.g., highlighting every occurrence of the words *too, two,* and *to*). Limited research with older students indicates that text-analysis programs do not supplant, but rather facilitate, children's learning and use of editing skills (Clements & Nastasi, in press).

Word processors have disadvantages, such as expense, complexity, and small screens. In one study, although learning disabled students benefited greatly from word processing, difficulties arose (MacArthur & Shneiderman, 1986). These difficulties included inefficiency (e.g., deleting several words to get back to a single minor mistake) and misconceptions (e.g., initially inserting numerous spaces to make room to add text instead of just inserting the text). Many students equate keyboard and screen with pencil and paper (Cochran-Smith et al., 1988). They may believe that they cannot insert words, or they may press "return" at the end of every line, not using the wrapping feature of word processors. This suggests the use of "what-you-see-is-what-you-get" word processors and a logical structure for commands (MacArthur & Shneiderman, 1986). Also, students need to build a clear conceptual model of word processing, giving specific attention to difficulties such as saving and loading, insertion and deletion, and proper use of returns for paragraphs and blank lines.

Perhaps more important is the teaching and learning environment in which word processing is embedded. In one project, parents taught their preschool children to compose with word processors (Rosegrant, 1986). They fundamentally affected their children's experiences. For example, Jessica wrote a letter to one of her grandmothers, mailing it when she got home. Several days later, her other grandmother called, demanding her own letter. Jessica loaded in the old computer letter, typed the second grandmother's name over the first, added a "P.S. How's your eye?" and promptly mailed out the "new" letter! Jessica's mother supported the clever use of the computer, joking, "My mother just got a form letter from her own grandchild!" On the other hand, Jane had to write 13 thank-you letters—all virtually identical—following her birthday party. She too thought of using the same basic "file," altered appropriately. Her mother refused to let her take that shortcut, forcing her to type the same letter 13 times.

For classroom use, too, benefits of word processors depend on the environment established (Cochran-Smith et al., 1988). Teachers in most recent projects are not only sensitive to the role instruction plays in combination with word processing, but also take care to create a setting in which the pedagogy is grounded in theory and research. They involve computers in the total composing process and work with computers for a year or more. Their findings are more positive as a result (Cochran-Smith et al., 1988; Hawisher, 1989). In sum, it appears that word processing can be successfully integrated into an early childhood process-oriented writing program. Such use can lead to interesting discoveries. One group of kindergartners discovered "magic letters." If they entered BCD into the computer, it said only "B C D." If they entered BAD, it pronounced the syllable, "BAD." That is, if a magic letter—a vowel—were in a string of letters, it would make a sound that was not a letter name, but a word (Clements & Nastasi, in press). They also discovered how to figure out what the words scrawled on the bathroom walls were!

Suggestions for maximizing the potential benefits of word processing include:

- Become familiar with the program yourself.
- Start simple, then add more commands to students' repertoires as they need them.
- Consider introducing word processing by writing a whole-class language-experience story.
- Work intensely with a small group to develop your first "experts," then have these experts help others.
- Continue presenting short lessons to the class followed by computer work in pairs.
- If few computers are available, rotate groups using the word processor for compositions. Have students write their first drafts in pencil, then sign up for a 20- to 30-minute computer session. Working in pairs, one student types in his or her own composition as a friend reads it, suggesting changes along the way. Then they switch places.
- Model the writing process yourself.
- Be a mentor, not a critic.
- Encourage children to be mindful in their writing.
- Avoid the pitfalls. For some children and some writing tasks, the screen can become "too public." Rearranging the setting can ameliorate this problem.
- Do not allow yourself to get carried away, overediting children's writing.
- Avoid viewing any printout (as nice as it may look) as a final draft.
- Consider your students' typing abilities. If they have insufficient typing skills, they may (at first) write less, be less spontaneous, or be loath to delete. Perhaps an adult can help enter the first draft.

Mathematics

The greatest gains in the use of drill CAI have been in mathematics for primary grade children (Lavin & Sanders, 1983; Ragosta et al., 1981). Even preschoolers have learned sorting and counting from computer programs, often more effectively than from a teacher (Corning & Halapin, 1989; Hungate, 1982). Of course, children should not work with such drill programs until they understand the concepts. In one study, CAI drill positively influenced total mathematics and computational skills more than other treatments, but the regular mathematics curriculum more effectively developed concept application skills (McConnell, 1983). So, teachers must carefully match students and goals with appropriate educational experiences.

Mathematics CAI appears especially effective in remedial situations and with students from schools serving lower socioeconomic populations (Lavin & Sanders, 1983; McConnell, 1983; Ragosta et al., 1981). It positively affects both achievement and attitudes (Mevarech & Rich, 1985).

Geometric and Spatial Thinking. With the ability to link pictures, words, and numbers, computers are especially suited to the development of geometric and spatial thinking. Kindergartners learn about shapes as effectively from a computer-based program as from a teacher-directed program (vonStein, 1982). Preschoolers learn about relational concepts such as above/below and over/under more effectively from computers than from television (Brawer, cited in Lieberman, 1985). More exciting, perhaps, is software that becomes a tool for spatial thinking. For example, computer drawing programs offer a new, dynamic way of exploring geometric concepts. Preschoolers drawing rectangles by stretching an electronic "rubber band" gain a different perspective on geometric figures (Forman, 1986b). Children also can fill closed regions with color; doing so leads the children to reflect on geometric properties, such as closure as the consequence of action rather than merely a characteristic of static shapes. The power of such drawing tools lies in the possibility that children will construct new mental tools by internalizing the processes.

Logo provides a potentially more powerful and extensible tool. Piaget demonstrated that young children do not learn about geometric shapes by passively taking mental snapshots of objects. Instead they learn from actions they perform on these objects. They internalize these actions and abstract the corresponding geometric ideas. For example, children can walk a rectangular path and then program the Logo turtle to draw it on the screen. The programming helps children link their intuitive knowledge about moving and drawing to more explicit mathematical ideas. In constructing series of commands to draw the rectangle, they analyze the visual components and make conclusions about its properties. Such activity helps them develop a more sophisticated level of geometric thinking (Clements & Battista, 1989, 1990).

As an example, a class of first graders had identified rectangles in the classroom and built them out of various materials such as blocks and clay. They then went to the computer lab and were making the turtle draw different rectangles. One child tried to be quite different. After making several rectangles, he attempted to draw a tilted one. He instructed the turtle to draw the first side using five FORWARD commands. He paused for quite some time as he came to the first turn, so the teacher asked him how much he had turned when he made his other rectangles. He said three RIGHTs (each RIGHT was 30 degrees) and hesitatingly tried three. It worked to his satisfaction and he drew the second side. He hesitated again, then tried three right turns. He thought out loud: "How far? Oh, it must be the same as its partner!" Effortlessly, he completed his rectangle. Even though this child had built several rectangles with sides horizontal and vertical, it was not obvious to him that the same commands would work for a tilted rectangle. The Logo environment provided him with the opportunity to analyze and reflect on the properties of a rectangle. It also encouraged him to pose challenges for himself (Clements & Battista, in press).

Logo and Mathematical Thinking. If used thoughtfully, Logo experience can help young children develop basic number sense, learn relationships between size of numbers and the length of a line drawn, apply arithmetic processes, and engage in high levels of mathematical discussion (Clements & Nastasi, in press). However, such benefits emerge only over time, and preschool children's conceptual difficulties with certain aspects of Logo (e.g., left and right, defining procedures) should not be underestimated. Certain specially designed Logo environments, however, can ameliorate these problems and enhance children's learning (Clements, 1983–84). There is no evidence that children must reach a certain age or stage (e.g., concrete operations) before successfully using Logo.

To use Logo thoughtfully, teachers must guide and mediate Logo work to help children form correct and complete mathematical concepts. They must help children build bridges between the Logo experience and their regular mathematics work (Clements, 1987b).

Quality Mathematics Software. These results suggest that there is a safe and easy way to use computers to teach mathematics to young children. Use of appropriate practice software about ten minutes a day will probably increase children's scores on achievement tests. On the other hand, if the goal is substantive increases in the quality of young children's mathematical experiences, try Logo and other programs that demand significant mathematical thinking, but be ready to work hard at it. Consider the following guidelines:

• Use software that challenges children to solve meaningful problems and that can be integrated with children's noncomputer mathematical experiences.

• Combine software use with use of manipulatives.

• Use software that does what textbooks and worksheets cannot do. For example, it should help students connect multiple representations and use animation appropriately.

• Use software that encourages multiple solution strategies.

• Plan for children's developmental growth in the use of powerful tools such as Logo.

Creativity and Problem Solving

Although most early childhood programs value creativity, few plan for or evaluate it. Students have repeatedly found that Logo programming increases creativity (Clements & Nastasi, in press; Roblyer et al., 1988). Following experience with Logo's turtle graphics, children's drawings are more fully developed in terms of completeness, originality, and drawing style (Horton & Ryba, 1986). Drawing on the computer screen and on paper are complementary, with each benefiting the other (Vaidya & McKeeby, 1984).

A recent study showed that Logo increased young children's scores on both the figural and verbal assessments, suggesting that processes involved in creative thinking were enhanced (Clements, in press). This and other studies show that the greatest benefits are not in flexibility or fluency but in originality, which may be the heart of creativity.

Problem-solving computer activities create a high level of motivation, which seems to encourage children as young as kindergarten age to make choices and decisions, alter their strategies based on feedback, and persist (Gélinas, 1986). The results are gains in reasoning and critical thinking (Riding & Powell, 1986, 1987).

Computer problem-solving activities complement concrete activities. For example, preschoolers thought more about process in a computer Smurf program and more about content in a concrete Smurf dollhouse (Forman, 1986a). In the computer program, children could see only one room at a time, so they had to reflect more because their choices had to be more deliberate. Also, ideas for using objects in the dollhouse seemed to flow from the physical manipulation of those objects. In comparison, ideas for use of the computer objects were planned ahead of time and often announced to others. In sum, the computer promoted planning, although the concrete dollhouse may have encouraged more playfulness.

Logo was created to develop problem-solving ability. While results from early studies were mixed (Clements & Nastasi, 1985), a recent meta-analysis showed a consistent substantial effect (Roblyer et al., 1988). Research specifically involving young children reveals that solving Logo programming problems is an engaging activity (Clements & Nastasi, 1988; Nastasi, Clements & Battista, 1990). Further, this activity increases problem-solving abilities in preschool to primary grade children (Clements & Nastasi, in press).

Especially promising is young children's growth in metacognitive or higher-order thinking skills. Both preschool and primary grade children have increased their ability to monitor their thinking processes—for example, to realize when they do not understand (Clements, 1986; Lehrer & Randle, 1986; Miller & Emihovich, 1986). This may reflect the prevalence of "debugging" in Logo programming. Logo also can develop children's ability to understand the nature of a problem, represent that problem, and "learn to learn" (Clements, 1990; Lehrer & Randle, 1986).

These benefits depend on the quality of teaching. Teachers should closely guide children's learning of basic Logo tasks, then encourage experimentation with opened-ended problems (Clements, 1990). They should always be active-questioning, prompting, and modeling. They should have pairs of children work together and talk about their work. Primary grade children should disagree and then resolve their conflicts (Nastasi et al., 1990). Such scaffolding encourages children to reflect on their own thinking behaviors and bring problem-solving processes to an explicit level of awareness.

USING TECHNOLOGY IN EARLY CHILDHOOD PROGRAMS

Computers vary from being among the most popular free-time activities to being slightly less popular than other activities (Clements & Nastasi, in press). Preschoolers spend about the same amount of time playing in the computer center as they do drawing, talking, or playing in the block or art centers (Hoover & Austin, 1986). Play in other important centers is usually unaffected by the presence of a computer. In one study, children's involvement in art centers diminished as they switched to involvement with computers, but this involved performing art activities on computer (Essa, 1987). In another study, dramatic play decreased in one classroom and increased in another, because only in the latter classroom did teachers make changes in the dramatic play center (Fein, Campbell & Schwartz, 1987). The computer is interesting to young children, but in balance with other activities. Differences in interests can be attributed to physical setup, teacher behaviors, software, and interesting varia- tions in the other activities (Clements & Nastasi, in press).

Social Behaviors

The influx of computers into schools first led to warnings of social isolation and visions of solitary children staring at computer screens (Barnes & Hill, 1983). There were also claims that computers were catalysts of positive social interaction (Papert, 1980). Actually, chil- dren prefer to use computers together rather than alone (Rosengren, Gross, Abrams & Perlmutter, 1985; Shade et al., 1986; Swigger et al., 1983; Swigger & Swigger, 1984). Even when working alone, young children consult their peers (Genishi et al., 1985; Hungate & Heller, 1984). They spontaneously teach and help each other in computer environments (Borgh & Dickson, 1986b; Paris & Morris, 1985; Wright & Samaras, 1986). In fact, they seem to prefer asking peers rather than an adult for help (Lieberman, 1985).

Children at the computer spend a great deal of time talking to others. Preschoolers spent 63 percent of their time with peers when working at the computer, compared to only 7 percent when working with puzzles (Muller & Perlmutter, 1985). When kindergarten and first grade children work with Logo, 95 percent of their talk is about the task, without conflict (Genishi et al., 1985). Primary grade children engage in a greater amount of collaboration on an assigned task while working on a computer than on paper-and-pencil activities (Clements & Nastasi, 1985). So the computer seems to encourage verbalization, communication, and cooperation.

The nature of children's interaction changes over time. Initially, children show an egocentric focus on turn taking. This gives way to a peer-oriented emphasis on helping and instructing, and finally to peer collaboration and independence from adult guidance. Interest- ingly, this same pattern occurs both across developmental levels and with greater experience with programs such as Logo (Clements & Nastasi, in press). Therefore, proper environments might facilitate this positive development.

Similar findings apply to the computer's impact on the classroom as a whole. Social participation is enhanced, not inhibited (Rosengren et al., 1985; Swigger & Swigger, 1984). New friendships are formed, and praise and encouragement of friends increase (Swigger & Swigger, 1984). Cooperative play is encouraged (Klinzing & Hall, 1985). So the computer fosters behavior consistent with the goals of preschool education.

In addition to fostering social interaction, computers may engender an advanced cognitive type of play among children. For example, "games with rules" was the most frequently occurring type of play among preschoolers working at computers (Hoover & Austin, 1986). In another study, the computer was the only activity that resulted in high levels of both language development and cooperative play (Muhlstein & Croft, 1986). Logo programming simultaneously increases prosocial and higher-order thinking behaviors (Clements, 1986; Clements, 1990; Clements & Nastasi, 1988; Nastasi et al., 1990). In sum, computer environments enhance both cognitive and social interactions, with each benefiting the other. Research is clear on one additional matter: Teachers make all the difference, facilitating the social use of computers by establishing rules, structuring the setting and the task, and encouraging collaboration.

Organizing the Computer Environment

Research suggests several guidelines for organizing young children's computer environments (Clements & Nastasi, in press; Muhlstein & Croft, 1986; Shrock, Matthias, Anastasoff, Vensel & Shaw, 1985).

Computer Centers. The youngest children in particular use the computer as a learning center. The following guidelines have been shown to be successful:

• Include a computer, turtle robot, mouse, and printer.
• Consider the ratio of computers to children. A 1:10 ratio might ideally encourage computer use, cooperation, and equal access for girls and boys.
• Choose software carefully to match your goals. Working with open-ended, problem-solving-oriented software such as Logo or word processing facilitates peer collaboration (Emihovich & Miller, 1988; Riel, 1985). More structured programs elicit teaching and turn taking (Bergin, Ford & Meyer-Gaub, 1986; Borgh & Dickson, 1986b).
• To encourage positive social interaction, place two chairs in front of the computer and one at the side for a teacher or aide. If more than two children work with a computer, they assert the right to control the keyboard frequently (Shrock et al., 1985).
• Place the center near an area requiring minimal supervision so that you can assist in the activity as needed. Preschoolers are more

attentive, more interested, and less frustrated when an adult is nearby (Shade et al., 1986).
- Consider use of a sign-up sheet.
- Involve administrators and parents. Show them what you are doing and enlist their support.

Computer Laboratories.   Some schools house the computers permanently in a computer laboratory. Such an arrangement makes for efficient use of limited computer resources and ensures availability of computers for each child during group lessons. The disadvantages include scheduling problems and—especially if someone other than the classroom teacher manages the computer laboratory—lack of integration with classroom work. The following suggestions may help:

- Utilize aides or parent helpers.
- Provide such helpers with an explicit list of directions, including: (1) how to turn on the computers, load programs, and care for equipment; (2) location of materials, including manuals; (3) expected behavior on the part of children; (4) procedures for selecting programs; and (5) most important, how to work with children, including when to intervene, how much assistance to give, how to give assistance (e.g., inquiry approaches rather than direct telling), how to provide encouragement, and how to achieve the conceptual and process goals of the program.
- Establish well-understood schedules, rules, and responsibilities.
- Provide room for desks so that children can work with noncomputer material, perhaps in conjunction with the computer work, as they await their turn on the computer. Teachers in the primary grades often find that splitting their classes between computer and noncomputer work allows them sufficient time to interact with small groups.

Suggestions for Teaching in Computer Environments.   Research indicates that teachers who use computers effectively with young children take a positive, exploratory approach and emphasize cooperation rather than correct answers and competition. Specific suggestions follow:

- Introduce computer work gradually. Initially, use only one or two programs at a time. Expect independent work from children gradually. Prepare them for independence, and increase the degree of such work slowly.

- Enhance sharing and peer teaching behaviors by encouraging children to use computers in pairs and by pairing children who would likely work well together.
- Provide substantial support and guidance initially, even sitting with children at the computer to encourage turn taking. Then gradually foster self-directed and cooperative learning.
- When necessary, teach children effective collaboration; for example, communication and negotiation skills. For young children, this might include such matters as what constitutes a "turn" in a particular game. However, do not mandate sharing the computer all the time. Especially with construction-oriented programs such as Logo, children sometimes need to work alone. If possible, make at least two computers available so that peer teaching and other kinds of interaction can take place, even if children are working on one computer.
- Be aware of developmental limitations. The limited perspective-taking abilities of young children may limit their ability to work collaboratively. For example, computers stimulate the social interaction of children as young as five in problem solving (Muller & Perlmutter, 1985). However, younger children's problem solving may be disrupted by social interaction. For them, the cognitive demands of solving a challenging problem and managing social relations may be too taxing. They may also find it too difficult to take the perspective of their partner.
- Monitor student interactions to ensure the active participation of all.
- Once children are working independently, provide enough guidance, but not too much. Intervening too much or at the wrong times can decrease peer tutoring and collaboration (Emihovich & Miller, 1988; Riel, 1985). On the other hand, without any teacher guidance, children tend to jockey for position at the computer and use the computer in the turn-taking, competitive manner of video games (Lipinski et al., 1986; Silvern, Countermine & Williamson, 1988).
- Avoid quizzing or offering help before children request it. Instead, prompt children to teach each other by physically placing one child in a teaching role or verbally reminding a child to explain his or her actions and respond to specific requests for help (Paris & Morris, 1985).
- Remember that preparation and follow-up are as necessary for computer activities as they are for any other. Do not omit critical whole-group discussion sessions following computer work. Consider using a single computer with a large screen or with overhead projector equipment.

• Research shows that the introduction of a microcomputer often places many additional demands on the teacher (Shrock et al., 1985). Plan carefully the use of computer programs that will substantially benefit your children.

REFERENCES

Bangert-Drowns, R. L. (1989, March). *Research on word processing and writing instruction*. Paper presented at the meeting of the American Educational Research Association, San Francisco.

Barnes, B. J., & Hill, S. (1983, May). Should young children work with microcomputers—Logo before Lego? *The Computing Teacher, 10,* 11–14.

Beeson, B.S., & Williams, R. A. (1985). The effects of gender and age on preschool children's choice of the computer as a child-selected activity. *Journal of the American Society for Information Science, 36,* 339–341.

Bergin, D., Ford, M. E., & Meyer-Gaub, B. (1986, April). *Social and motivational consequences of microcomputer use in kindergarten*. Paper presented at the meeting of the American Educational Research Association, San Francisco.

Borgh, K., & Dickson, W. P. (1986a). *The effects on children's writing of adding speech synthesis to a word processor*. Unpublished manuscript, University of Wisconsin, Madison.

Borgh, K., & Dickson, W. P. (1986b). Two preschoolers sharing one microcomputer: Creating prosocial behavior with hardware and software. In P. F. Campbell & G. G. Fein (Eds.), *Young children and microcomputers* (pp. 37–44). Reston, VA: Reston Publishing.

Britten, R. M. (1988, April). The effects of instruction on keyboarding skills in grade 2. *Educational Technology, 28,* 34–37.

Christensen, C. A., & Cosden, M. A. (1986). The relationship between special education placement and instruction in computer literacy skills. *Journal of Educational Computing Research, 2,* 299–306.

Clements, D. H. (1983–84). Supporting young children's Logo programming. *The Computing Teacher, 11*(5), 24–30.

Clements, D. H. (1985). *Computers in early and primary education*. Englewood Cliffs, NJ: Prentice Hall.

Clements, D. H. (1986). Effects of Logo and CAI environments on cognition and creativity. *Journal of Educational Psychology, 78,* 309–318.

Clements, D. H. (1987a). Computers and literacy. In J. L. Vacca, R. T. Vacca & M. Gove (Eds.), *Reading and learning to read* (pp. 338–372). Boston: Little, Brown and Company.

Clements, D. H. (1987b). Longitudinal study of the effects of Logo programming on cognitive abilities and achievement. *Journal of Educational Computing Research, 3,* 73–94.

Clements, D. H. (1989). *Computers in elementary mathematics education*. Englewood Cliffs, NJ: Prentice Hall.

Clements, D. H. (1990). Metacomponential development in a Logo program-
    ming environment. *Journal of Educational Psychology, 82,* 141–149.
Clements, D. H. (in press). Enhancement of creativity in computer environ-
    ments. *American Educational Research Journal.*
Clements, D. H., & Battista, M. T. (1989). Learning of geometric concepts in
    a Logo environment. *Journal for Research in Mathematics Education,
    20,* 450–467.
Clements, D. H., & Battista, M. T. (1990). The effects of Logo on children's
    conceptualizations of angle and polygons. *Journal for Research in Math-
    ematics Education, 21,* 356–671.
Clements, D. H., & Battista, M. T. (in press). Geometry and spatial
    reasoning. In D. A. Grouws (Ed.), *Handbook of research on mathematics
    teaching.* Reston, VA: National Council of Teachers of Mathematics/
    Macmillan.
Clements, D. H., & Mcloughlin, C. S. (1986). Computer-aided instruction in
    word identification: How much is enough? *Educational and Psychologi-
    cal Research, 6*(3), 191–205.
Clements, D. H., & Nastasi, B. K. (1985). Effects of computer environments
    on social-emotional development: Logo and computer-assisted instruc-
    tion. *Computers in the Schools, 2*(2–3), 11–31.
Clements, D. H., & Nastasi, B. K. (1988). Social and cognitive interactions
    in educational computer environments. *American Educational Re-
    search Journal, 25,* 87–106.
Clements, D. H., & Nastasi, B. K. (in press). Computers and early childhood
    education. In T. Kratochwill, S. Elliott & M. Gettinger (Eds.), *Advances
    in school psychology: Preschool and early childhood treatment directions.*
    Hillsdale, NJ: Erlbaum.
Cochran-Smith, M., Kahn, J., & Paris, C. L. (1988). When word processors
    come into the classroom. In J. L. Hoot & S. B. Silvern (Eds.), *Writing with
    computers in the early grades* (pp. 43–74). New York: Teachers College
    Press.
Corning, N., & Halapin, J. (1989, March). *Computer applications in an
    action-oriented kindergarten.* Paper presented at the meeting of the
    Connecticut Institute for Teaching and Learning Conference, Wallingford,
    Connecticut.
Dickinson, D. K. (1986). Cooperation, collaboration, and a computer: Inte-
    grating a computer into a first–second grade writing program. *Research
    in the Teaching of English, 20,* 357–378.
Emihovich, C., & Miller, G. E. (1988). Talking to the turtle: A discourse
    analysis of Logo instruction. *Discourse Processes, 11,* 183–201.
Essa, E. L. (1987). The effect of a computer on preschool children's activities.
    Early Childhood Research Quarterly, 2, 377–382.
Fein, G. G., Campbell, P. F., & Schwartz, S. S. (1987). Microcomputers in the
    preschool: Effects on social participation and cognitive play. *Journal of
    Applied Developmental Psychology, 8,* 197–208.
Forman, G. (1986a). Computer graphics as a medium for enhancing reflec-

tive thinking in young children. In J. Bishop, J. Lochhead & D. N. Perkins (Eds.), *Thinking* (pp. 131–137). Hillsdale, NJ: Erlbaum.

Forman, G. (1986b). Observations of young children solving problems with computers and robots. *Journal of Research in Childhood Education, 1,* 60–74.

Gélinas, C. (1986). *Educational computer activities and problem solving at the kindergarten level.* Quebec City, Quebec: Quebec Ministry of Education.

Genishi, C., McCollum, P., & Strand, E. B. (1985). Research currents: The interactional richness of children's computer use. *Language Arts, 62*(5), 526–532.

Goodwin, L. D., Goodwin, W. L., & Garel, M. B. (1986). Use of microcomputers with preschoolers: A review of the literature. *Early Childhood Research Quarterly, 1,* 269–286.

Goodwin, L. D., Goodwin, W. L., Nansel, A., & Helm, C. P. (1986). Cognitive and affective effects of various types of microcomputer use by preschoolers. *American Educational Research Journal, 23,* –356.

Haugland, S. W., & Shade, D. D. (1990). *Developmental evaluations of software for young children.* Albany, NY: Delmar.

Hawisher, G. E. (1989). Research and recommendations for computers and composition. In G. E. Hawisher & C. L. Selfe (Eds.), *Critical perspectives on computers and composition instruction* (pp. 44–69). New York: Teachers College Press.

Hess, R., & McGarvey, L. (1987). School-relevant effects of educational uses of microcomputers in kindergarten classrooms and homes. *Journal of Educational Computer Research, 3,* 269–287.

Hoover, J., & Austin, A. M. (1986, April). *A comparison of traditional preschool and computer play from a social / cognitive perspective.* Paper presented at the meeting of the American Educational Research Association, San Francisco.

Horton, J., & Ryba, K. (1986). Assessing learning with Logo: A pilot study. *The Computing Teacher, 14*(1), 24–28.

Hungate, H. (1982, January). Computers in the kindergarten. *The Computing Teacher, 9,* 15–18.

Hungate, H., & Heller, J. I. (1984, April). *Preschool children and microcomputers.* Paper presented at the meeting of the American Educational Research Association, New Orleans.

Klinzing, D. G., & Hall, A. (1985, April). *A study of the behavior of children in a preschool equipped with computers.* Paper presented at the meeting of the American Educational Research Association, Chicago.

Kuschner, D. (1985, June). *A study of the possibilities for reversible actions in software for young children.* Paper presented at the meeting of the Fifteenth Annual Symposium of the Jean Piaget Society, Philadelphia.

Lavin, R., & Sanders, J. (1983). *Longitudinal evaluation of the C/A/I Computer Assisted Instruction Title 1 Project: 1979–82.* Chelmsford, MA: Merrimack Education Center.

Lehrer, R., & deBernard, A. (1987). Language of learning and language of computing: The perceptual-language model. *Journal of Educational Psychology, 79,* 41–48.

Lehrer, R., Levin, B. B., DeHart, P., & Comeaux, M. (1987). Voice-feedback as a scaffold for writing: A comparative study. *Journal of Educational Computing Research, 3,* 335–353.

Lehrer, R., & Randle, L. (1986). Problem solving, metacognition and composition: The effects of interactive software for first-grade children. *Journal of Educational Computing Research, 3,* 409–427.

Lewis, C. (1981). A study of preschool children's use of computer programs. In D. Harris & L. Nelson-Heern (Eds.), *Proceedings of the National Educational Computing Conference* (pp. 272–274). Iowa City, IA: National Educational Computing Conference.

Lieberman, D. (1985). Research on children and microcomputers: A review of utilization and effects studies. In M. Chen & W. Paisley (Eds.), *Children and microcomputers: Research on the newest medium* (pp. 59–83). Beverly Hills, CA: Sage.

Lipinski, J. M., Nida, R. E., Shade, D. D., & Watson, J. A. (1986). The effects of microcomputers on young children: An examination of free-play choices, sex differences, and social interactions. *Journal of Educational Computing Research, 2,* 147–168.

MacArthur, C. A., & Shneiderman, B. (1986). Learning disabled students' difficulties in learning to use a word processor: Implications for instruction and software evaluation. *Journal of Learning Disabilities, 19,* 248–253.

Malone, T. W. (1980). What makes things fun to learn? A study of intrinsically motivating computer games. *Dissertation Abstracts International, 41,* 1955B. (University Microfilms No. 8024707)

McConnell, B. B. (1983). *Evaluation of computer instruction in math. Pasco school district. Final report.* Pasco, WA: Pasco School District 1.

McCormick, L. (1987). Comparison of the effects of a microcomputer activity and toy play on social and communication behaviors of young children. *Journal of the Division for Early Childhood, 11,* 195–205.

Mevarech, Z. R., & Rich, Y. (1985). Effects of computer-assisted mathematics instruction on disadvantaged pupil's cognitive and affective development. *Journal of Educational Research, 79,* 5–11.

Miller, G. E., & Emihovich, C. (1986). The effects of mediated programming instruction on preschool children's self-monitoring. *Journal of Educational Computing Research, 2*(3), 283–297.

Muhlstein, E. A., & Croft, D. J. (1986). *Using the microcomputer to enhance language experiences and the development of cooperative play among preschool children.* Cupertino, CA: De Anza College.

Muller, A. A., & Perlmutter, M. (1985). Preschool children's problem-solving interactions at computers and jigsaw puzzles. *Journal of Applied Developmental Psychology, 6,* 173–186.

Nastasi, B. K., Clements, D. H., & Battista, M. T. (1990). Social-cognitive interactions, motivation, and cognitive growth in Logo programming and CAI problem-solving environments. *Journal of Educational Psychology, 82,* 150–158.

Norton, P., & Resta, V. (1986). Investigating the impact of computer instruction on elementary students' reading achievement. *Educational Technology, 26*(3), 35–41.

Papert, S. (1980). *Mindstorms: Children, computers, and powerful ideas.* New York: Basic Books.

Paris, C. L., & Morris, S. K. (1985, March). *The computer in the early childhood classroom: Peer helping and peer teaching.* Paper presented at the meeting of the Microworld for Young Children Conference, Cleege Park, MD.

Prinz, P. M., Nelson, K., & Stedt, J. (1982). Early reading in young deaf children using microcomputer technology. *American Annals of the Deaf, 127,* 529–535.

Prinz, P. M., Pemberton, E., & Nelson, K. E. (1985). The ALPHA interactive microcomputer system for teaching reading, writing, and communication skills to hearing-impaired children. *American Annals of the Deaf, 130,* 444–461.

Ragosta, M., Holland, P., & Jamison, D. T. (1981). *Computer-assisted instruction and compensatory education: The ETS/LAUSD study.* Princeton, NJ: Educational Testing Service.

Riding, R. J., & Powell, S. D. (1986). The improvement of thinking skills in young children using computer activities: A replication and extension. *Educational Psychology, 6,* 179–183.

Riding, R. J., & Powell, S. D. (1987). The effect on reasoning, reading and number performance of computer-presented critical thinking activities in five-year-old children. *Educational Psychology, 7,* 55–65.

Riding, R. J., & Tite, H. C. (1985). The use of computer graphics to facilitate story telling in young children. *Educational Studies, 11,* 203–210.

Riel, M. (1985). The Computer Chronicles Newswire: A functional learning environment for acquiring literacy skills. *Journal of Educational Computing Research, 1,* 317–337.

Robinson, M. A., & Uhlig, G. E. (1988). The effects of guided discovery Logo instruction on mathematical readiness and visual motor development in first grade students. *Journal of Human Behavior and Learning, 5,* 1–13.

Roblyer, M. D., Castine, W. H., & King, F. J. (1988). *Assessing the impact of computer-based instruction: A review of recent research.* New York: Hearth Press.

Rosegrant, T. J. (1985, April). *Using a microcomputer to assist children in their efforts to acquire beginning literacy.* Paper presented at the meeting of the American Educational Research Association, Chicago.

Rosegrant, T. J. (1986, April). *Adult-child communication in writing.* Paper presented at the meeting of the American Educational Research Association, San Francisco.

Rosegrant, T. J. (1988). Talking word processors for the early grades. In J.

L. Hoot & S. B. Silvern (Eds.), *Writing with computers in the early grades* (pp. 143–159). New York: Teachers College Press.

Rosengren, K. S., Gross, D., Abrams, A. F., & Perlmutter, M. (1985, September). *An observational study of preschool children's computing activity.* Paper presented at the "Perspectives on the Young Child and the Computer" conference, University of Texas at Austin.

Shade, D. D., Nida, R. E., Lipinski, J. M., & Watson, J. A. (1986). Microcomputers and preschoolers: Working together in a classroom setting. *Computers in the Schools, 3,* 53–61.

Shade, D. D., & Watson, J. A. (1987). Microworlds, mother teaching behavior, and concept formation in the very young child. *Early Child Development and Care, 28,* 97–113.

Shrock, S. A., Matthias, M., Anastasoff, J., Vensel, C., & Shaw, S. (1985, January). *Examining the effects of the microcomputer on a real world class: A naturalistic study.* Paper presented at the meeting of the Association for Educational Communications and Technology, Anaheim, CA.

Silvern, S. B., Countermine, T. A., & Williamson, P. A. (1988). Young children's interaction with a microcomputer. *Early Childhood Development and Care, 32,* 23–35.

Sivin, J. P., Lee, P. C., & Vollmer, A. M. (1985, April). *Introductory computer experiences with commercially-available software: Differences between three-year-olds and five-year-olds.* Paper presented at the meeting of the American Educational Research Association, Chicago.

Swan, K., Guerrero, F., Mitrani, M., & Schoener, J. (1989, March). *Honing in on the target: Who among the educationally disadvantaged benefits most from what CBI?* Paper presented at the meeting of the American Educational Research Association, San Francisco.

Swigger, K., & Campbell, J. (1981). Computers and the nursery school. In D. Harris & L. Nelson-Heern (Eds.), *Proceedings of the National Educational Computing Conference* (pp. 264–268). Iowa City: National Educational Computing Conference.

Swigger, K. M., Campbell, J., & Swigger, B. K. (1983, January/February). Preschool children's preferences of different types of CAI programs. *Educational Computer Magazine, 3,* 38–40.

Swigger, K. M., & Swigger, B. K. (1984). Social patterns and computer use among preschool children. *AEDS Journal, 17,* 35–41.

Vaidya, S., & McKeeby, J. (1984, September). Computer turtle graphics: Do they affect children's thought processes? *Educational Technology, 24,* 46–47.

vonStein, J. H. (1982). An evaluation of the microcomputer as a facilitator of indirect learning for the kindergarten child. *Dissertation Abstracts International, 43,* 72A (University Microfilms No. DA8214463).

Watson, J. A., Chadwick, S. S., & Brinkley, V. M. (1986). Special education technologies for young children: Present and future learning scenarios with related research literature. *Journal of the Division for Early Childhood, 10,* 197–208.

Weir, S., Russell, S. J., & Valente, J. A. (1982, September). Logo: An approach to educating disabled children. *BYTE, 7,* 342–360.

Wright, J. L., & Samaras, A. S. (1986). Play worlds and microworlds. In P. F. Campbell & G. G. Fein (Eds.), *Young children and microcomputers* (pp. 73–86). Reston, VA: Reston Publishing.

CHAPTER 7

Moving From Here to There

RETHINKING CONTINUITY AND TRANSITIONS IN EARLY CARE AND EDUCATION

Sharon L. Kagan

George Bernard Shaw once noted that there are two tragedies in life: One is to gain one's heart's desire, the other is to lose it. The field of early care and education is facing such a conundrum. On the one hand, convinced that investing in young children is cost-effective, legislators, governors, and corporate executives have worked to increase services for young children and their families. On the other hand, as programs proliferate, deep-seated problems are exacerbated by such growth. Practitioners, facing increasing numbers of piece-meal programs, a myriad of funding streams, and inconsistent regulations, ardently attempt to link services so that children will experience continuity and services will be more efficient and cost-effective. Empiricists, who question why cognitive gains attained in high-quality preschool programs are not sustained as children move into school, are also disquieted by the lack of continuity. Sadly, despite efforts to optimize the field's knowledge and the public's dollars, continuity remains illusive as the field attempts to deal with expansion and effectiveness simultaneously.

The current proliferation of services for young children and their families beckons a reexamination of continuity. This chapter delineates why intense concern about continuity and "transition" efforts to achieve it have resurfaced now. In reviewing historic attempts to achieve continuity in federal, state, and local efforts, the chapter suggests that despite good intentions, real continuity has not been achieved because our conceptualization has been too narrow, our efforts too brief. Following a redefinition of *continuity,* the author posits recommendations for practice and policy.

THE RATIONALE FOR INTEREST IN
CONTINUITY AND TRANSITION

Although interest in continuity and transition in the early care and education field is not new, it has commanded considerable attention recently. At the national level, impressive legislation (Labor and Human Resources Committee, 1990) has funded a series of demonstration projects that assist parents and children as they make the transition from preschool to elementary school. The United States Department of Education has funded a national study of transition efforts and, with support from the Department of Health and Human Services, is stimulating work on transition within the Office of Educational Research and Improvement (OERI) Centers. Moreover, these departments have formed a joint Head Start/Compensatory Education Task Force with the explicit goals of (1) strengthening the transition from Head Start to school; (2) sustaining gains made by Head Start and other preschool programs during the early years in school; and (3) fostering coordination of Head Start with compensatory education programs, especially the Chapter 1 and Even Start programs (J. MacDonald, personal communication, July 1990). Similar cross-program enthusiasm is manifest in hundreds of early care and education collaborations at the state and local levels, where exciting work to ease children's transitions is being conducted. Though diverse, activities being generated throughout the nation affirm that interest in fostering continuity among and between programs and services for young children is high.

The Current Impetus

The current explosion of interest in continuity and transition emanates from several sources. To be sure, one important impetus is the proliferation of complex social problems coupled with the establishment of diverse programs to address them. Young children and families are increasingly being served in nonfamilial settings by multiple institutions, each having distinct goals and service orientations. To minimize fragmentation and to maximize the benefit of the interventions, cross-agency communication, team meetings, case management, and/or transition strategies are being launched. In particular, transition activities among agencies serving the same young children and their families but offering different services are growing rapidly.

A second impetus for the current interest in transition reflects a new ethos emerging in the heretofore separate fields of child care and early childhood education. Historically, child care and early education evolved as distinct services, sponsored by different agencies, usually education or human services. Formed with different goals and sometimes based on different approaches to child development theory, child care and early education remained quite separate until fairly recently when common principles and practices were codified through the publication of *Developmentally Appropriate Practices* (Bredekamp, 1987). The evolution of the National Association for the Education of Young Children's (NAEYC) accreditation program also served to unite the field. Different professional requirements for day care versus public school teachers, different salary scales, and different images of the field (custodial versus educational) that were previously accepted are now questioned. Care and education are being united. A single word, *educare,* advanced by Bettye Caldwell, reflects the field's new alignment. Training, data collection, and joint purchasing of goods and services are being carried out across agencies (Project Giant Step, 1986). Community councils are being established to forge effective transitions for children as they move from program to program (Kagan, Rivera & Lamb-Parker, 1990). And though not planned as systematic links, professionals—as they move from one program to another to capitalize on the employment opportunities offered by newly funded programs—cross-fertilize the ideological soil, creating better understanding and more effective links between care and education.

A third impetus for renewed interest in transition emanates from a quiet, though growing, concern regarding the need to sustain gains made by low-income youngsters in their preschool years. The "fade-out" phenomenon—the falling off of test scores in the middle years following intervention—continues to plague researchers and practitioners (Lally, Mangione & Honig, 1988). If the benefits of early intervention are to be sustained, it is clear that a one-year inoculation—however robust—is insufficient. Links must be made among the systems that surround the child, namely the family and the school.

The fourth impetus is built upon the recognition that parents are their children's first and most important teachers, making continuity between family and institutions a critical need. New efforts that support parents in this critical role have emerged (Kagan, Powell, Weissbourd & Zigler, 1987; Wandersman, 1987; Weiss & Seppanen, 1988). Parent education, parent support programs, and state commitments to involve parents are burgeoning, fostering smooth transitions between these new efforts and schools, between homes and institutions, and between parents and caregivers or teachers. Efforts to evaluate the efficacy of these programs are mounting as well (Henderson, 1987; Powell, 1989).

Historical Antecedents

However strong the current momentum for transition, it would be erroneous to conclude that such interest is new or unique. Concern about continuity and effective transitions has been a bond linking child psychologists and educators for decades. Dewey (1902) reminds us, "The child's life is an integral, a total one. He passes quickly and readily from one topic to another . . . but is not conscious of transition or break. . . . Classification is not a matter of child experience; things do not come to the individual pigeonholed" (pp. 5–6). Dewey and countless reformers advocate active learning in which children are engaged in activities that integrate curriculum areas. Integrated days, unit approaches to curriculum, and the primary unit represent strategies to enhance continuity for young children.

Beyond curricular strategies, continuity has other faces. In discussing the application of well-known and well-researched child development principles to program practice, Zigler and Kagan (1982) affirm that children benefit if they experience a sense of continuity between (1) the time periods of their lives and (2) the spheres of their lives. This principle suggests vertical and horizontal interpretations of continuity, with the former inferring the importance of continuity between the ages (time periods of their lives) and the latter among home, school, and community (spheres of their lives).

Although past theoretical efforts have recognized the importance of the multiple dimensions of continuity, most practice has focused primarily on assuring curricular continuity within programs and often within classrooms. Because the concept of continuity has become more holistic and because the field is changing so rapidly, a single focus on curricular continuity will no longer be sufficient. Visions of the 1960s, while important, need to be reassessed in light of knowledge amassed in the interim 30 years and in light of future directions.

DEFINING THE CONTENT AND INTENT OF CONTINUITY

While there is little consensus regarding the definition of continuity in the child development and early intervention literature, widely held beliefs and assumptions prevail (Peters & Kontos, 1987; Powell, 1989). Some scholars and practitioners assume that continuity is inherently good and discontinuity inherently bad for children, irrespective of the lack of empirical data that firmly substantiate that assumption (Peters & Kontos, 1987). Others argue that in a world characterized by inconsistencies and turbulence, continuity for children may be counterproductive, since their adult lives are likely to be hallmarked by discontinuity. Such concerns demand that new conceptions of continuity take context into consideration. Stated simply, we need to ask continuity of what, and continuity for what?

Most conventional approaches to continuity do not address questions of both content and intent. In addressing the content question, for example, the historical focus has been on pedagogical approaches to continuity, often omitting concerns about continuity in philosophy or in structure. In addressing the intent question, past work has again been too narrowly focused. This analysis suggests that for continuity to be optimized, we need to first recognize that continuity is not synonymous with transition. *Continuity* is a principle of development, while *transitions* are strategies used to overcome discontinuity. Second, we need to expand the content of continuity beyond a pedagogical focus and discern subtle differences in the intent of continuity.

The Content of Continuity

The content of continuity has three major properties: philosophical, pedagogical, and structural. The philosophical property is the base upon which subsequent efforts are built. Although the underlying values and beliefs that constitute professional ideology do not have to be in full agreement, there must be an understanding of philosophic similarities and differences among the groups striving to achieve continuity. For example, the lack of continuity between preschool and school is often attributed to different philosophies—one rooted in child psychology and child study, the other in educational pedagogy and curriculum. One starts with the learner; the other with the content. Weber (1971) sums up the problem:

> Child development thinking . . . remained isolated from application in the major mass institutions. While it influenced nursery schools, university demonstration schools, experimental private schools, and parent education, developmental thinking within state education—in kindergartens or in the few Dewey schools—suffered from restriction, narrowness of application and lack of influence. (pp. 236–237)

Weber is joined by others in early childhood education (Elkind, 1981;

Katz, 1977; Sigel, 1987) who lament the lack of connectedness between principles of child psychology and educational practice.

Reaching broad philosophic agreement does not mean that all must view the child or the content of curriculum in the same manner. For example, we accept and appreciate different views of child development—maturational, cognitive, behavioral. Philosophical agreement *does* mean acknowledging that young children process information and experiences differently from their older counterparts. For continuity to flourish, there must be basic agreement that because young children learn differently, their learning needs are different.

Philosophical continuity transcends these child and curriculum issues. It must also embrace common values and commitment to the roles of parents and community in the care and education of young children. Parents are not adults to be blithely tolerated; they are the *sine qua non* of early care and education, the critical lens through which young children develop their sense of self and of the world. Real agreement on the appropriate role of parents in early education is the cornerstone of philosophical continuity.

A second property of continuity is that of pedagogy—the content and process of instruction. Less an issue for the elementary grades, where curriculum content is heavily influenced by sequenced subject area texts and basal readers, pedagogical and curricular continuity is more difficult to define in preschool and kindergarten. How broad is early childhood pedagogy? Are health, nutrition, and parent education components? Although reaching consensus on differing conceptions of pedagogy and different curricular strategies has been particularly challenging, there is general agreement that early childhood pedagogy must transcend particular curricula and must embrace more than the cognitive domain, thus including social, emotional, and health domains.

Continuity within and among early childhood services is dramatically shaped by a third property—structure. Structures that influence continuity and transition efforts include agencies of auspices, funding and program regulations, and the ornate legislative and bureaucratic apparatus that forms policy and influences practice. Because of its fragmented history and multisystem modes of funding (Scarr & Weinberg, 1986; Kagan, 1989), early childhood, more than many other fields, is particularly vulnerable to discontinuity. Structural continuity across and between systems was, until fairly recently, lacking. To redress structural discontinuities, innovative efforts are being launched, including interagency councils, community collaboratives, integrated services, and case management.

In summary, the content of early childhood continuity has several properties—philosophical, pedagogical, and structural. Philosophical continuity refers to the values and beliefs that undergird practice; pedagogical continuity refers to the content of curriculum and the process of instruction; and structural continuity refers to the systems, regulations, and policies that shape services. The continuity that children and families experience is contingent upon all three properties. None exists independently; all are inextricably linked. The consequence is that any renewed definition of continuity must embrace all three.

The Intent of Continuity

As a construct, continuity is defined not only by the content it addresses, but also by its intent. Recent work has attempted to discern between various ends, between continuity, consistency, and congruity (Peters & Kontos, 1987; Pettygrove, 1987). For example, using Bronfenbrenner's (1979) ecological systems model, Peters and Kontos (1987) suggest that consistency be reserved for within-unit or -system analyses and that continuity be used for between-system analyses. The term *congruity* is used across systems. Using slightly different nomenclature, Pettygrove (1987) suggests that *consistency* refers to the delivery of services at a level and for a duration necessary to sustain family functioning; *continuity* refers to shared values or expectations; *congruity* refers to the relationship between societal expectations and family needs.

More generic in nature, the *Random House Dictionary* (1980) uses congruence to imply the state of agreeing or reaching harmony. The intent, then, is commonality of understanding. Continuity implies the state of being continuous, without being the same. Its intent is not complete isomorphism, but the existence of a whole and completeness, of which one stage is a part. Consistency implies holding together or retaining the form, thereby suggesting the linkage of separate parts. Though sometimes subtle, the distinctions in terminology as well as the attention accorded the definitional dilemmas by scholars suggest that the single term *continuity* may be too simplistic to describe the array of intents it conjures. As a more precise definition is needed to delineate the content of continuity, so is precision needed to delineate its various intents.

Linking Content and Intent

I have suggested that the content of continuity is multifaceted and manifest in at least three distinct but interactive properties:

philosophy, pedagogy, and structure. In addition, I have suggested that more precision is needed in discerning intent, discerning among congruence, continuity, and consistency. However interesting, the above discussion remains oblique and academic until the concepts are linked, as follows: Our goals should be to achieve congruence of philosophy, continuity of pedagogy, and consistency of structure.

Congruence of Philosophy. Before we can ever hope to effect transitions that make a difference for children and families, we need to address the lack of philosophical harmony. Considering the value we accord diversity in our heterogeneous society and the multiple disciplines that shape early care and education, each with its own culture, language, and traditions, our goal can never be philosophical isomorphism; nor should it be. Nonetheless, transitions for children and families would be better facilitated if philosophy were at least congruent.

Continuity of Pedagogy. Continuity implies a state of being connected and whole, but not being precisely the same. This is our pedagogical goal. Children at various developmental levels should not be learning precisely the same things in precisely the same way. Rather, instructional content and process should vary, but should be part of a continuous whole. Ideas should be introduced and revisited so that, as Bruner's (1962) spiral curriculum suggests, the same concepts are taught but at increasingly complex levels. Building upon a congruent philosophical base—one that respects differences—pedagogy must be continuous, but not the same.

Consistency of Structure. Consistency acknowledges the existence of separate parts and implies striving for agreement among them. Given the extant structure of early care and education, one that is likely to remain divided into separate parts, our goal should be consistency, not congruence or continuity, of structure. We should acknowledge different components of the early childhood structure and strive for agreement, not integration, among them.

CONGRUENCE, CONTINUITY, AND CONSISTENCY: THE PRIMARY GOALS?

Given the different components of the early care and education system, I have suggested that our goals for transition efforts should not be lodged solely with pedagogical continuity, but should be directed to the congruence of philosophy and the consistency of structure as well. Such a position accords positive value to the concept of continuity. Alternatively, continuity might better be considered as value-neutral, with value premised on that which is being continued. For example, if inappropriate practices are happening in preschool classes, is the value accorded to continuity the same as if the activities were appropriate? No. Rather than propagating continuity, the emphasis should be on improving quality. Commitment to continuity must not exist in the abstract; continuity is a relative construct that must be considered within the context of quality. If quality exists, then continuity may be the goal; conversely, if quality does not exist, then quality—not continuity—must become the primary goal.

As suggested earlier, a second concern related to continuity as a primary goal is its utilitarian value for the future. Naisbitt and Aburdene (1990) and others predict that we will be living in a world of flux and change. Should children be taught to deal with these inconsistencies and irregularities, rather than focus on continuity? Conventional responses suggest that by establishing high-quality environments where children experience continuity of caregivers (Whitebook, Howes & Phillips, 1990) and curricular continuity, they will be better able to cope with the discontinuous lives they are apt to lead. Continuity, therefore, cannot be fostered in isolation from quality or context. Practical efforts to achieve continuity—discussed below as transitions—are not the primary goal; they are means to ends.

LESSONS FROM PAST WORK ON CONTINUITY AND TRANSITIONS

Examining major federally funded initiatives and ground-breaking efforts at state and local levels provides an informative lens through which to frame 1990s transition efforts. This analysis suggests that while research results are mixed, lessons from past efforts can guide future work.

Federal Initiatives

Although a plethora of data now confirms the efficacy of high-quality early intervention, particularly in the lives of low-income children, this was not the case in the mid to late 1960s when Head Start and Follow Through began. Reflecting the optimism and ethos of the era, Head Start began rapidly, and data collection followed quickly. Datta (1979) described three waves of findings: the first between 1965 and 1968 as generally positive; the second between 1969 and 1974 as negative—the winter of disillusion; and the third, since 1975, considerably more optimistic. Yet even during the first wave, rumblings about the efficacy of Head Start surfaced. Belief in the malleability of IQ was rampant and as early as 1966, studies showed that Head Start children made substantial gains on IQ tests and other measures while they were in the program. However, Head Start effects disappeared as children moved into the early grades of school (Holmes & Holmes, 1966). Though very preliminary, and questioned by some, these early findings led President Lyndon Johnson to propose the Follow Through program in 1967. Its goal was to build on Head Start by providing continuing help to Head Start children as they entered regular school (Rivlin & Timpane, 1975). So began the first federally sponsored effort to promote continuity between preschool and elementary school—or so it appeared.

Originally, Follow Through was designed to be a national program like Head Start (Weisberg, 1973), but due to funding constraints, the program became a limited planned variation experiment to determine whether various curriculum models would have differential effects on low-income children. Never large by Head Start standards, Follow Through involved at its zenith 22 sponsors working with 173 local projects serving about 84,000 children in 50 states (Hodges et al., 1980).

Enmeshed with Follow Through, Head Start launched the Head Start Planned Variation Program (HSPV) in 1969. A limited number of communities participating in Follow Through were invited to join HSPV so that the Follow Through sponsor would also sponsor an HSPV model, ostensibly making it feasible to follow children involved in the same curriculum from preschool through the early grades. HSPV evaluation results indicated that HSPV children showed substantially greater test gains than children not enrolled in any preschool. However, HSPV youngsters did not do significantly better than comparison children in regular Head Start, nor did particular HSPV models emerge as significantly better than others (Rivlin & Timpane, 1975).

Similarly, Follow Through results were mixed and badly confounded by implementation and research realities—noncomparable treatment and control groups, tests not equally reflecting the goals of all the models, unrefined and underdeveloped program models, mobile children and teachers, and insufficient sites, particularly in the early years. As Kennedy (1978) indicated, the "Follow Through study was more likely to fail than to succeed" (p. 10). Underscoring the complexity of administering a large-scale demonstration and evaluation effort, Hodges (1981) and others have offered inventive design alternatives.

In addition to its evaluation complexities, Follow Through, despite its stated intent, was never implemented as a comprehensive transition program, replicating the array of support services offered by Head Start. It changed from a service to a demonstration program, from a comprehensive effort to one focused primarily on curriculum. Reflecting this ethos, little attention was accorded transition in the national evaluation studies. Love (1988), drawing on Stebbins et al. (1977), points out that "the only reference made to the issue appeared in an examination of the relationship of program impacts to child characteristics, in which it was found that two of the Follow Through models were more effective with Head Start children than with children who had attended some other preschool or no preschool at all" (p. 16).

Overall, the data regarding the benefits of transition were not sufficiently convincing. Sustaining the gains remained a challenging issue to which the Office of Child Development (OCD), now the Administration for Children, Youth and Families (ACYF), responded. In 1974, OCD launched Project Developmental Continuity (PDC) with the explicit goals of assuring continuity of experiences for children from preschool through the early primary years and of developing models for developmental continuity that could be implemented on a wide scale in Head Start and other child development programs and school systems (Love, Granville & Smith, 1978). Two models were advocated—one that created a new administrative structure in communities where Head Start and the schools were under separate auspices, and a second that established an early childhood school where Head Start programs operated in the public schools. A conceptually significant initiative, PDC addressed the comprehensive domains in which transition needed attention—administrative coordination, curriculum, pre- and in-service training, developmental support services, parent involvement, and services for handicapped and bilingual, multicultural children. Unlike its worthy predecessors, PDC was crisply visioned to address the continuity dilemma.

Although different in vision and breadth, PDC research experienced the same problems of other national demonstration efforts. Despite an unusually thorough evaluation and lead time for program planning, research results were inconclusive. It was difficult to retain pure "no-treatment" conditions in PDC communities because control sites heard about and anxiously implemented the PDC strategies in non-PDC sites. Therefore, the evaluation found no significant differences favoring PDC children. In some sites, however, PDC children showed more positive learning attitudes or styles during the elementary years (Bond, 1982). On the positive side, despite limited outcome findings, the PDC experiment suggested that with attention and resources, it is possible to implement transition efforts that link preschool and school. On the negative side, the challenge of assessing quality outcomes prevailed.

Still concerned about the transition issue, the national Head Start office launched two other initiatives: (1) Basic Educational Skills, primarily a curricular strategy, in the late 1970s, and (2) the Head Start Transition Project in 1986. In 1986, all Head Start programs were encouraged to initiate transition activities, with 15 programs receiving special grants to do so. The impetus for the 1986 effort came from ACYF Commissioner Dodie Livingston's desire "to respond to key findings of the Head Start Synthesis Project which showed children achieving dramatic cognitive and socio-emotional success in Head Start which declined once they entered school" (Hubbell, Plantz, Condelli & Barrett, 1987, p. 8). Results obtained from a random sample of Head Start programs concluded that transition grantees were more likely to provide transition activities than regular Head Start grantees, although many of the latter did implement transition strategies. The more frequently teachers participated in transition activities, the higher they rated the preparedness of Head Start children and the lower the child stress during the first month of school as reported by parents. Further, children in the transition grantees showed the greatest resilience through the first months of school when self-confidence levels typically drop off (Hubbell et al., 1987).

The study also yielded information regarding strategies that worked—written agreements, mandates for transition, ongoing transition activities, visits to kindergartens by Head Start children, training parents to deal with the schools, support groups for parents as their children made the transition to school, and summer book lists and activity calendars to help parents ease their children's transition. Important barriers to transitions were identified—"different educational approaches of Head Start and the schools . . . failure to transfer records of all Head Start children . . . the inability of some parents to deal successfully with the schools . . . the inability of some Head Start children to meet the academic demands of the school . . . and the hostile, competitive or patronizing attitudes of Head Start or school staff toward each other" (Hubbell et al., 1987, p. 6).

State and Local Initiatives

Several important efforts have also occurred at the state and local levels. The Brookline (MA) Early Education Project, though not specifically designed to focus on continuity-transition activities, offered support to children and families as the children moved into kindergarten (Pierson, Walker & Timan, 1984). As a result of a comprehensive intervention strategy, the youngsters had significantly fewer classroom behavior problems and less difficulty in reading. The Kramer School in Little Rock under the direction of Bettye Caldwell adopted vertical and horizontal continuity, in that high-quality services were extended through the day (horizontal) and efforts were made to support children and parents as they moved from grade to grade (vertical) (Caldwell, in press). Older children were given roles to play with younger children, and a child development unit for children in grades four through six was implemented. Continuity became part of the fabric of school life for all children.

Transition efforts undertaken by the New Jersey Department of Education (Glicksman & Hills, 1981) focused on communication and emphasized who should be involved in the transition, when it should take place, and what activities best link participants. New Jersey's Urban Pre-kindergarten Program builds upon this effort. Recognizing the importance of continuity, the New York City Project Giant Step Program mandated "continuity of programming through kindergarten" (Project Giant Step, 1986). Teachers develop continuity plans for children and participate in ongoing in-service activities with public school teachers. Preliminary research suggests significant child gains and high levels of parent satisfaction (Layzer, Goodsen & Layzer, 1990).

IMPLICATIONS AND RECOMMENDATIONS

Though brief, this review of transition work indicates that many efforts have addressed the need to build effective links between preschool and school. It also suggests that despite major national and inventive local efforts, we are somewhat stymied empirically, strategically, and conceptually. We have comparatively scant empirical data affirming improved and robust child outcomes given the presence of effective transition efforts. We remain uncertain about who needs and benefits most from transition efforts and why. Do low-income children need transition efforts more than upper-income children, and what does this say about equity of public education? Heuristically, we are impelled to promote continuity and transition efforts, yet we acknowledge little the indictment this plea unleashes.

Strategically, we have learned about the difficulties of implementing transitions. We know that different institutional cultures and missions developed over time complicate easy solutions. Yet we do not know precisely which activities yield the greatest benefit or whether a single effort can achieve the same or comparable impact as multiple activities. We do not fully understand if placing preschool programs in public schools facilitates more effective transitions or more beneficial child outcomes than placing programs in non-school-based settings. We do not understand if and how the educational press for restructuring will influence transition activities, and we know little about the real potential of community collaboration as a vehicle for promoting continuity among programs and between programs and schools.

Conceptually, we remain uncertain of how to think about transition. Past efforts have fluctuated between those focused on curricular interventions and those designed to include other strategic alterations. They have lacked a guiding conceptual framework, as evidenced in the multiple strategies and definitions advanced. Many of our transition efforts were intentionally inductive experiments from which we hoped to derive conclusions. Though conceived with good intentions, many were short-term activities: continuity plans, episodic joint training, the passing on of records, and child and staff visits to the next grades. Few were sustained over time and few addressed deep-seated attitudinal and structural discontinuities that undergird early care and education. Almost like Band-Aids, designed only to cover the wounds, the efforts rarely got beneath the surface to address deep and ongoing systemic problems. Some of the programs tried different kinds of curricular Band-Aids to see if they would work better, and indeed we gained important, but not sufficient, insights. Nonetheless, with the possible exception of Project Developmental Continuity (although it was limited to Head Start), our transition efforts remain conceptually too narrow and too shallow in implementation to answer the complex questions we have posed. In short, empirically, the verdict on transitions is still out.

To that end, next-stage transition efforts should be

reconceptualized to reach beyond isolated activities. Using the framework suggested earlier—congruence of philosophy, continuity of pedagogy, and consistency of structure—we turn to specific recommendations for more robust and productive efforts.

Recommendations Regarding the Congruence of Philosophy

People who work with young children irrespective of site and specific age of the children must share basic philosophies about how young children develop. They must understand and be able to articulate how young children's vulnerabilities affect the nature and content of pedagogy. There must be congruence in their attitudes and values regarding the role of expectation and motivation in learning. They must share an understanding of the role of the teacher and the parent in the educational process. Such shared values and attitudes do not emerge overnight or from single-session in-service workshops. Consequently, we must reexamine the content and structure of teacher preparation programs to discern what modifications need to be made in pre-service education to foster congruence of philosophy among those trained across disciplines to work with children from birth to age eight. We must also better understand how sustained in-service training should be structured to promote cross-grade and cross-setting understanding. Before real philosophical congruence can be achieved, a comprehensive rethinking of pre- and in-service training must take place.

Recommendations Regarding the Continuity of Pedagogy

Ideally, teachers serving cohorts of children over time should agree on pedagogy and on instructional and disciplinary principles. Although young children should not have to encounter drastically different approaches to instruction from year to year, curriculum content can vary. Indeed, research indicates that many curriculum approaches produce positive results.

Within communities serving cohorts of children, there should be pedagogical accountability. Teachers should be aware of instructional goals and of the practices predecessors have used to meet them. Multiage grouping (Katz, Evangelou & Hartman, 1990) and early childhood units (National Association of State Boards of Education, 1988) should be considered. Beyond pedagogical agreement across grades and settings, there should be agreement regarding how children will be observed and how progress will be recorded. Although standardized tests for young children are not appropriate, more benign strategies should be agreed upon.   Time must be allocated for those working directly with children across the age span to meet, discuss, and create.   Pedagogical continuity should be considered and implemented by those closest to children.

Those working with young children must focus on continuity as a critical pedagogical dimension. Understanding children's home cultures and values demands a revitalized commitment to working and communicating with parents. This may take the form of parent visits, workshops, or materials sharing. Establishing mechanisms so that parents can support one another through informal networks or buddy-to-buddy programs proved effective in the Head Start transition study. Understanding what children have experienced before they come to school demands new outreach by educators to colleagues in the field.

Recommendations Regarding the Consistency of Structure

If pedagogical continuity has been the most frequently addressed property of continuity efforts to date, structural consistency has been the least. Regulations vary not simply from state to state but within locales, with schools often being exempt from any licensure. Structural consistency that makes all centers or school-based environments comparable is a badly needed first step toward continuity. Credentialing requirements for staff among institutions serving young children vary dramatically and, along with grave salary differentials, precipitate staff turnover.   Though complex, these structural anomalies must be addressed as we tackle continuity. Finally, we need to acknowledge that teacher/child ratios and group size are among the most critical variables in delivering high-quality services for preschool-aged youngsters. Comparable attention must be accorded these variables at the school level, and promising data are revealing that ratio reduction through the realignment of Chapter 1 dollars may be effective at promoting positive child outcomes (Slavin, Karweit & Madden, 1989).

Discontinuity is not solely a curricular concern; it will not be eradicated by the elimination of discordant curriculum guides. It is bred from different philosophies and basic inequities that pervade all early care and education. Addressing the core issues—congruence of philosophy, continuity of pedagogy, and consistency of structure—is the requisite preamble to instituting effective transition activities.

Returning to Shaw, the tragedy of our field's past life seems to have been not conceptualizing the challenge of transition sufficiently broadly. Despite gaining our heart's desire—badly needed support and attention—the tragedy of our next life may be not using the opportunity to effectively address the continuity/transition challenge. It is hoped that this will not be the case; instead, buoyed by past efforts and renewed public support, we will create a system of early care and education in which high-quality, equitable, and continuous programs render the need for separate transition efforts extinct.

NOTE

The author is indebted to Robert Egbert, Jenni Klein, and John Love for being (and accessing) helpful resources in the preparation of this chapter.

REFERENCES

Bond, J. T. (1982). *Project Developmental Continuity evaluation. Final report: Vol. 1. Outcomes of the PDC intervention.* Ypsilanti, MI: High/Scope Educational Research Foundation.

Bredekamp, S. (Ed.) (1987). *Developmentally appropriate practice in early childhood programs serving children from birth through age 8.* Washington, DC: National Association for the Education of Young Children.

Bronfenbrenner, U. (1979). *The ecology of human development.* Cambridge, MA: Harvard University Press.

Bruner, J. S. (1962). *The process of education.* Cambridge, MA: Harvard University Press.

Caldwell, B. (in press). Continuity in the early years: Transitions between grades and systems. In S. L. Kagan (Ed.), *The care and education of America's young children: Obstacles and opportunities. The ninetieth yearbook of the National Society for the Study of Education.* Chicago: University of Chicago Press.

Datta, L. (1979). Another spring and other hopes: Some findings from national evaluations of Project Head Start. In E. Zigler & J. Valentine (Eds.),*Project Head Start: A legacy of the war on poverty* (pp. 405–433). New York: Free Press.

Dewey, J. (1902). *The child and the curriculum.* Chicago: University of Chicago Press.

Elkind, D. (1981). *The hurried child.* Reading, MA: Addison-Wesley.

Glicksman, K., & Hills, T. (1981). *Easing the child's transition between home, child care center & school: A guide for early childhood educators.* Trenton, NJ: New Jersey Department of Education.

Henderson, A. (1987). *The evidence continues to grow: Parent involvement improves student achievement.* Columbia, MD: National Committee for

Citizens in Education.

Hodges, W. (1981). *Instructional models, model sponsors, and future Follow Through research* (NIE-P-80-0177) (ED 244 740). Washington, DC: National Institute of Education.

Hodges, W., Branden, A., Feldman, R., Follins, J., Love, J. M., Sheehan, R., Lumbley, J., Osborn, J., Rentfrow, R. K., Houston, J., & Lee, C. (1980). *Follow Through: Forces for change in the primary schools.* Ypsilanti, MI: High/Scope Educational Research Foundation.

Holmes, D., & Holmes, M. B. (1966). Evaluation of two associated YM-YWCA *Head Start programs of New York City: Final report.* New York: Associated YM-YWCAs of New York City.

Hubbell, R., Plantz, M., Condelli, L., & Barrett, B. (1987). *The transition of Head Start children into public school. Final report: Vol. 1.* Alexandria, VA: CSR, Inc.

Kagan, S. L. (1989). *Early care and education: Are we tackling the tough issues? Phi Delta Kappan, 70*(6), 433–439.

Kagan, S. L., Powell, D. R., Weissbourd, B., & Zigler, E. (Eds.). (1987). *America's family support programs: Perspectives and prospects.* New Haven, CT: Yale University Press.

Kagan, S. L., Rivera, A., & Lamb-Parker, F. (1990). *Collaborations in action: Reshaping services for young children and their families.* New Haven, CT: Yale Bush Center in Child Development and Social Policy.

Katz, L. (1977). Education or excitement. In L. Katz (Ed.), *Talks with teachers* (pp. 107–114). Washington, DC: National Association for the Education of Young Children.

Katz, L., Evangelou. D., & Hartman, J. A. (1990). *The case for mixed age grouping in early education.* Washington, DC: National Association for the Education of Young Children.

Kennedy, M. (1978). Findings from the Follow Through planned variation study. *Educational Researcher, 7*(6), 3–11.

Labor and Human Resources Committee. (1990). Human Services Reauthorization Act. Washington, DC: U.S. Government Printing Office.

Lally, J. R., Mangione, P. L., & Honig, A. S. (1988). The Syracuse University family development research programs: Long-range impact on an early intervention with low-income children and their families. In D. R. Powell (Ed.), *Parent education as early childhood intervention: Emerging directions in theory, research, and practice: Vol. 3. Advances in applied developmental psychology* (pp. 79–104). Norwood, NJ: Ablex.

Layzer, J. I., Goodsen, B. D., & Layzer, J. A. (1990). *Evaluation of Project Giant Step. Year two report: The study of program effects.* Cambridge, MA: Abt Associates.

Love, J. M. (1988). *Study of public school programs designed to ease the transition of children from preschool to kindergarten: Study overview and conceptual framework.* Hampton, NH: RMC Research Corporation.

Love, J. M., Granville, A. C., & Smith, A. G. (1978). *A process evaluation of Project Developmental Continuity: Final report of the PDC feasibility study, 1974–1977.* Ypsilanti, MI: High/Scope Educational Research Foundation.

Naisbitt, J., & Aburdene, P. (1990). *Megatrends 2000: Ten new directions for the 1990's.* New York: William Morrow and Company, Inc.

National Association of State Boards of Education. (1988). *Right from the start: The report of the NASBE task force on early childhood education.* Alexandria, VA: Author.

Peters, D. L., & Kontos, S. (1987). Continuity and discontinuity of experience: An intervention perspective. In D. L. Peters & S. Kontos (Eds.), *Continuity and discontinuity of experience in child care. Annual advances in applied developmental psychology: Vol. 2 (*pp. 1–16). Norwood, NJ: Ablex.

Pettygrove, W. B. (1987). Moving from consistency to congruence in child care policy: The state's role. In D. L. Peters & S. Kontos (Eds.), *Continuity and discontinuity of experience in child care. Annual advances in applied developmental psychology: Vol. 2* (pp. 169–187). Norwood, NJ: Ablex.

Pierson, D. E., Walker, D. K., & Timan, T. (1984). A school-based program from infancy to kindergarten for children and their parents. *Personnel and Guidance Journal, 62*(8), 448–455.

Powell, D. R. (1989). *Families and early childhood programs.* Washington, DC: National Association for the Education of Young Children.

Project Giant Step. (1986). *Program guidelines and requirements.* New York: Office of the Mayor.

Random House Dictionary of the English Language. (1980). New York: Random House.

Rivlin, A. M., & Timpane, P. M. (1975). Planned variation in education: An assessment. In A. Rivlin & P. M. Timpane (Eds.), *Planned variation in education: Should we give up or try harder?* (pp. 1–21). Washington, DC: The Brookings Institution.

Scarr, S., & Weinberg, R. (1986). The early childhood enterprise: Care and education of the young. *American Psychologist, 41*(10), 1140–1146.

Sigel, I. (1987). Early childhood education: Developmental enhancement or developmental acceleration? In S. L. Kagan & E. Zigler (Eds.), *Early schooling: The national debate.* New Haven, CT: Yale University Press.

Slavin, R. E., Karweit, N. L., & Madden, N. A. (1989). *Effective programs for students at risk.* Boston: Allyn & Bacon.

Stebbins, L. B., St. Pierre, R. G., Proper, E. C., Anderson, R.B., & Cerva, T. R. (1977). *Education as experimentation: A planned variation model: Vol. IV-A. An evaluation of Follow Through.* Cambridge, MA: Abt Associates.

Wandersman, L. P. (1987). New directions in parent education. In S. L. Kagan., D. R. Powell, B. Weissbourd & E. Zigler (Eds.), *America's family support programs: Perspectives and prospects* (pp. 207–227). New Haven, CT: Yale University Press.

Weber, L. (1971). *The English infant school and informal education.* Englewood Cliffs, NJ: Prentice Hall.

Weisberg, H. I. (1973). *Short-term cognitive effects of Head Start Programs: A report on the third year of planned variation, 1971–1972.* Cambridge, MA: Huron Institute.

Weiss, H. B., & Seppanen, P. (1988). States and families: A new window of opportunity for family support and education programs. *Family Resource Coalition, 7*(3), 15–17.

Whitebook, M., Howes, C., & Phillips, D. (1990). *Who cares? Child care teachers and the quality of care in America.* Oakland, CA: Child Care Employee Project.

Zigler, E., & Kagan, S. L. (1982). Child development knowledge and educational practice: Using what we know. In A. Lieberman & M. McLaughlin (Eds.), *Policy making in education. Eighty-first yearbook of the National Society for the Study of Education.* Chicago: University of Chicago Press.

CHAPTER 8

Informal Social Support and Parenting

UNDERSTANDING THE MECHANISMS OF SUPPORT

Joseph H. Stevens, Jr.

In recent years, a new early childhood program has emerged: the family support program (Kagan, Powell, Weissbourd & Zigler, 1987; Powell, 1989). These are prevention programs whose primary clients are adults—the parents of young children. This chapter outlines the key components of family support programs, describes the empirical base of this movement, proposes a framework for understanding the mechanisms underlying the giving and receiving of informal social support in parenting, and identifies implications for the curriculum of support programs.

These community-based programs are designed to provide education and support to parents in their roles as socializers and caregivers. They are intended to provide these services in ways that empower parents and promote their interdependence, rather than increase their helplessness and dependence (Weissbourd & Kagan, 1990). Typically, programs provide parent education and support groups, home visitation, drop-in services, warmlines and hotlines, information and referral, lending libraries, health/nutrition services, and child care when parents are otherwise engaged at the center. That family support programs have become a significant component in the array of early childhood programs is most clearly evidenced by the development of state-funded programs in Minnesota, Missouri, South Carolina, Kentucky, Maryland, Connecticut, and Oklahoma (Weiss, 1990).

Weissbourd and Kagan (1990) have identified four principles that underlie service delivery in these programs:

1. The long-range goal of programs is prevention rather than treatment.

2. The parent, rather than the child, is the primary client.
3. Service delivery takes into account the developmental characteristics of the parent.
4. Social support is assumed to be of universal benefit to individuals, especially during life transitions (e.g., the transition to parenthood, the child's transition into school, or the transition for the new parent back to the world of work).

THE EFFICACY OF SOCIAL SUPPORT IN PARENTING

Behavioral scientists who study these support phenomena have typically defined the structure of interest as the individual's social network (or circle of intimates), while the function of these ties or networks has been the provision and availability of social support. Network support has been shown to vary directly with network size; larger networks provide more support (Hall & Wellman,1985; Vaux, 1988). Network density influences support utilization; typically, more dense or close-knit networks discourage utilization of support from sources outside the network compared to less dense networks (Gottlieb & Pancer, 1988; McKinlay, 1973). And more heterogeneous networks have been shown to facilitate complex problem-solving tasks such as job searches (Granovetter, 1974).

A social network has typically been defined as one's circle of intimates, or that group of friends, family, or workmates that means something to the individual (Hall & Wellman, 1985). At least three types of social support have been the focus of research: informational, instrumental, and emotional (Cohen & Wills, 1985; House & Kahn, 1985). Informational support involves sharing of information and advice—often about the management of particular situations. Concrete help, gifts, and money are frequent types of instrumental support. Emotional support consists of expressions of attachment, affection, and confidence in one's worth as a person. Informational support and instrumental support buffer the individual against the debilitating effects of stress, while emotional support has beneficial effects, across the board, irrespective of the presence of stress (Burton & Bengston, 1985; Cohen & Wills, 1985; Cutrona, 1989; House, Landis & Umberson, 1988; Slaughter & Dillworth-Anderson, 1985).

If similar relationships between types of social support and parenting behavior hold as outlined above, one would predict that emotional support enhances the ability of the parent to be accessible and responsive to the child, irrespective of the current life circumstances. But when the parent is confronted by a challenge or stress (e.g., the transition to parenthood, a developmentally at-risk child, a temperamentally difficult infant), informational or instrumental support directly related to that particular stressor would be most likely to enhance functioning, coping, and problem solving.

THE RELATIONSHIP OF INFORMAL SOCIAL SUPPORT
TO PARENTING BEHAVIOR

Let us examine the empirical evidence of the effects of social support on parents' child rearing. In a study of Australian working-class mothers, Cotterell (1986) found that the mothers who provided more stimulating home environments were those who received greater informational support about child rearing from social network members, lived in communities with more women at a similar stage in life, and received greater support from their husbands. Child-rearing information from network members (particularly from relatives), along with other factors, seemed to enhance the mothers' parenting abilities.

Dunst and Trivette's research (1988) on parents of handicapped children showed that greater social support (whether informational, emotional, practical, or tangible) was predictive of more positive interactive behavior during free-play episodes with their young children. Mothers receiving greater support were more encouraging, more attentive to their children, and more likely to assist their children's engagement with objects.

Stevens (1988) examined the relationship of social support and personal control to parenting behavior in three groups of low-income mothers. In two of the three groups studied (black teens and white adults), mothers' information and assistance with child-rearing problems from extended family members were predictive of more positive parenting behavior.

Weinraub and Wolf (1983, 1987) found that among both single- and two-parent families, middle-class Caucasian mothers who received more parenting support showed more positive interactive behavior with their preschoolers. Parenting support was defined as the extent to which mothers valued the parenting beliefs of their intimate associates as well as the degree of parenting support received from groups and organizations. The more parenting support they received, the more positive their interactive behavior with the child: positive maternal control, encouragement of the child to act maturely, greater nurturance, and positive verbal and nonverbal communication.

Similar relations were evident in a study of white middle-class mothers (Crnic, Greenberg, Ragozin, Robinson & Basham, 1983; Crnic & Greenberg, 1987). Mothers who reported more intimate support and more community support showed more positive affect in interaction with their infants. They demonstrated more enjoyment of the interaction and greater responsivity.

In a study of working-class Hispanic families (Feiring, Fox, Jaskir & Lewis, 1987), mothers receiving more tangible support from the father and from the social network showed more proximal, stimulating caregiving and less distal interaction. Certainly this proximal engagement with the infant should promote infant emotional and intellectual development (Bradley, Caldwell & Rock, 1988; Gottfried, 1984; Lamb, 1988).

In Zarling, Hirsch, and Landry's study (1988), no relationship between new mothers' ratings of support (informational, emotional, or tangible) and maternal sensitivity to the infant at six months was found. However, measures of support may not have been sensitive to differences in the variations in support provided around the child-rearing enterprise, but were likely reflective of global social support.

The majority of these studies demonstrate that social support to parents from network members provided substantial benefits to the family system—particularly when that support is specific to the child-rearing enterprise. If informal social support does produce benefits to individual functioning, then perhaps programs for parents can facilitate their ability to construct and utilize such network relationships.

Understanding Social Support Processes

How does the exchange of social support operate to influence parenting behavior? What are the specific dynamics of such exchange, and how do these bring about changes in parenting behavior and beliefs? We might conceptualize this problem as one focused on the social transmission of parenting. Viewed in this manner, parenting is transmitted from one member of the social network to another through exchanges of informational support, emotional support, and perhaps tangible aid or assistance.

Social learning theory provides one framework for thinking about these transmission mechanisms. Based on Bandura's social learning view (1977), we might project that network members influence the child-rearing beliefs and strategies of parents in at least three ways: modeling, direct teaching (e.g., tuition), and direct reinforcement.

Consider these mechanisms as you read this informal comment made by one of the individuals interviewed in the Stevens studies (1984, 1988). A grandmother living with a teen mother comments:

> I'm patient—that's what it takes—patience! I be showing her [Peaches, the infant] different thing. She hear a truck, I'll say truck. She see a dog, I'll tell her doggy. She talks over the phone and if you don't hand the phone to her, she'll be mad. But her mother will spank her. Sandra's is young. The younger they is, the less patience. I tell her NO, you don't do that. She just have to reminds [Peaches]. I put Peaches on the pot and put her some food there and if she eat she'll have a move. And when she got through eating, she have a BM and pee-pee. She was hardly walking and other people tell me you have really brought that baby out [Peaches].

The grandmother uses direct reinforcement when she tells her daughter, "No, you don't do that!" She goes beyond simply criticizing this parenting strategy to directly teaching another: "just reminds Peaches!" And she used the third strategy as well: modeling. She puts Peaches on the pot, gives her some food, waits until she has a bowel movement. Then she says, these (and her verbal stimulation) strategies "have really brought [Peaches] out!"

In a recent study we examined whether these mechanisms do influence the parenting behavior of young parents (Stevens & Bakeman, 1990). We followed 15- to 17-year-old black teens, pregnant for the first time, from the last trimester of pregnancy to their infants' first birthdays. We videotaped the play interaction of teen mother, infant, and grandmother and transcribed the verbal behavior of participants. Our hope was to tap exchanges like those that probably naturally occur in the home, while grandmothers and mothers interact, and when one adult talks with the other about some significant incident involving the infant. Let us examine the transcript of such an episode.

Play Interactions

The Griffith family, including teen mother (TM), Janice; her 12-month-old infant, Carrie; and the infant's grandmother (GM), Doris, were videotaped in an eight-by-ten-foot playroom containing two chairs and the following toys: Playskool house, nesting bird (water toy), Sesame Street pop-up friends, plasticene ball with butterfly, busy box for infants, and musical bird.

During the entire free-play period Janice and her infant played together on the floor, while Doris, the grandmother, watched from a chair. Following is a transcript of the verbal interaction observed during this laboratory play episode.

TM (to infant): No. What you got—mirror. See yourself. Look Boo. Look Boo. Look right here. Right there.

GM (to TM): Roll her sleeve up a little bit. (Laughs.) Her skirt could be pulled up a little bit, Janice.

TM (to GM): (Laughs.) Mama.

Infant: [De da.]

GM (to infant): Yea.

TM (to infant): Where you going?

GM (to infant): You gone bring it to Granny? Say, "Now I see something else I want to play with."

TM (to infant): You see yourself in the mirror (points at mirror)? Say "Boo Boo."

TM (to others): She scared of balloons. (Laughs.)

TM (to infant): Say "dog." Say "it's so many stuff, so much stuff in here, I don't know what to play with." Say "dog." Put this on here. See look. Right.

GM (to TM): You should let her do it the way she want.

TM (to infant): (Laughs.) You like the little duck?

TM and GM (to infant): (Laugh.)

GM (to TM): She say "When I get through looking at one thing, I see another one."

TM (to infant): Say, "choo-choo."

Infant: [De da.]

TM (to infant): Yeah.

GM (to TM): I rolled it too far.

TM (to infant): Wait a minute. Say "train." Ball. Ball. Ball.

GM (to TM): I think the ball's too big 'cause it won't stay still. (Laughs.)

TM (to GM): (Laughs.) She watching the film.

TM and GM (to infant): (Laugh.)

TM (to infant): You suppose to roll it, Boo. See.

GM (to infant): Well, never mind about that. I think I'll pull the man out of the socket. (GM speaks as if she is the infant.)

TM (to infant): Man. Man. Here, put your finger on it. (TM places infant's finger on the choo-choo train's button to make noise.)

Infant: (Pushes button.)

TM (to infant): You don't wanna play with the chain. No. (TM takes small doll out of infant's mouth.) Ball.

GM (to TM): I don't think she's really seen herself in the mirror, Janice.

TM (to GM): Uh-uh. She haven't.

TM (to infant): Look in the mirror. See?

GM (to TM): Push it around in the front of her. She love a mirror.

TM (to infant): (Laughs.) Open it up. There you go. You see yourself in the mirror? Put it in the hole right here. Look, right there. Put it in there. You don't want to. Look in the mirror. No. (Laughs.)

How does one caregiver in this situation influence the parenting behavior and beliefs of the other? How might parenting be transmitted from one to the other in social situations like this one? We will explore three such mechanisms: modeling, direct teaching, and reinforcement.

With the modeling mechanism, one caregiver shows the other how to do something with the infant. This may be either intended or unintended. In the Griffith family interaction above, the grandmother interacts very little with the infant, and consequently does little modeling of interactive strategies. She does, however, model other behavior: careful observation of the infant's behavior. She is oriented toward the infant and the teen mother, and is quite attentive to their behaviors. We will see in another excerpt examples of how a grandmother may model for a teen mother (as well as vice versa).

The reinforcement mechanism is also not much in evidence among the Griffith family. However, we will see slightly more reinforcement behavior in a subsequent episode.

A more apparent mechanism demonstrated here is direct teaching, or tuition. Using this mechanism, one caregiver tells the other about something, points out a behavior, an event, or a phenomenon, and tells the other about its significance. There are three basic strategies the Griffiths appeared to use to teach each other: coaching, interpreting, and evaluating.

Coaching is direct, may be intrusive, but is typically a communication about the adult's behavior, urging the other to do something or to act in a particular manner. Interpreting is often indirect, frequently less intrusive but no less instructive, and typically is a comment focused on the infant's behavior. Evaluating is also indirect, but is generally a comment about an aspect of the physical environment rather than about either the adult's or the infant's behavior. All three of these tuition strategies probably serve to transmit knowledge about both infants and parenting.

In the Griffith excerpt we see several examples of coaching on the part of the grandmother. She coaches when she suggests that Janice roll up the child's sleeve, or pull up her skirt. Likewise, when Janice is attempting to show the infant how to put the rings together, the grandmother says, "You should let her do it the way she want." This may be a rather intrusive comment that sidetracks the mother's teaching attempt and could undermine her attempt to guide the infant's behavior. However, on reviewing the videotape several times, we found that the grandmother appeared to say this the instant after the baby could be seen to pull her piece away and swipe against (or towards) the mother with the other hand. The grandmother may, in fact, have picked up on the baby's interest in doing it her own way. Coaching is a strategy we see used by both grandmothers and teens to influence the other's behavior. This again points to the importance of examining bidirectional socialization influences.

The interpreting strategy is also apparent in this play interaction. There appear to be several ways that caregivers engage in such direct teaching, depending on whom their verbalization is addressed to. First, the parent might describe what the infant is thinking, doing, or feeling and verbalize this while interacting with the infant— perhaps directing it to the infant herself, as in "You like the little duck," or "You want to play with the ball?" Second, the parent might speak as if she or he is the infant, as in "It's so much stuff in here, I don't know what to play with." Third, the parent might speak directly to the other adult, interpreting what the child is doing or assigning meaning to the child's behavior, as in "I don't think she's really seen herself in that mirror." Each of these three types of interpretive acts likely teaches the other adult about the infant, about her behavior, and about her underlying feelings or intentions.

Not only should these types of interpretive acts teach the other caregiver about infant developmental characteristics and their importance, but they should also enhance the ability of the other to take the role of the infant—to understand the infant's point of view, her intentions, feelings, and thoughts. For very young parents who are often insensitive to the infant's point of view, such tuition strategies probably are quite beneficial.

The third tuition strategy, evaluating, appears to constitute sharing information about the physical environment. The grandmother does this at least once. Toward the end of the play episode, after they see the infant reach for the ball and try (unsuccessfully) to pull it closer, the grandmother says, "I think the ball's too big 'cause it won't stay still." This comment tells the teen that this ball may not be developmentally appropriate for infant Carrie, and may not be something one would want to purchase or really spend much additional time encouraging the infant to play with (in the absence of a great deal of support and assistance).

Let us examine another grandmother-teen-infant triad and how they use the same materials. But in this situation, the grandmother interacts much more directly with the infant.

GM (to infant): Ooh. Look a there! Look a there! Umm. Look a there. Come on. Look at the toys.

TM (to GM): She gotta think about it first. (Laughs.)

GM (to infant): Look Aisha. Let's play with this, come on. Yeah.

TM (to infant): Let me see.

GM (to infant): No, you can't take it back out the door now. You used to taking the toys out one room and taking it to the next. Look a there (as TM shows infant the musical toy).

GM (to TM): Make him bounce, Terry. Put him on the floor and make him bounce . . .

GM (to infant): Look a there. Look (GM pushes button on train). Look at the train. Look, look. Push it. Push it. Don't pick it up. This way, look. Look here. Look. See. Yeah (infant pushes train).

TM (to GM): That's what she like. (Laughs.)

GM (to TM): She likes to be able to push things.

GM (to infant): Now bring it back this way. Get something else. Look. Look Aisha (GM tries to show infant the house). Look here. Aisha. Aisha. Look at this. Look. Look. Come get this.

TM (to infant): (Laughs.) Hmm (rolls ball to infant).

GM (to infant): Roll me the ball.

TM (to GM): She love a ball . . .

TM (to infant): (Whispers.) Get that ball, look.

TM (to GM): She don't want this ball. Huh.

GM (to infant): You wanna take it to him? Push it to him, ha?

TM (to infant): Let me see. See that? (TM dials phone on train.) You do it.

GM (to TM): Don't hold her hand. Let her do it on her own.

TM (to infant): See that?

TM (to GM): She say yeah. (Laughs.)

TM (to infant): Look (TM squeezes birdie).

GM (to TM): Let her have it. She will squeeze it.

GM (to infant): Squeeze it. We didn't say chew it. Squeeze it. Take it . . . uh-uh. No, no, no.

TM (to GM): That's got spit on it. (Laughs.)

TM (to infant): Oh Aisha. Look at this. Look at the house.
GM (to TM): You can put it to the side of that; she trying to play
    with it and can't.
TM (to GM): Hmmn?
TM (to infant): Look (TM shows infant mirror on house).
GM (to infant): Look Aisha (GM pushes train). Look.
TM (to infant): You ain't gone say nothing?
GM (to TM): She got to think of how to take them apart.

Again in this excerpt we see several instances in which one
caregiver teaches the other about infants and their behavior. First let
us consider the instances of teaching in which one caregiver inter-
prets the infant's behavior to the other. For example, when the
grandmother says to the infant, "you can't take it back out the door.
... You used to taking toys out one room and taking it to the next." She
restricts the infant's behavior, but attributes the behavior to the
infant's usual habit of carrying toys freely around the house. This
comment directed to the infant teaches the other adult about the
infant. This infant's behavior is predictable. She demonstrates
preferences in her style of interaction with play materials: picking
them up and carrying them from room to room. The grandmother also
communicates an acceptance of this behavior; however, the infant
just can't do it now.

Elsewhere both teen and grandmother comment to the other that
the infant enjoys acting on objects—pushing them. Other instances
of interpretation include recognition of infant preferences, as in, "She
loves a ball." These interpretive remarks suggest that adults are
observing what the infant is doing and assigning meaning to it; given
these interpretations, the adults act to encourage object exploration
and play (as in, "You can put it to the side of that; she trying to play
with it and can't").

The above comments provide clear examples of another related
teaching strategy—coaching. These are instances in which the
grandmother encourages the teen to act in particular ways, such as
letting the infant use it the way she wants to. Also consider the
example in which the grandmother encourages the teen to "Let her
have it. She will squeeze it." This prediction is not confirmed, as the
infant puts it in her mouth and the grandmother tells the infant "No,
no, no" (not in your mouth!).

A second of our hypothesized mechanisms of social transmission—modeling—is illustrated in the preceding episode. This grandmother models two optimal parent-infant interactive strategies: use

of positive feedback with the infant and use of elaborated language. There are several instances in which the grandmother provides the infant with positive feedback about her efforts: "Yeah," when the infant imitates and pushes the train. This grandmother models the use of more elaborate language by naming objects that the infant plays with or watches: "Look a there . . . look at the train"; "Roll me the ball"; and "Look at those toys."

In these excerpts we see examples of how parenting individuals talk with one another about the infant and about their own parenting behavior. It appears that these exchanges of information and viewpoints are probably similar to those that would naturally occur in homes or other behavior settings shared by mothers and grandmothers. And it seems logical to expect that these exchanges influence the parenting beliefs and behaviors that these caregivers subsequently evidence.

IMPLICATIONS FOR CURRICULUM DEVELOPMENT

The research relating social support to parenting behavior and the typology of social transmission mechanisms presented here provide guidance for the design of family support programs. Two major implications can be identified.

First, family support programs would be wise to rely heavily on group parent education strategies to strengthen families' informal social networks and to enhance the social support that these networks provide. The research reviewed here indicates that through strengthening parents' social network relationships and the informational and emotional support they receive, parents' child-rearing capacities will be enhanced. An effective strategy for achieving this is group parent education, in which parents of young children meet to discuss child-rearing issues and to try alternative strategies for interacting with and rearing children. These group consultation methods assist parents in building additional informal social networks (Powell, 1989).

In most group parent education programs, parents meet with others who have children at similar developmental levels. Consequently, these ongoing groups provide an effective setting in which child-rearing information relevant to the parents' particular concerns can be dealt with. Powell & Leif's (1990) study of middle-income parents enrolled in a two-year group parent education program sponsored by the Minnesota Early Learning Design (MELD) demonstrated that participants developed significantly more new friendships with other parents of young children than did parents who were not enrolled in such a parent support program. They also evidenced greater child development knowledge than did nonparticipants at the end of the second program year.

Second, family support programs might consider use of some of the mechanisms of transmission outlined here: modeling, coaching, interpreting, and evaluating. Although there is, as yet, an absence of empirical evidence about the salience of these mechanisms for the social transmission of parenting, they appear to have some validity. Family support programs would probably do well to provide opportunities for groups of parents and children to engage in joint play opportunities. In these settings, some of the mechanisms outlined here are likely to operate most effectively. It is in these joint play settings where parents would have the opportunity to observe one another utilize alternative play and teaching strategies with their children, and where parents might engage in the tuition strategies of coaching, interpreting, and evaluating. It is especially likely that these interpreting and evaluating exchanges—during which parents discuss child behavior and its meaning and critique play materials and physical environmental stimuli—will be especially beneficial. And these settings are ideal for group leaders or parent consultants to utilize coaching as a strategy to help parents consider alternative play and interactive strategies with their children, as well as to employ modeling to demonstrate how a particular interactive technique is executed.

REFERENCES

Bandura, A. (1977). *Social learning theory.* Englewood Cliffs, NJ: Prentice Hall.

Bradley, R. H., Caldwell, B. M., & Rock, S. L. (1988). Home environment and school performance: A ten year follow-up and examination of three models of environmental action. *Child Development, 59,* 852–867.

Burton, L. M., & Bengston, V. L. (1985). Black grandmothers: Issues of timing and continuity of roles. In V. L. Bengston & J. F. Robertson (Eds.), *Grandparenthood* (pp. 61–78). Beverly Hills, CA: Sage.

Cohen, S., & Wills, T. A. (1985). Stress, social support and the buffering hypothesis. *Psychological Bulletin, 98,* 310–357.

Cotterell, J. L. (1986). Work and community influences on the quality of child rearing. *Child Development, 57,* 362–374.

Crnic, K., & Greenberg, M. (1987). Maternal stress, social support, and coping: Influences on the early mother-infant relationship. In C. F. Z. Boukydis (Ed.), *Research on support for parents and infants in the postnatal period* (pp. 25–40). Norwood, NJ: Ablex.

Crnic, K. A., Greenberg, M. T., Ragozin, A. S., Robinson, N. M., & Basham, R. B. (1983). Effects of stress and social support on mothers and premature and full-term infants. *Child Development, 54*, 209–217.

Cutrona, C. E. (1989). Ratings of social support by adolescents and adult informants: Degree of correspondence and prediction of depressive symptoms. *Journal of Personality and Social Psychology, 57,* 723–730.

Dunst, C. J., & Trivette, C. M. (1988). A family systems model of early intervention with handicapped and developmentally at-risk children. In D. R. Powell (Ed.), *Parent education as early childhood intervention: Emerging directions in theory, research and practice* (pp. 131–180). Norwood, NJ: Ablex.

Feiring, C., Fox, N. A., Jaskir, J., & Lewis, M. (1987). The relation between social support, infant risk status, and mother-infant interaction. *Developmental Psychology, 23*, 400–405.

Gottfried, A. W. (Ed.) (1984). *Home environment and early cognitive development.* New York: Academic Press.

Gottlieb, B. H., & Pancer, S. M. (1988). Social networks and the transition to parenthood. In G. Y. Michaels & W. Goldberg (Eds.), *The transition to parenthood: Current theory and research* (pp. 235–269). Cambridge, MA: Cambridge University Press.

Granovetter, M. (1974). *Getting a job.* Cambridge, MA: Harvard University Press.

Hall, A., & Wellman, B. (1985). Social networks and social support. In S. Cohen & S. L. Syme (Eds.), *Social support and health* (pp. 23–42). Orlando, FL: Academic Press.

House, J. S., & Kahn, R. L. (1985). Measures and concepts of social support. In S. Cohen & S. L. Syme (Eds.), *Social support and health* (pp. 83–108). Orlando FL: Academic Press.

House, J. S., Landis, K. R., & Umberson, D. (1988). Social relationships and health. *Science, 241,* 540–545.

Kagan, S. L., Powell, D. R., Weissbourd, B., & Zigler, E. F. (Eds.) (1987). *America's family support programs.* New Haven, CT: Yale University Press.

Lamb, M. E. (1988). Social and emotional development in infancy. In M. H. Bornstein & M. E. Lamb (Eds.), *Developmental psychology: An advanced textbook* (2nd ed.) (pp. 357–410). Hillsdale, NJ: Erlbaum.

McKinlay, J. (1973). Social networks, lay consultation, and help-seeking behavior. *Social Forces, 51*, 275–292.

Powell, D. R. (1989). *Families and early childhood programs.* Washington, DC: National Association for the Education of Young Children.

Powell, D. R., & Leif, K. (1990, October). *Information and social support in the transition to parenthood: A study of MELD.* Paper presented at the biennial meeting of the Family Resource Coalition, Chicago.

Slaughter, D. T., & Dillworth-Anderson, P. (1985, April). *Child care of sickle cell anemia children.* Paper presented at the Society for Research in Child Development, Toronto, Ontario, Canada.

Stevens, J. H., Jr. (1984). Black grandmothers and black adolescent mothers; knowledge about parenting. *Developmental Psychology, 20,* 1017–025.

Stevens, J. H., Jr. (1988). Social support, locus of control, and parenting in three low-income groups: Black adults, white adults and black teenagers. *Child Development, 59,* 635–642.

Stevens, J. H., Jr., & Bakeman, R. (1990, March). *Continuity in parenting among black teen mothers and grandmothers.* Paper presented at the biennial meeting of the Society for Research on Adolescence, Atlanta.

Vaux, A. (1988). *Social support: Theory, research, and intervention.* New York: Praeger.

Weinraub, M., & Wolf, B. M. (1983). Effects of stress and social supports on mother-child interactions in single and two-parent families. *Child Development, 54,* 1297–1311.

Weinraub, M., & Wolf, B. (1987). Stress, social supports and parent-child interactions: Similarities and differences in single-parent and two-parent families. In C. F. Z. Boukydis (Ed.), *Research on support for parents and infants in the postnatal period* (pp. 114–138). Norwood, NJ: Ablex.

Weiss, H. B. (1990). State family support and education programs: Lessons from the pioneers. *American Journal of Orthopsychiatry, 59,* 32–48.

Weissbourd, B., & Kagan, S. L. (1990). Family support programs: Catalysts for change. *American Journal of Orthopsychiatry, 59,* 20–31.

Zarling, C. L., Hirsch, B. J., & Landry, S. (1988). Maternal social networks and mother-infant interactions in full term and very low birthweight, preterm infants. *Child Development, 59,* 178–185.

CHAPTER 9

The Influence of Standardized Tests on the Early Childhood Curriculum, Teachers, and Children

Lorrie A. Shepard

The educational reform movement of the 1980s created a new purpose for standardized testing in public schools and thus dramatically shifted the debate about the effects of testing. In the past, controversy associated with testing focused primarily on the fairness and validity of tests used to make decisions about individuals, such as college admission decisions or placement of children in special education. Standardized measures of educational achievement were administered routinely to monitor programs and report to parents, but their use was largely uncontroversial because they received so little notice. Educational reformers changed the use of achievement tests by adopting tests as the instruments of reform. Rather than including tests as part of reform legislation to gather data about the effects of other substantive reforms, the tests themselves were used to leverage change in schools. By administering highly public measures of student outcomes it was expected that educators would shape up and do whatever was necessary to improve student performance on the important skills measured by the tests.

Thus it can be argued that standardized tests mandated as accountability measures were intended to dictate curriculum. At the close of the decade, innumerable accounts documented that tests were indeed determining what was taught. Contrary to the vision of the reformers, however, there is evidence that test-driven curricula have reduced the quality of education and opportunities to learn. In its position statement on standardized testing of young children aged three through eight, the National Association for the Education of Young Children (NAEYC) criticized the adoption of inappropriate teaching practices as a consequence of testing: "Children are being taught to provide the one 'right' answer on the answer sheet, but are not being challenged to think" (NAEYC, 1988, pp. 42–43).

What if accountability tests have had a perverse effect on teaching and learning because they acted as a policing agent to enforce bad instructional practices? How could it happen that intense efforts to raise standards would actually produce less student learning? The purpose of this chapter is to examine the influence of standardized testing on early childhood curriculum, with particular attention to the irony of good intentions turned bad. Although there are numerous position statements decrying the negative effects of testing, this chapter provides a more extended discussion of the research evidence and an analysis of how politically important tests determine the nature of instruction, not just the content to be covered.

I do not pretend that this analysis is a neutral treatment of the positive and negative effects of testing on teaching and learning. Given the evidence and having concluded that highly politicized testing has had pervasively detrimental effects, I focus primarily on the negative case. To acknowledge the other side—although not to give it equal time—two preliminary sections are offered. In these sections, I recapitulate the arguments in favor of measurement-driven instruction and summarize the evidence for positive effects from high-stakes testing. In the central section of the chapter I consider the direct negative effects of high-stakes accountability tests on curriculum. Following that I present three other categories of negative influence: indirect effects on curriculum, effects on children, and effects on teachers.

GOOD INTENTIONS OF
MEASUREMENT-DRIVEN INSTRUCTION

Test-based reforms in the 1980s were an extension of the back-to-basics and competency testing movements of the mid and late 1970s. The sense of urgency associated with recent reform efforts has been much greater, however, because of the economic argument that connected poor student achievement with the loss of U.S. competitiveness in world markets (*A Nation at Risk,* 1983). In addition to their declining test scores, American students consistently fare poorly in international comparisons. Although the *Nation at Risk* report specifically criticized minimum competency examinations that had allowed minimums to become maximums, it nevertheless encouraged the use of standardized achievement tests to set rigorous

and measurable standards. Governors and state legislators endeav-
oring to pass reform legislation and increase public expenditures for
education saw testing as a means of setting higher standards and
ensuring taxpayers of accountability.

Within the framework created by the politics of reform, measurement specialists who believed in the behaviorist instructional model
of test-teach-test provided the rationale for using tests to improve
achievement. Popham (1987) argued that measurement-driven instruction (MDI) was a more effective improvement strategy and
markedly less expensive than hiring "a host of well-paid, highly
skilled teachers" (p. 679). "Measurement-driven instruction occurs,"
he said, "when a high-stakes test of educational achievement, because of the important contingencies associated with the students'
performance, influences the instructional program that prepares
students for the test" (p. 680). High-stakes tests include either those
used to make important decisions, such as student promotion and
teacher merit pay, or those that receive considerable media attention.

Popham went on to specify several attributes of a good measurement-driven instructional program. The instructional targets must
be clearly described by means of criterion-referenced tests, and the
tests must assess defensible content and be limited to a manageable
number of targets. For example, "a number of high-stakes tests in
reading assess only five or six truly essential skills, such as finding
the 'main idea' and drawing the correct inference" (p. 680). It was
Popham's explicit intention that the discriminations required of
students by well-crafted multiple-choice test questions would clarify
for teachers exactly what the targets of their instruction should be.
Finally, MDI must be accompanied by instructional support materials, including illustrative test items and an analysis of how each skill
might be taught. In answer to the criticism that MDI constrains what
is taught, Popham responded that, to the contrary, high-stakes
testing causes teachers to waste far less time. "Creative teachers can
efficiently promote mastery of content-to-be-tested and then get on
with other classroom pursuits" (p. 682).

There is some indication that proponents who first installed
testing programs based on these rhetorical claims are having second
thoughts. For example, Texas is replacing its TEAMS (Texas Educational Assessment of Minimum Skills) program with a somewhat
broader TAAS (Texas Assessment of Academic Skills) program because:

Concerns are being raised that in many districts the TEAMS
objectives have become "the curriculum" and that these "mini-

mums" have become "maximums." . . . Teachers are experiencing a
great deal of stress to raise TEAMS scores, and in some cases, the
instruction o f "essential elements" not measured directly on TEAMS
has suffered. (Texas State Board of Education, 1988, p. 1–2)

Nonetheless, the model of using tests to leverage educational
improvement continues to have wide appeal, as evidenced by the
recently enacted educational reform in Indiana. Its leading provision
for increasing student achievement was a statewide testing program
for students in grades 1, 2, 3, 6, 8, 9, and 11 (Indiana Department of
Education, 1988).

POSITIVE EFFECTS FROM HIGH-STAKES TESTING

When proponents of measurement-driven instruction are asked
to produce evidence of learning gains from high-pressure testing
systems, they turn to the steeply rising scores on the accountability
tests themselves. For example, Popham, Cruse, Rankin, Sandifer,
and Williams (1985) reported on "four success stories" for MDI using
data such as the following:

> The percentage of Maryland students who pass the reading test has
> risen consistently. When the test was first administered in the fall
> of 1980, 78% of the students passed. In 1981 the pass rate was 83%;
> in 1982, 89%; and in 1983, 94%. Much of this consistent improve-
> ment appears to stem from the increasing familiarity of Maryland
> educators with the test specifications for the skills being assessed.
> (p. 634)

In 1987 Popham demonstrated the "substantial improvements
in student mastery of basic skills" (p. 682) attributable to testing
programs by showing the increased passing rates over time for tests
in six states. He emphasized that these data proved clearly that
students who previously had not mastered fundamental skills were now
acquiring them.

It is possible, however, to raise test scores without necessarily
improving learning. If students are provided with extensive practice on
materials that closely resemble the test questions, it is likely that test
performance will improve without there being a more generalized
increase in students' understanding of the concepts underlying test
content. There is evidence that after narrowly focused coaching on one
type of test question students will not be able to answer correctly if the
same skill is tested in even a slightly different way (Shepard, 1988).

The more politicized the climate for testing, the more worrisome it is to use the same test to assess the effects of testing. The Cannell report released in 1987, debunking the claim that all 50 states are above average, drew public attention for the first time to the possibility that euphoric test score gains might be fraudulent. In a systematic follow-up of the Cannell study, Linn, Graue, and Sanders (1990) concluded that, indeed, nearly all states and a disproportionate number of districts report more than 50 percent of their students to be above the national median. Furthermore, achievement trends based on commercial standardized tests appear to be increasing more dramatically than can be corroborated by parallel comparisons using data from the National Assessment of Educational Progress (NAEP). Thus it appears that some portion of the gains claimed on high-stakes standardized tests might be inflated or spurious.

If high-stakes tests are corruptible as measures of student achievement, then what is needed is an independent evaluation of student learning. The NAEP provides the best available external check on what students know. Because the NAEP tests are broader measures of content areas and are secure, they typically do not fall victim to teaching to the test. Therefore NAEP results supply much more convincing evidence (although not so dramatic) to support Popham's claims that mastery of basic skills has increased during the period of high-stakes testing. In fact, NAEP data provide both the good news and the bad news about the effects of measurement-driven instruction and highly focused basic skills instruction. At each of the age levels tested by the NAEP, there has been an increase in performance in low-level skills but no gain or a decrease in higher-order, advanced skills. For example, from 1971 to 1988 the percentage of 9-year-olds with rudimentary reading skills increased by 2.5 points, while the percentage of 17-year-olds with advanced reading and interpretive skills declined by 1.8 points (Mullis & Jenkins, 1990). Similarly, the gains in mathematics achievement from 1973 to 1986 occurred predominantly in lower-order skills. Students do not seem to be developing the conceptual understanding necessary to apply their computational skills. In addition, authors of the NAEP mathematics report drew a connection between students' limited problem-solving abilities and survey data showing that the pervasive method of mathematics instruction is for teachers to tell students what to do and then have them practice in rote fashion (Dossey, Mullis, Lindquist & Chambers, 1988).

NAEP data confirm the claims of measurement-driven instruction by demonstrating gains in fundamental skills, but also provide fuel for the counterclaims that are developed in the following sections of the chapter. I argue that massive effort has produced small gains in rote skills at the expense of teaching students to reason and apply what they have learned.

DIRECT NEGATIVE EFFECTS OF TESTING ON CURRICULUM

Test-driven reforms have accomplished exactly what they set out to do. They require teachers to devote concerted effort to teaching material covered on the test. Therefore, high-stakes standardized tests have influenced curriculum in the early grades by more or less becoming the curriculum. When pressure is great enough, the list of skills to be tested is the list of skills to be taught. But if this is so, why should teaching to tested skills be deleterious? Most obviously, tests refocus attention away from nontested content. However, when tests become the templates for instruction, they harm learning of even the tested skills because teachers adopt testlike formats as the means to drill students on essential skills. As can be shown by findings from the last 20 years of research in cognitive psychology, the model of learning that advocates postponing the development of higher-order thinking abilities until building-block skills have been acquired by rote is fundamentally flawed.

Instruction Redirected to Tested Skills to the Exclusion of Nontested Content

The issue of narrowing the curriculum is the more familiar argument against too much emphasis on tests. For example, critics of testing have argued that it causes minimums to become maximums, ignores higher-order thinking skills, and fosters endless drill in reading and mathematics to the exclusion of science, social studies, art, and affective educational goals. To these complaints, Popham and others have answered (1) that the tested skills are the most important (i.e., if only limited content can be covered, this should be it), and (2) that efficient teaching of essential skills allows time later for less central content. Previously these claims and counterclaims were largely rhetorical. Now, however, we are beginning to have access to data that belie the efficiency argument. In high-stakes contexts, teachers never finish teaching the basics.

In interviews with 50 state testing directors and a nationally representative sample of 50 district testing coordinators, respondents were asked, "Do you think that teachers spend more time teaching the specific objectives on the test(s) than they would if the tests were not required?" Eighty percent at the state level and 70 percent at the district level answered yes; furthermore, there was an association between the importance and pressure ascribed to the testing program and the extent to which it was seen to redirect teaching effort (Shepard, 1990a, 1990c). Many of those interviewed believed that this refocusing of instruction was a positive benefit of accountability efforts; they saw the neglect of other subjects as a necessary trade-off. Others expressed concern about the extent to which the test curriculum had taken over, and some were looking for new tests of critical thinking skills to redress the overemphasis on basics.

From interviews with teachers, Darling-Hammond and Wise (1985) found that tests used as external control mechanisms caused a narrowing of curriculum. High stakes create incentives to teach "the precise content appearing on the test rather than the concepts underlying the content, . . . to teach tested areas of knowledge at the expense of untested areas and to teach skills as they are to be tested rather than as they are used in the real world" (Darling-Hammond & Wise, 1985, p. 320). After an extensive 18-month observational study in two schools, Rottenberg and Smith (1990) concluded that because of the joint effects of a crowded curriculum and external testing, most teachers had given up on reading real books, writing in authentic contexts, longer-term integrative unit projects, and the like. They were filling all available time with word recognition, recognition of errors in spelling, language usage, punctuation, and arithmetic operations.

Distortion of the Way Basic Skills Are Taught

Those who argue that narrowing of curriculum is acceptable because of the paramount importance of basic skills have not considered what happens to children's learning in reading, mathematics, and language arts when instruction is dominated by testlike worksheets. As tests take on greater importance and teachers are encouraged to monitor subskill by subskill any deficiencies in student performance, classroom instruction increasingly takes on the look of tests. In particular, test-driven curriculum encourages the teaching of skills in isolation; the testlike format of materials elicits different cognitive processes than if teachers address intended learning goals directly. For example, students are asked to read artificially short texts and to recognize one right answer rather than invent either their own questions or possible answers. Even in the early grades, they practice finding mistakes rather than writing and learn to guess by eliminating wrong-answer choices.

According to Darling-Hammond and Wise's interview data from teachers, the tendency is to reformat instruction to resemble testing even though teachers recognize that children are being cheated of more appropriate learning experiences:

> I've changed my teaching behavior. . . . I do not use as many essay tests as I did before, because I try to give them things which they are apt to meet on standardized tests. I feel that it is hurting the children, rather than helping them because they don't have to write their own sentences. (Darling-Hammond & Wise, 1985, p. 320)

Consider the following examples of tests becoming the templates for early grade instruction—not just for the two weeks before testing, but every day throughout the school year. Fiske (1988) reported these observations of a no-nap kindergarten:

> For part of the day, the youngsters march to the ring of a kitchen timer. Every 13 minutes, the timer goes off and the students move to a different table. Some practice beginning word sounds. Others, prompted by flashcards and worksheets, add and subtract on their fingers, filling in circles beneath correct answers in preparation for standardized testing that will be scored by a computer. (p. B-1)

The teacher of this classroom estimated that possibly a fourth of the kindergarten population was not ready for such an academic push and needed a different pace, namely a two-year kindergarten program. Harman (1990) gives a similar characterization of the typical first grade classroom. Instead of engaging in real reading, where the idea is to enjoy the story, reading instruction is devoted to disembodied segments of the reading "task":

> [Reading] means drawing lines from the picture of the ball to the letter B, finding the word sat in a list of three sits and a sat, circling the words with the sound of E as in egg, filling in the missing final consonants, dividing words into syllables, and "bubbling in" answers to the five "comprehension" questions taken from a six-line "story." (p. 111)

An in-depth case study of two very different schools by Smith, Edelsky, Draper, Rottenberg, and Cherland (1990) (summarized in Rottenberg & Smith, 1990) provided extensive documentation of the specific changes made in basic skills teaching to conform to the expectations of standardized tests. The two schools shared the same state-mandated Iowa Test of Basic Skills (ITBS) and two district-mandated objectives-based, mastery-level tests. However, Hamilton had a direct-instruction phonics-based reading program, while Jackson followed a whole-language approach (school names are pseudonyms). Because of negative district reactions to less than a year's growth on the language subtest of the ITBS, Hamilton's principal instituted a program of daily systematic review of "language."

> This consisted of exercises that required pupils to identify or supply the correct answer to multiple-choice questions on grammar, usage, punctuation, and capitalization. Alternative methods of improving language, such as providing increased opportunities for pupils to write, inservice for teachers that would better prepare them to teach language or writing, aides to help grade papers, or a different text or set of teaching materials were not considered. As a result of Systematic Review, there was less time for the teachers to pursue alternative teaching forms. (Rottenberg & Smith, 1990, pp. 8–9)

Further, in January (in anticipation of April testing), several Hamilton teachers asked to be excused from the *Expressive Writing* and *Writing and Thinking* programs because of the discordance between the content of these programs and the format of important external tests. And *Math Their Way* was given up in favor of "memorizing math facts, subtraction with regrouping and speed drills on simple addition and subtraction problems" (Smith et al., 1990, p. 53).

Jackson Elementary School had received permission to participate in a pilot program that would allow it to satisfy the district requirement for ongoing basic skills testing in language arts by using teacher judgment rather than standardized tests. Thus Jackson students were excused from one of three mandated tests for language arts. Initially the teachers were enthusiastic because the alternative assessment would be more compatible with their holistic instructional approach. However, by midyear Jackson had abandoned the pilot program and reinstated the standardized measures for quarterly testing because standardized formats would better prepare students to take the ITBS and minimum-competency tests that would be given at the end of the year. The teachers at Jackson also chose to use *Scoring High on the ITBS,* which is an extensive package of test preparation materials consuming several weeks of instructional time. According to Smith et al. (1990), the teachers were willing to adopt test coaching strategies that violated their philosophy of education as a protection for their whole-language program, which might be threatened if scores were unacceptably low.

The data from 18 months of observation at Hamilton and Jackson are especially important because they provide concrete examples of the substantive shifts in basic skills instruction that occur because of testing, and they demonstrate how pervasive the effects of antici- pated tests are on instruction throughout the school year. "Prepara- tion" for standardized tests is not limited to the three weeks of review just before each test.

The Harm of Fill-in-the-Blank Rote Instruction

To most experts in child development and early childhood educa- tion, it is obvious that instruction conceived in the format of multiple- choice tests is incompatible with how children learn. However, for accountability enthusiasts who favored the tests in the first place, drill on each skill until mastered seems to be just what is needed. Therefore, more information is required to explain why repeated drill will not lead to better educational outcomes. I present here, in brief, arguments that are best articulated by Resnick (1987) and Resnick and Resnick (in press).

The test-teach-test model of instruction derives from behaviorist theory, which assumed that all learning could be broken down into constituent elements and learned one piece at a time. According to Skinner (1954), "The whole process of becoming competent in any field must be divided into a very large number of very small steps, and reinforcement must be contingent upon the accomplishment of each step" (p. 94). Then, after practicing each skill in isolation, it was assumed that complex understandings could be put together like a piece of machinery from prefabricated parts. Resnick and Resnick (in press) labeled these as the *decomposibility* and *decontextualization* assumptions of early learning theories.

Adherence to this conception of learning has several implications for instructional practice, as manifest in countless contemporary classrooms. In addition to encouraging rote drill on isolated skills, belief in rigidly sequenced hierarchies of skills has caused teachers to postpone efforts to teach thinking and reasoning—so-called higher- order skills—until after basic skills have been mastered (Shepard, 1990c). As a consequence, poor students receive a disproportionate share of dull and largely meaningless instruction because they never do well enough at the basics to be allowed to go on to "the good stuff," which, ironically, would give them some context to use to make sense of the skills they have been unable to memorize (Shepard, 1990b). This underlying hierarchical model explains, for example, why good readers receive instruction focused on comprehension and come to understand that comprehension is the purpose of reading, while poor readers receive instruction focused on decoding and come to believe that oral fluency is the purpose of reading (Allington, in press; Borko & Eisenhart, 1986).

Finally, criterion-referenced testing, which derives from behaviorism, has created a logic and rhetoric that makes it acceptable to "teach to the test" because it is believed that all of the elemental steps in a learning hierarchy can be exhaustively specified and tested for; therefore, behaviorists do not acknowledge that there could be any disjuncture between a well-conceived test and what we want children to know (Shepard, 1990c).

Unfortunately, the research evidence gathered to support the existence of learning hierarchies was post hoc and never actually tested whether sequential learning worked. Because experts in a subject area nearly always possess both complex understandings and rudimentary skills, and novices can perform only basic skills, it was assumed that experts acquired their knowledge one skill at a time in building-block fashion. In fact, a model of learning that delays thinking until later stages is refuted by the last 20 years of research in cognitive psychology. As summarized by Resnick and Resnick (in press), Glaser (1984), and others: All learning involves thinking. Learning of even the simplest skill, like counting, requires that children actively construct their own mental representations of concepts and relations; however, if instruction is geared to have children memorize the string of numbers from one to ten, it is conceivable that they could pass a "counting" test without understanding that eight is more than seven. Reading of even the most basic text requires inference and making sense; and as good readers know, reading entails rereading and making extra interpretive effort when comprehension fails, that is, when the text does not make sense. Good instruction fosters learning by helping children see relations and connect new understandings to background experiences.

There is a natural progression in the development of children's learning, but it is not from memorized facts to thinking. Rather, learning occurs as children's mental schemas, their understandings, grow from simple to complex. Regrettably, a test-driven curriculum aimed at a list of skills does not focus on the development of children's reasoning; nor does it treat children as problem solvers, because the right answer always exists and only has to be recognized among three wrong answers. Given the insights from current research and cognitive theory, it was entirely predictable that today's skills-dominated instructional practices (reinforced by tests) would produce the kinds of results cited earlier from the NAEP—that is, where student performance has increased nationally on routine skills but declined on higher-order thinking tasks.

One last example serves to illustrate how reliance on test content to determine curricular emphases deprives children of the most important kinds of learning experiences—those that help to develop language and thinking abilities. Stallman and Pearson (1990) conducted a content analysis of reading-readiness tests and found them to be dominated by isolated skills rather than tasks that would ask children to behave like readers. The cognitive processing required by test items was recognition, not production or even word identification in context. Furthermore, "what dominates the whole enterprise when children actually take the test is test-taking behavior—filling in bubbles, moving the marker, making sure everyone is in the right place" (p. 38). Stallman and Pearson's analysis also showed the close similarity between the readiness tests used today and the original versions developed in the 1930s, exemplifying the learning theories prevalent at that time.

If Stallman and Pearson were concerned that children would be given a misleading orientation to real literacy while taking a 90-minute readiness test, what might their concerns be if one of these same tests became the format for daily literacy instruction in kindergarten? Based on nonsystematic observations and comments from early childhood educators in several states, there appears to be an increasing trend to select "at-risk" kindergartners for extended-day placements using developmental screening tests and readiness tests like those analyzed by Stallman and Pearson. Then in many instances, as illustrated in the sites studied by Graue (1990), two instructional consequences follow: (1) Children are tracked with all low-readiness children placed in the same classroom, and (2) instruction conforms to the skills on the readiness measure. In Graue's study, the EPSF (Early Prevention of School Failure) curriculum was used in the extended-day program for at-risk kindergartners. In these classrooms, instruction was oriented toward so-called prereading skills (e.g., visual, auditory, language, and fine and gross motor skills), in contrast to the district curriculum, which was developed with a content area focus. For example, one of the district objectives eschewed as too advanced for the EPSF children was this reading objective: "The student will demonstrate an understanding of the concept of 'reading' as a communications process" (Graue, 1990, p. 203). Although the one extended-day teacher studied intensively by Graue supplemented the readiness curriculum with other language development and story experiences, the EPSF curriculum by itself addresses only practice on isolated skills without any attempt to foster children's emergent literacy or awareness that print contains meaning. It is not farfetched to speculate that a vicious cycle has developed whereby children who are measured to be low on readiness skills because they have had few literacy experiences at home are then placed in instructional settings where they are given fewer integrated literacy experiences than "normal" children.

The tendency to deprive children of language and literacy experiences in the name of skill instruction is not always limited to low-track children, however. Durkin's (1987) more general finding was that kindergarten instruction is predominated by workbook drill on phonics, with no effort being made to convey to children that the purpose for learning letter sounds is to unlock what words say.

To be fair, standardized test makers did not create the faulty learning theory that now governs so much of early grades instruction. It is fair to say, however, as shown by Resnick and Resnick (in press) and Stallman and Pearson (1990), that both norm-referenced and criterion-referenced tests are based fundamentally on outmoded learning theories that the tests now carry forward. And because of the power of the tests, these flawed theories have a pervasive and exaggerated effect on instruction today—an effect that mastery learning and programmed instruction never enjoyed in their heyday. Furthermore, no matter how much is known by researchers and practitioners about more appropriate ways to teach young children, the political clout of the tests is often too great to permit any deviation from the curriculum they dictate. Thus it can be argued that accountability tests intended to improve education have become impediments to change and the enforcers of bad instructional practice.

INDIRECT NEGATIVE EFFECTS OF TESTING ON CURRICULUM

The direct negative effects of testing described in the preceding section occur most obviously in classrooms where high-stakes tests are administered each spring. However, in many schools testing has a pervasive effect on what is taught and how it is taught even in grade levels where there is no official test. This section presents arguments that accountability testing has subtle systemic effects on educational climate, attitudes, and the organization of curriculum. Specifically, testing reinforces a lockstep organization of early grades curriculum, contributes to the escalation of narrow academic demands, and leads to the rejection of a high percentage of children as abnormal or misfitting.

The evidence documenting these influences is necessarily correlational data. Therefore, it cannot be said that testing is the primary cause of the observed associations. To the contrary, it might even be argued that whatever the nominal importance of external tests, certain principals, groups of teachers, or school communities might choose to give tests greater salience in their schools because of other beliefs and values that share an affinity with a test-driven curriculum; for example, they might subscribe to the sequential learning theory discussed previously. Regardless of the direction of causation, it is important to describe the character of curriculum and instruction in schools where testing is of paramount importance.

In previous work aimed at understanding the context of kindergarten retention practices, we discovered systematic differences between schools with very high kindergarten retention rates and schools that seldom retained children in kindergarten (Shepard & Smith, 1988; Smith & Shepard, 1988). High-retaining schools shared features that we later characterized as an "accountability culture." These schools were consistently more bureaucratic and rule-governed. They were characterized by greater grade segregation and inflexibility of grade expectations. Although extra grades (developmental kindergartens and transitional first grades) were created ostensibly to respond to developmental differences, there was no evidence of adaptation of instruction to individual pupil's needs within grades. Rather the one-time special placement was expected to take care of children who could not keep pace with the highly regimented grade structure; and within the special grades a considerable amount of instructional time was spent teaching the rules of behavior required for the next level of instruction.

Thus high-retaining schools had developed a lockstep early grades curriculum with rigid exit requirements governing promotion from one grade to the next. Although all teachers within a school participated in maintaining the rigid system, for example, by retaining children who were not ready for the next grade, they pointed to external causes of age-inappropriate curricular demands, namely parent pressure and standardized tests. Shepard and Smith (1988) traced the apparent sequence whereby third grade standardized test requirements were translated by teachers into third grade entrance requirements. Then, if second grade teachers had to ensure these exit requirements, they imposed their own entrance requirements, and so on down the line, until kindergarten teachers were taught explicitly (in teachers' meetings; see also Graue, 1990) or implicitly (by children being sent back from first grade) that they must not promote children who were not ready for instruction that commenced at a fixed point. Others have likened this type of school organization to an assembly line or factory model of education, such that the amount of learning to be added at each stage is exactly specified. The lockstep organization of grades is a logical extension of learning hierarchies and the skills approach applied within grades. Our observation that standardized testing is an integral feature of this model of education is consistent with the findings of Hatch and Freeman (1988). Their analysis of interview data identified five categories of explanations for the shift to increasingly academic kindergarten programs: "(1) changes in children, (2) expectations of parents, (3) accountability to the district and state, (4) proliferation of published materials, and (5) expectations of society" (p. 146).

Although it is logically possible to distinguish between the problems of a lockstep grade structure and the age-inappropriateness of content within a grade, these two features were entwined in the high-retaining schools we studied. Field work was completed prior to our knowledge of the NAEYC guidelines for developmentally appropriate practice. In retrospect, however, it was as though instructional practices in these schools rejected both dimensions of the NAEYC's definition of developmental appropriateness—that curriculum should be age appropriate and individually appropriate (Bredekamp, 1987). Therefore, we came to see a natural correlation in practice between rigid adherence to a common set of requirements for all children and focusing of instruction on a narrow set of reading and numeracy skills. In our research we concluded that the downward translation of next-grade expectations had contributed to both lockstep organization and the escalation of academic demands in kindergarten. For example, first-grade teachers in schools marked by a bureaucratic or accountability culture were no longer willing to teach prereading skills or to accept children who were not ready to begin a reading program the first week of school (Shepard & Smith, 1985). Other analyses have led to similar conclusions. For example, Cunningham (1989) attributed the "trickle down" of academic expectations from elementary grades into kindergarten to accountability pressure and the increased "quantitative assessment of academic skills for children of all ages" (p. 19).

Last, it should be obvious that this system of fixed and inappropriate demands leads to the rejection of a large number of children as unready for normal progress through the grades, hence the need for grade retentions or extra-year programs. The patterns we identified in a sample of high-retaining schools in Colorado closely resemble findings from the California School Readiness Task Force, which were summarized as follows:

> There has been a trend in California (and the nation) to "push down" an overemphasis on specific skills in the curriculum. This has been at the expense of programs tied to the developmental stages of the learner and despite what many kindergarten teachers know about how children learn. As a result of this individually-inappropriate and often age-inappropriate curriculum, many children are not advancing as rapidly as they could and many other children are failing in their first school experience. The retention rate for kindergarten children is increasing in the state. And . . . we have seen an increase in assessment for placement of kindergarten children. (California State Department of Education, 1988, p. v)

How much has standardized testing contributed to this trend toward an aversive early grades curriculum, which some have likened to the procrustean myth (i.e., where children are lopped off if they do not fit the immovable school structure)? We know that many other factors have contributed to the gradual escalation of kindergarten and first-grade expectations, including "Sesame Street," preschool, universal participation in kindergarten, published workbooks, parental demands, and the increasing age of kindergartners (which, ironically, is both a response to and a cause of increasing demands)(Shepard & Smith, 1988). We also know from our comparative study that not all schools responded in the same way as the high-retaining schools to the same externally mandated third grade tests. Low-retaining schools shared a different culture in contrast to the accountability culture of high-retaining schools. In these schools, teachers in different grades worked cooperatively and had more flexible attitudes about grade-level boundaries. For example, they used cross-age peer tutoring and had children moving back and forth between grades for accelerated or remedial instruction. Teachers responded to individual differences with the expectation that the next-grade teacher would pick up where they had left off, and because they did not have rigidly conceived ideas about what constituted grade-level curriculum, they did not judge individual children as misplaced in their grades. In the observational and interview data from low-retaining schools, standardized testing did not arise as an explanation for what teachers did (Smith & Shepard, 1988).

Although our study, which was designed to have equal numbers of high-retaining and low-retaining schools, produced evidence that teachers and schools can sometimes resist creation of a bureaucratic skill-driven curriculum, the California study cited previously suggests that the great majority of schools are affected by rigid, age-inappropriate curriculum in the early grades, leading to special placements for many children. The Hatch and Freeman (1988) study, as well, argues that the pattern we observed in high-retaining schools is the more pervasive one and is influenced by accountability demands.

The inference that accountability pressures generally and standardized tests in particular bear some appreciable share of the blame for the current state of affairs is supported by both formal and informal evidence, such as specific instances from our research and informal responses from teachers at national and regional conferences. For example, in response to the Shepard and Smith study (1985), first grade teachers in one school defended their need to admit only children with advanced prereading skills by pointing to inquiries from their principal whenever any one of their first graders was not above the national norm on the district-administered standardized tests. In various meetings conducted by organizations such as the National Research Council's National Forum on the Future of Children and Their Families and the National Association of State Boards of Education, classroom teachers have provided testimony singling out standardized tests and district-mandated textbooks as the major impediments to changing toward more developmentally appropriate practice. In some respects it does not matter whether teachers could ignore the tests and other pressures without serious consequences (as evidenced by exceptions to the trend), so long as the perception predominates that teachers are powerless to change the imposed system.

NEGATIVE EFFECTS OF TESTING ON CHILDREN

A discussion of the influence of standardized testing would be incomplete without mention of the effects of testing on children and teachers. For children, the degree of harm caused by standardized testing is in direct proportion to the test's control of learning opportunities. As previously described, all children are hurt by a test-driven curriculum because of its lifeless focus on skills rather than thinking, reasoning, language and literacy development, problem solving, and the like. This means that even gifted children are harmed if they are taught the basics by rote without seeing that the purpose of classroom "work" is to develop conceptual understanding and the ability to apply skills to solve real problems.

The more serious harm occurs, however, for children who fail because of the lockstep curriculum or are measured to be incompetent by readiness tests. One way to interpret the data in the previous section is to conclude that the bureaucratic structure of schools has made teachers much less willing to be responsible for hard-to-teach children. Therefore, there are more "rejects" sent to readiness rooms and special education under the onus of accountability. Children are labeled inadequate because of an inadequacy on the part of the school, and they are assigned to extra-year kindergarten programs, kindergarten retention, or segregated kindergartens for at-risk children. In these cases, tests control 100 percent of a child's learning opportunities by virtue of the special placement; yet the 16 controlled studies now available on extra-year programs such as transitional first grade do not show a positive effect on children's learning. They do show some negative social-emotional effects (Shepard, 1989). There are no studies that evaluate the consequences of placing all at-risk kindergartners in the same class (usually because of limited resources for extended-day programs). However, a long record of research on tracking suggests that we can expect a social stigma and watered-down instruction from full-time segregated arrangements.

NEGATIVE EFFECTS OF TESTING ON TEACHERS

In a study intended to document the nature of kindergarten instruction in Ohio, Hatch and Freeman (1988) discovered that teachers are themselves victims of the push for accelerated and narrow academics in kindergarten. Although teachers were the direct agents of worksheet, skill-based programs, 67 percent reported considerable distress because of the discord between the instructional methods they were forced to adopt and their own training and beliefs about children's learning needs. Hatch and Freeman likened the systematic stress and role conflict that they encountered among kindergarten teachers to Walberg's (1970) review findings from research on beginning teachers who were denied professional autonomy. The likelihood is that the most intellectually able teachers and those with the greatest sense of professional identity will leave teaching because of the conflict, and those who remain are likely to protect themselves from the dissonance by caring less about their teaching and their students.

Hatch and Freeman's findings are no surprise to sociologists and policy analysts who have studied the effects of top-down reforms on the professional role of teachers. As explained by Darling-Hammond (1988), the very conception of bureaucratic accountability is intended to remove control from the judgments of individual teachers, hence the notion of "teacher-proof" curricula. According to this view of education, which derives from the century-old idea of scientific management, all of the important factors governing teaching—curriculum, instructional methods, textbooks, tests, promotion standards, and the like—can be adopted and standardized outside the classroom and then merely handed to the classroom teacher to implement. Teachers are not expected to be experts in child development or pedagogy.

Bureaucratic accountability (which Darling-Hammond contrasts with professional accountability) begets exactly what it assumes, namely less skilled professionals who take less responsibility for the instructional needs of their students. In an extensive field study, McNeil (1988) documented among high-school teachers some of the same stifling of professionalism that Hatch and Freeman found with kindergarten teachers. In McNeil's study, teachers responded to a school structure that rewarded procedural controls over educational substance by developing similar controls over their own students. They "deliberately presented simplified, fragmented bits of information to their students in the hope that students would comply with minimum requirements and leave the teacher in charge of the pacing of the course" (p. 480). McNeil entitled her study "Contradictions of Control." One of the contradictions that she observed was the extent to which two reforms, proficiency-based testing of students and an assessment of teacher behaviors, actually reinforced the dynamics of low-quality, mechanistic instruction. Similarly, Rottenberg and Smith (1990) found that teachers were both degraded and deskilled by a high-stakes testing environment. Teachers felt ashamed and embarrassed by low scores even when they recognized the influence of socioeconomic factors on school rankings and the mismatch of the test content to instructional goals. And teachers were deskilled because their decisions to align instruction with the tests impoverished their teaching repertoires and ultimately limited their own conceptions of what should be taught.

CONCLUSION

Test-driven educational reform in the 1980s has had a pervasively negative effect on teaching and learning because the content and format of standardized tests now determine the character of elementary school curriculum. Most specifically, the political importance of accountability tests has cemented and exaggerated the worst features of a skills-oriented conception of instruction and a bureaucratic, lockstep organization of the early grades.

Reformers intent on improving educational outcomes never stopped to examine the substance of standardized tests to decide whether they would be adequate as the exclusive targets of instruction, day in and day out. Nor did they recognize that traditional achievement tests (both norm-referenced and criterion-referenced) are based on an outmoded learning theory that postpones thinking and problem solving until after students have mastered the basics. Reformers also failed to anticipate the negative side effects of an inappropriate, test-driven curriculum on children and teachers. Many more children are made to fail by narrow academic drill in kindergarten and first grade and are relegated to ineffective instructional placements such as extra-year programs and special tracks for "at-risk" children. Teachers are demoralized and deskilled by an external accountability system that had as its purpose eliminating teacher judgment and control over important educational decisions. As a consequence, teachers take less responsibility for hard-to-teach children and accept their powerlessness to teach in developmentally appropriate ways because of the need to keep instruction closely aligned to external tests.

What are the remedies or alternatives to this distressing picture? Some of these problems are beginning to be understood, and important position statements about the testing of young children have been articulated in a forum that is likely to influence some policy makers (NAEYC, 1988; NASBE, 1988). However, there is still a disproportionate share of the old rhetoric abiding—as evidenced by calls for more testing and legislators wanting to keep children out of school until they are ready to learn, rather than letting them in so they can learn—making it unlikely that the juggernaut of external accountability demands will topple soon. Therefore, at the grassroots level the solution is for groups of teachers to meet and decide to make their classroom instruction more developmentally appropriate and to refuse to pattern daily instruction after the format of tests.

Often the repercussions that teachers fear from not teaching to the
tests, such as losing their jobs or getting less desirable teaching
assignments, are imagined. For example, in the Hatch and Freeman
(1988) study, principals denied that they were directly exerting the
pressure that teachers reported. But whether the repercussions are
imagined or real, they are better withstood by a group of teachers in
a school than by an individual, especially if the group has developed
a well-articulated, professional statement that justifies curricular
decisions in terms of the learning needs of children. Notice that these
teacher-initiated actions accomplish two purposes: They redirect
instruction in a way that is more conducive to student learning, but
they also take the first step in reestablishing the professional role of
teachers and the responsibility of teachers for making important
instructional decisions within their classrooms.

At the policy level, two courses of action should be taken to break
the cycle of dreary instruction followed by poor student performance,
followed by more testing and even more deadly drill and practice.
First, a moratorium on standardized testing in the early grades
should be called in each jurisdiction. Although the negative effects of
standardized testing can be documented at all grade levels, they are
most intensely felt in the early elementary grades where paper-and-
pencil fill-in-the-blank tasks are most at odds with how children
learn. There should be no publicly reported multiple-choice testing of
children before third grade. Then, once the distorting effects of
standardized testing have been halted, policy makers should consider
instituting exemplary performance or "authentic" assessments that
would be more respectful of children, teachers, and important educational goals (see Resnick & Resnick, in press; Wiggins, 1989).

Rather than lead instruction in the wrong direction, accountability assessments should be the embodiment of best practice. Assessments that include oral reading, story retelling, interviews about
science projects, portfolios of students' work, and construction of
models to represent mathematical problems are considered authentic
because they engage students in exactly the kinds of challenging
tasks that we want them to be able to do. If teachers were to copy these
kinds of tasks and teach to authentic assessments there would be, in
theory at least, no harm to student learning. Measurement specialists are aware, however, that even performance assessments can be
corrupted if the stakes are high enough, and the assessment tasks are
necessarily a limited sample from intended learning goals. Therefore, the most important lesson to be learned from the accountability
"madness" of the 1980s is that reforms will fail if they try to take

important day-to-day instructional decisions out of the hands of classroom teachers.

Test-leveraged reform is only as good as the test-turned-to-mandated curriculum. Given that there cannot be a perfect test, curriculum reform and teacher training hold greater promise for positive change.

NOTE

Research reported herein was supported in part by a grant from the Office of Educational Research and Improvement, Department of Education (OERI/ED). However, the opinions expressed are those of the author and do not reflect the position or policy of the OERI.

REFERENCES

Allington, R. L. (in press). Children who find learning to read difficult: School responses to diversity. In E. Hiebert (Ed.), *Literacy for a diverse society: Perspectives, programs, and policies.* New York: Teachers College Press.

Borko, H., & Eisenhart, M. (1986). Students' conceptions of reading and their reading experiences in school. *Elementary School Journal, 86,* 589–611.

Bredekamp, S. (Ed.) (1987). *Developmentally appropriate practice in early childhood programs serving children from birth through age 8.* Washington, DC: National Association for the Education of Young Children.

California State Department of Education. (1988). *Here they come ready or not: A report of the School Readiness Task Force.* Sacramento, CA: Author.

Cannell, J. J. (1987). *Nationally normed elementary achievement testing in America's public schools: How all 50 states are above the national average.* Daniels, WV: Friends for Education.

Cunningham, A. E. (1989). *Eeny, meeny, miny, moe: Testing policy and practice in early childhood.* Paper prepared for the National Commission on Testing and Public Policy, University of California, Berkeley.

Darling-Hammond, L. (1988). Accountability and teacher professionalism. *American Educator, 12,* 8–13, 38–43.

Darling-Hammond, L., & Wise, A. E. (1985). Beyond standardization: State standards and school improvement. *The Elementary School Journal, 85,* 315–336.

Dossey, J. A., Mullis, I. V. S., Lindquist, M. M., & Chambers, D. L. (1988). *The mathematics report card: Are we measuring up?* Princeton, NJ: Educational Testing Service.

Durkin, D. (1987). A classroom-observation study of reading instruction in kindergarten. *Early Childhood Research Quarterly, 2,* 275–300.

Fiske, J. (1988, May 8). Kindergarten: The rules have changed. *The Press-Enterprise*, pp. B-1, B-3.

Glaser, R. (1984). Education and thinking: The role of knowledge. *American Psychologist, 39,* 93–104.

Graue, M. E. (1990). *Socially constructed readiness for kindergarten in three communities.* Unpublished doctoral dissertation, University of Colorado at Boulder.

Harman, S. (1990). Negative effects of achievement testing in literacy development. In C. Kamii (Ed.), *Achievement testing in the early grades: The games grown-ups play.* Washington, DC: National Association for the Education of Young Children.

Hatch, J. A., & Freeman, E. B. (1988). Who's pushing whom? Stress and kindergarten. *Phi Delta Kappan, 69,* 145–147.

Indiana Department of Education. (1988). *Indiana statewide testing for educational progress, ISTEP: Program manual.* Indianapolis, IN: Author.

Linn, R. L., Graue, M. E., & Sanders, N. M. (1990). Comparing state and district test results to national norms: The validity of claims that "everyone is above average." *Educational Measurement: Issues and Practice, 9,* 5–14.

McNeil, L. M. (1988). Contradictions of control, part 3: Contradictions of reform. *Phi Delta Kappan, 69,* 478–485.

Mullis, I. V. S., & Jenkins, L. B. (1990). *The reading report card, 1971–88.* Princeton, NJ: National Assessment of Educational Progress.

A Nation at Risk. (1983). Washington, DC: The National Commission on Excellence in Education.

National Association for the Education of Young Children. (1988). NAEYC position statement on standardized testing of young children 3–8 years of age. *Young Children, 43,* 42–47.

National Association of State Boards of Education. (1988). *Right from the start: The report of the NASBE Task Force on Early Childhood Education.* Washington, DC: Author.

Popham, W. J. (1987). The merits of measurement-driven instruction. *Phi Delta Kappan, 68,* 679–682.

Popham, W. J., Cruse, K. L., Rankin, S. C., Sandifer, P. D., & Williams, P. L. (1985). Measurement-driven instruction: It's on the road. *Phi Delta Kappan, 66,* 628–634.

Resnick, L. B. (1987). *Education and learning to think.* Washington, DC: National Academy Press.

Resnick, L. B., & Resnick, D. P. (in press). Assessing the thinking curriculum: New tools for educational reform. In B. R. Gifford & M. C. O'Connor (Eds.), *Future assessments: Changing views of aptitude, achievement, and instruction.* Boston: Kluwer Academic Publishers.

Rottenberg, C., & Smith, M. L. (1990, April). *Unintended effects of external testing in elementary schools.* Paper presented at the annual meeting of the American Educational Research Association, Boston.

Shepard, L. A. (1988, April). *Should instruction be measurement-driven? A debate.* Paper presented at the annual meeting of the American Educational Research Association, New Orleans.

Shepard, L. A. (1989). A review of research on kindergarten retention. In L. A. Shepard & M. L. Smith (Eds.), *Flunking grades: Research & policies on retention.* London: Falmer Press.

Shepard, L. A. (1990a). Inflated test score gains: Is the problem old norms or teaching the test? *Educational Measurement: Issues and Practice, 9,* 15–22.

Shepard, L. A. (1990b). Negative policies for dealing with diversity: When does assessment and diagnosis turn into sorting and segregation? In E. Hiebert (Ed.), *Literacy for a diverse society: Perspectives, programs, and policies.* New York: Teachers College Press.

Shepard, L. A. (1990c, April). *Psychometricians' beliefs about learning.* Paper presented at the annual meeting of the American Educational Research Association, Boston.

Shepard, L. A., & Smith, M. L. (1985, March). *Boulder Valley kindergarten study: Retention practices and retention effects.* Boulder, CO: Boulder Valley Public Schools.

Shepard, L. A., & Smith, M. L. (1988). Escalating academic demand in kindergarten: Counterproductive polices. *The Elementary School Journal, 89,* 135–145.

Skinner, B. F. (1954). The science of learning and the art of teaching. *Harvard Educational Review, 24,* 86–97.

Smith, M. L., Edelsky, C., Draper, K., Rottenberg, C., & Cherland, M. (1990). *The role of testing in elementary schools.* Los Angeles: Center for Research on Evaluation, Standards, and Student Testing.

Smith, M. L., & Shepard, L. A. (1988). Kindergarten readiness and retention: A qualitative study of teachers' beliefs and practices. *American Educational Research Journal, 25,* 307–333.

Stallman, A. C., & Pearson, P. D. (1990). Formal measures of early literacy. In L. M. Morrow & J. K. Smith (Eds.), *Assessment for instruction in early literacy.* Englewood Cliffs, NJ: Prentice Hall.

Texas State Board of Education. (1988, June). *Rationale for the development of the student assessment program: 1990–1995.* Austin, TX: Author.

Walberg, H. J. (1970). Professional role discontinuities in educational careers. *Review of Educational Research, 40,* 409–420.

Wiggins, G. (1989). Teaching to the (authentic) test. *Educational Leadership, 46,* 41–47.

CHAPTER 10

Searches for Validity in Evaluating Young Children and Early Childhood Programs

Douglas R. Powell
Irving E. Sigel

This chapter examines the problems and recent progress in improving the validity of evaluations of young children's development and early childhood programs. Since the 1960s, there has been an unprecedented growth in research on the effects of early intervention and child care programs, largely in response to questions about the wisdom of investing resources in programs for young children. There has been a concomitant increase in the practice of evaluating young children as part of outcome studies of early childhood programs and as part of ambitious screening and testing programs aimed at placing children in appropriate educational environments. The consequences of these evaluations for social policy, program planning, theory building, and ultimately the lives of young children are considerable.

Validity is a construct involving high stakes. The increase in evaluation activities rests on the proposition that the instruments employed to assess children and other program outcomes are valid procedures. If the measures are valid, then it would follow that a lack of anticipated level of functioning among children is due to either the nature of the child or the inadequacy of the program in which the child is a participant. On the other hand, it may well be that the program is adequate and the children do profit, but that the assessment procedures are irrelevant to the program experiences or are invalid indicators of the construct reportedly being measured. Instruments used in child screening and testing programs also are presumed to be valid. If child assessment instruments are valid, then it follows that a child's developmental functioning is accurately described, providing a solid foundation for making an informed decision about an appropriate educational placement. On the other hand, invalid measures lead to inaccurate descriptions of child functioning and probably to inappropriate educational placements, a matter of no small consequence to the child and his or her future.

The three major points at which consideration of validity is critical in evaluating young children and early childhood programs are (1) the identification of program outcome variables, (2) the development and use of valid measures of child functioning, and (3) the use of evaluation findings to inform public policy and program design decisions. Different types of validity are considered from the perspective of whether a test or study assesses what it purports to assess, and whether certain inferences from an evaluation of children and/or a program are appropriate or meaningful. Readers are referred to Cronbach and Meehl (1967) and Messick (1974) for detailed treatments of approaches to validity.

DETERMINING VALID PROGRAM OUTCOME VARIABLES

Evaluations of early childhood programs have made some progress in the past two decades in identifying outcome variables that are compatible with program goals and methods. The match or close correspondence between program and outcome variables may be referred to as *program validity* (or instructional validity; see Seppanen & Love, 1990). A logical assessment of early childhood programs involves tapping variables that are directly related to program experience. The logic is the same as that employed in evaluations of other educational programs in which the criterion measures are connected to program inputs in theory and in practice. One sign of progress in evaluations of early childhood programs is the broadening of outcome variables beyond IQ scores. Progress also is seen in policy directives such as the National Association for the Education of Young Children's (NAEYC) position statement on standardized testing of young children, which calls for assessments to match "the locally determined theory, philosophy, and objectives of the specific program" (NAEYC, 1988, p. 46). Nonetheless, as discussed below, the search for valid representations of program effects has not proceeded without conceptual and methodological difficulties.

IQ Scores

Without question, the IQ score was the most frequently used outcome variable in evaluations of early childhood intervention programs in the 1960s and 1970s. The hypothesis being tested was that an increase in IQ should occur as a result of experience in an early childhood program. The popularity of IQ scores stemmed from several sources. Standard IQ tests are tried-and-true measures with well-documented psychometric properties. They are relatively easy to administer, especially if evaluators employ a brief test that has a high correlation with a full-fledged IQ test. Of no less importance, IQ scores have consistently been found to be strong predictors of school success. This fact makes the IQ score an especially appealing outcome variable among those who view early childhood education as preparation for later school performance.

In spite of this seemingly rational basis for using IQ scores in assessing the effects of early childhood programs, they have increasingly been criticized as inadequate and irrelevant indicators of the efficacy of a child's preschool program experience. Criticism of the use of IQ scores in evaluating early childhood programs was particularly pronounced in the 1970s, as investigators expanded the empirical understanding of what IQ scores represent. For example, data indicated that IQ changes resulting from preschool intervention programs reflected motivational changes that influenced test performance rather than changes in actual cognitive functioning (Zigler, Abelson & Seitz, 1973). IQ scores also were found to have a modest relation to everyday performance in life in the postschool period (McClelland, 1973).

Social Competence

The construct of social competence was enthusiastically proposed as a promising area for assessing early childhood program outcomes in the 1970s, primarily due to a widespread view of social competence as a broader and therefore more valid indicator of program effects. The construct proved to be difficult to define in precise terms, however. One notable attempt to generate a useful definition yielded some 29 indicators of social competence, each in need of greater refinement (Anderson & Messick, 1974). Another effort to define the components of a social competence index included four areas: physical health and well-being, formal cognitive ability, achievement, and motivational and emotional indices (Zigler & Trickett, 1978). Presently, the concept of social competence may be more of a generic umbrella encompassing a range of diverse measures of children's social behavior than a practical guide for test construction (Clarke-Stewart & Fein, 1983). Of necessity, recently developed measures falling within the social competence rubric have employed less comprehensive definitions. For example, the Bronson executive skills profile assesses children's planning and decision-making skills in such areas as use of time (Bronson, 1975, 1985), and the Howes peer play scale defines social competence as behavior that reflects successful social functioning with peers (Howes, 1980, 1987).

Social Indicators

In recent years, social indicators have surfaced prominently as outcome variables in evaluations of early childhood programs (Consortium for Longitudinal Studies, 1983; Berreuta-Clement, Schweinhart, Barnett, Epstein & Weikart, 1985). These indicators include school attendance, retention in grade, placement in special education, use of public welfare services, and juvenile delinquency as measures of the long-term effects of early education. Distinctive advantages of social indicators include their ease in communicating evaluation results to the lay public and their connection to widespread societal values (e.g., youth should not commit delinquent acts). Positive findings do not lend themselves to easy interpretation, however. Grade retention and placement in special education, for instance, are likely to be affected by school policies and other external factors that might cloud their interpretation as measures of long-term individual functioning (Travers & Light, 1982). Clarke-Stewart and Fein (1983) set forth central questions: If program children do not differ from nonprogram children on measures of school achievement, but do differ from one another on measures of grade retention or assignment to special education, does it mean that children are retained in grade or placed in special education for reasons other than academic criteria? If so, what might these criteria be, and how do children enrolled in preschool manage to meet them?

Progress in identifying outcome variables that are linked to program goals and operations, then, has led to crucial questions about the meaning of indices that presumably tap individual well-being. The lack of conceptual clarity surrounding social competence and social indicators probably is no greater than the field's ambiguous understanding of what a traditional IQ test actually measures. Nevertheless, the issues and questions posed above deserve the thoughtful attention of researchers.

DEVELOPING VALID MEASURES OF CHILD FUNCTIONING

The young child poses many measurement challenges. In this section, we examine two sets of key issues pertaining to the development of valid assessment procedures for young children: the mismatch between developmental processes and traditional child assessment strategies, and the relation of context to a child's performance in an assessment situation. Implications of these issues for the evaluation of young children are also addressed.

Measurement and the Developmental Process

Young children are not good candidates for taking traditional tests. The reliability and validity of test results are greatly compromised by the child's rapid changes in development, fluctuations in the intensity and focus of interests, and the unfamiliarity of the assessment situation. Measurement is especially difficult in the first years of life because there are relatively few stable functions.

The search for validity has required that phenomena be examined objectively, usually through standardized tests involving quantification, in order to reduce idiosyncratic interpretation and to communicate results objectively. The irony is that meeting these measurement objectives has necessitated the violation of a number of psychological principles related to a conceptualization of the child as a dynamic living organism locked into a system of transformational change.

Stability, Continuity, or Transformation. Measurement presumes that the characteristic being measured is stable and that the relationship obtained among variables is independent of temporal relationships. For a developmental psychologist, this perspective is nonsense, because a static state is a nonreal phenomenon at any age. Change permeates all living matter. With children, in whom change is dramatic and often apparent but unpredictable, we are faced with a ticklish measurement problem when using repeated measure designs. How long a temporal interval should be used? If a child is tested at period 1 and retested at period 2, what are the parameters of this time span—a day, a week, a month—to be considered as a test of reliability? After what time period do we consider it no longer an issue of reliability of the test, but rather the stability of the behavior in question? The distinction between reliability of the measure and stability of the individual becomes somewhat blurred and can be judged only on the basis of the knowledge we have of the developmental process; this then becomes a validity issue. Validity and reliability begin to blend because the consistency over time may be reliable, but one needs to question whether it is, in fact, consistency. If the relative position of individuals within a group is maintained on a retest, but the scores are higher, is the test reliable and also valid?

The question is: Does a test (controlled for difficulty, of course) measure the same variable at each point in the course of development? If, for example, the child is given a sorting task with familiar objects, does it measure classification ability each time it is used, or does it measure different things at different times? At issue here is the conceptualization of developmental change. Are traits consistent over time, which means that they function and are identifiable in the same form from one time epoch to another; or are they similar in form but different in meaning from one time epoch to another; or are they different in form and in meaning from one time epoch to another; or are they similar in form and in meaning from one time epoch to another?

Each of these is possible. For example, does aggression mean the same thing when manifested by a three-year-old as by a five- or ten-year-old? Does the same act appearing at age three differ in significance when expressed at age ten, since the child at this older age knows different things about social behavior? The problem of measurement in the personal-social domain is that the behaviors defined at one age level can be similarly defined at another age level, but the function of that behavior may vary from one point to another. The issue in the cognitive area is similar. At one age level, for example, there is no evidence of conservation; at another, the child is a conserver. Is this discontinuous or continuous change?

There is no question that the issue of continuity, stability, or transformation forms the crucial challenge to developmental measurement. Similarities in form do not necessarily mean similarities in function. That is, in terms of traits or abilities, the appearance of something that looks like something else on a manifest level may in fact not function in an identical way. For example, memory for digits for the very young child may be an index of comprehension of ordering numbers, whether arbitrary or not, while at an older level it may appear as a rote memory task. On a draw-a-person task, some children at young age levels may in fact draw a conception of man, while an older child may well draw an idealized image, not really a reflection of the child's own perceptions of reality. Wohlwill (1973) was among the first to seriously address these issues (see also Emmerich, 1966; Kagan, 1969), and his perspective offered nearly twenty years ago continues to be a relevant argument for a clearer conceptualization of continuity:

> The field of stability and continuity is one strewn with roadblocks
> of the investigator's own making, arising from the purely correla-
> tional sense in which the terms are typically taken, combined with
> the all too human tendency to lose sight of the limitations in
> discussion of the subject. (Wohlwill, 1973, p. 373)

Continuity poses particular problems for evaluation. For some phenomena, continuity in the sense of incremental gains (e.g., better skill in mathematics) suggests the appropriateness of assessments that are cumulative, in that the items are of the same class but get more difficult. For other phenomena, continuity is conceptualized as correlated with subsequent behavior, but the correlated behaviors are not expressed in the same form; that is, a transformation has taken place. This type of apparent discontinuity with underlying continuity would suggest different types of items and tasks.

Assessing Learning Potential.   Another needed modification in our assessment procedure pertains to the type of tasks employed. It is commonplace to comment on the static quality of test items. Typically, children are asked to tell what they know, not to show what they can learn or how they learn. The assumption is that if an individual has a large fund of information, it can be assumed that the individual is a good learner. This may not be the case. From scores on these instruments, we know only how much they know, not their competence in acquiring that knowledge.

There is a lack of clarity in the field today regarding the purposes and limits of tests that measure knowledge acquisition versus learning potential. A case in point is the substitution of readiness tests for developmental screening tests (see Meisels, 1984, 1985, 1987). The key difference between developmental screening tests and school readiness tests is the distinction between skill acquisition and the ability to acquire skills. The purpose of developmental screening tests is to identify children who may have a learning problem or handicapping condition that could affect their developmental potential, including success in school. Readiness tests focus on current skill achievement and performance. Readiness tests should be used to facilitate curriculum planning on the basis of the information a readiness test yields about a child's preparedness to benefit from a specific program. Readiness tests generally lack predictive validity and therefore should not be used to identify children who may need special services or intervention. They describe the entry characteristics of children and are not intended to predict child outcomes.

What is often needed in assessments of young children is information on the child's learning potential. Tests need to provide sources of information on how the child learns. For example, the inclusion of mini-learning tasks would permit the evaluation of errors, length of time to learn a task, and the style in which the child approaches the task. Coupling this information with what the child knows, as assessed by traditional test items, affords a broader picture of the child's competencies. Yet it must be kept in mind that these data are still collected within the confines of a one-to-one learning situation and may not be representative of the way the child learns in the classroom. Observation of the child in a classroom setting would constitute another type of information for improving an understanding of the child's learning abilities.

Types of Test Responses. Another issue that arises when considering testing situations is the type of response expected. Reviewing the major intelligence tests in the field, one finds that responses to items are essentially of the convergent-thinking type. All require the child to give a single right-wrong answer. Elaborations are not systematically required. If elaborations are made, the examiner may or may not record them; if they are recorded at all, they are recorded as impressions and not systematically employed in the scoring or analysis.

If the approaches of Piaget and Werner regarding the developmental cognitive structure are taken seriously, there might well be a discrepancy between what the child says and what the child understands. If this is true, convergent-type tasks provide only a limited source of information. First, they tell us little if anything about process; second, they tell us little about the range of the child's mental approach to tasks; and third, they tell us little about the child's conceptualizations. In effect, precious little is learned about the processes involved in intellectual or social functioning when there is reliance on tasks demanding convergent-type responses.

Proposals for altering traditional tests to allow for children's elaborations and for the inclusion of other process data are often deemed antithetical to standardization, precluding the use of comparative information. Yet we argue that the kinds of knowledge we typically amass on a child are limited and not valid indicators of competence. If given the opportunity, children often provide interesting verbal elaborations of their experiences and the meaning of items in the course of performing tasks.

Analysis of Errors in Test Performance. A related issue is the handling of errors in the child's test responses. It is not a novel idea to be concerned with errors, especially for early childhood professionals working within a constructive perspective (Forman & Fosnot, 1982), but more attention needs to be given to this aspect of test behavior among children. Errors appear to be systematic, which is not surprising if one accepts the assumption that all behavior on a test has some basis in the respondent's reality. If behavior has purpose, then an error is an expression of purpose. The error is, in fact, the child's expression of what he or she thinks is a right answer. Consequently, an error can provide some insight into the child's interpretation of the item.

Child Performance: Typical Behavior or Situationally Determined?

Psychologists have long emphasized the need to consider the setting in which individuals are observed and tested (e.g., Lewin, 1951; Barker, 1963). The task is to understand the significance of the various settings in which a child functions and then attempt to identify salient interactions within these settings, examining how they influence the kind and the quality of ongoing behavior. Unfortunately, the traditional rationale and procedures for testing children do not take into account the manifest differences in behavior from one setting to another. Tests are presumed to transcend the specific situation, have general predictive value, and allow for predictions to situations in general. Rarely do assessments of young children include observations or testing in more than one setting (e.g., home and school), and rarely do results specify the situation for which a prediction is being made. There is a tacit assumption of contextual irrelevance (Bronfenbrenner, 1989). Yet validity is improved when relevant dimensions of the setting are specified from the child's perspective.

Same Person, Different Settings. In the past two decades, interest in relations between setting characteristics and individual behavior has focused primarily on the ecological validity of child evaluation procedures. The interest has been stimulated and refined in part by Bronfenbrenner (1979, 1989), who proposed two conditions for a research setting to be ecologically valid: an investigation of the psychological and social meaning of the subject's experience in the setting, and a correspondence between the research situation and the everyday life or environmental experience to which the evaluator wishes to generalize. Attention to ecological validity in the evaluation of young children has focused primarily on the latter condition. Recently, for instance, questions have been raised about the ecological validity of the Strange Situation (Ainsworth, Blehar, Waters & Wall, 1978), a procedure often used to assess the effects of out-of-home child care on infants. Clarke-Stewart (1988) has argued that the Strange Situation has elements that may be familiar to infants of working mothers, and therefore the procedure may not be equally stressful for infants of working and nonworking mothers. Infants of working mothers may well be accustomed to features of the Strange Situation: The infant plays in a room that is not his or her own, is left with a woman in the mother's absence, and plays with and is comforted by that woman in the mother's absence; then the mother returns to pick up the infant (Clarke-Stewart, 1988).

Concern about ecological validity has been fueled by criticisms of IQ tests as primarily measures of middle-class Anglo values and attitudes that should not be imposed in the assessment of children from low-income and ethnic minority populations (Laosa, 1982). Because most preschool programs that undergo evaluation typically enroll populations of considerable sociocultural diversity, a critical question is the extent to which outcome measures are pluralistic in nature and hence able to gauge performance that is genuinely related to the child's past and future life experiences.

Laboratories as Contexts.   A primary target of interest in ecological validity has been the laboratory setting where one-on-one testing of children generally is carried out. To be sure, the setting is likely to be unusual if not unreal from the child's point of view. Other than with a physician, the child rarely engages in a one-on-one encounter with a relatively unfamiliar adult. The strangeness of the situation probably is heightened if the adult expresses the wish to play games with the child. Is this not a strange role for an adult? Rarely if ever does a parent make this announcement and then proceed to take the child away, perhaps from an enjoyable activity, into a room where the two of them play so-called games, with the agenda determined by the adult. This is a very atypical game-playing experience for the child.

In the 1970s, a misguided but prevalent response to criticisms of one-on-one laboratory testing was to abandon individual assessment and/or the laboratory setting and to assume that any testing or observation of children carried out in a naturalistic setting such as the home was a superior method of gathering information about child development and functioning (see Bronfenbrenner, 1979). The fact that results obtained in a laboratory differ from those secured in the home does not lead logically to the interpretation that the home is a more ecologically valid context for data collection. The laboratory, home, and other real-life settings represent different ecological contexts that vary in their appropriateness for assessing certain aspects of children. Moreover, intrusions into the home for data-gathering purposes—such as a visit from a white middle-class observer to a low-income African-American home—may create ecological distortions in the real-life situation that attenuate a child's test performance (see Seitz, Abelson, Levine & Zigler, 1975). Comparisons of results obtained across diverse settings provide an opportunity to determine the ecological validity of a measure or set of measures and data used to generalize about child functioning.

Developmental Validity.   Most evaluations of young children and early childhood programs that gather data on children in multiple settings seek to determine whether a child's developmental functioning transcends setting characteristics. This goal is in contrast with the research aim of examining the interactional nature of relations between child behavior and setting variables. To determine that developmental change has occurred, it is necessary to demonstrate that a change in a person's conceptions and/or activities carries over to other settings and other times. Bronfenbrenner (1979) refers to such a demonstration as *developmental validity.* Knowing whether a child's behavior is typical or situationally determined is problematic in a number of ways, as indicated above. One key set of variables that often goes ignored pertains to child characteristics. The trans-situational stability of child functioning is likely to be highly variable, partly as a function of child variables; some children will consistently demonstrate competence in a task in both one-to-one situations and in the classroom, while other children will show stronger performance in the classroom than in one-to-one situations, and vice versa.

Thus, situational differences as well as child responses to the demand characteristics of situations may partly account for inconsistencies in child behaviors across settings. Teachers' ratings of children on behaviors similar to those assessed in a test situation might not be highly correlated, for example. To disregard the teacher ratings or test data solely on the basis of presumed inadequacies of a measure or procedures offers an incomplete conception of variability in individual behavior. The "fault" may not lie with the examiner/rater or the instrument, but with an interaction of child characteristics and situational factors that constrains or enhances child functioning. We concur with Bronfenbrenner's (1989) argument that context should be included as an essential element in defining competence. Recent studies by Ceci and his colleagues have demonstrated that both child and adult cognitive processes vary in complexity and efficiency as a function of the context in which they are embedded (Ceci, in press; Ceci & Bronfenbrenner, 1985; Ceci & Liker, 1986). The context is not "simply an adjunct to the cognition, but a constituent of it" (Ceci, Bronfenbrenner & Baker, 1988, p. 243). The assessment of competence, then, must be interpreted in the light of the culture or subculture in which the child has been or is being reared (Bronfenbrenner, 1989).

Implications for the Assessment of Young Children.   The basic principles that affect the validity of assessment procedures may be summarized as follows:

1. Individuals are variable, and their variation expresses their own competence levels.
2. Fragmenting behaviors, without taking contingencies and other contextual factors into account, limits the understanding of the individual and subsequent validity of assessment.
3. Individuals vary in the degree to which they are consistent from one setting to another; hence, valid assessment must include the assessment of comparable behaviors across settings, or limit generalizations to settings.
4. Irrespective of setting, task variables must be considered in discussions of validity. Analyses of errors should be made systematic, since errors are psychologically systematic behaviors, assuming that people act for reasons. The format of a response must allow for elaboration and process expression if there is to be an understanding of the dynamics of performance.

Predicting a Developmental Course.   Given a developmental view of the child as a rapidly changing organism whose behaviors are inextricably tied to culture and specific settings, a worst-case scenario for assessment procedures is to use data from a single *acontextual* measure administered at one point to predict the course of development at a later point in a child's life. In many ways, such a situation exists today for growing numbers of children who are subjected to evaluations used to make decisions about school entry and grade level placement.

A serious problem is that the predictive validity of many screening tests is unknown or inadequate. The accuracy of information about predictive validity is critically important because of the risk of misidentifying and placing children in inappropriate settings. Accordingly, the American Psychological Association's (1985) technical standards for screening or placement tests are more rigorous than for readiness tests. Yet there has been a proliferation of screening tests, many developed by local school districts, that lack credible evidence on validity and reliability (Meisels, 1987). Further, the predictive validity of even the most well-developed screening tests is often examined through inadequate procedures (e.g., correlations) that do not clearly compare the screening test results to later levels of individual functioning through classification analysis (see Meisels, 1984).

One test used widely in the United States for both readiness and developmental screening is the Gesell School Readiness Screening Test (Ilg & Ames, 1972). The test is designed to assess a child's developmental functioning, using tasks derived from Arnold Gesell's norms of development and theory of maturational readiness. Unfortunately, there is no evidence to indicate that the behaviors measured by the Gesell test accurately predict subsequent development. A recent study found the Gesell test to have a small positive relationship to first grade report card grades, modest predictive validity for standardized tests, and low validity for teacher judgment of performance in first grade (Graue & Shepard, 1989). Graue and Shepard note that in two earlier studies on the predictive validity of the Gesell tests (Ilg, Ames, Haines & Gillespie, 1978; Wood, Powell & Knight, 1984), the test results were contaminated with the criterion variable (e.g., Gesell test results used to make placement decisions, then grade placement used as a validity criterion).

In a thorough review of developmental screening instruments, Meisels (1984) concluded that available screening tests are neither definitive nor comprehensive. Many predict well for the short term but are weak in the accuracy of long-term identification of children at risk. Developmental screening tests should be used as indicators, to signal the need for intensive follow-up assessments that provide more detailed information and have greater predictive power.

It is an open question whether the long-term predictive validity of child assessment tools can be improved substantially. Adding data about influences on development, such as family conditions, may contribute to predictive accuracy; for instance, information on parent circumstances and the home environment has been found to improve the predictive validity of the Strange Situation procedure for measuring mother-infant attachment (Thompson, Lamb & Estes, 1982) and of an index for identifying infants at risk (Siegel, 1982). Researchers have a long way to go in specifying family variables and measures that could be incorporated into assessment tools with both efficiency and empirical confidence. Further, environments are not static entities immune to change over time (Bronfenbrenner, 1989). Tapping the dynamic quality and multiple levels of person-environment interaction in assessment procedures is likely to enhance the validity of evaluations of young children. Major progress in the improvement of validity, however, also hinges on conceptual and methodological advances regarding the previously discussed developmental issues of continuity, stability, and transformation.

Integrating an Array of Information. In the past several decades there has been growth in the development and use of assessments tied to expected knowledge acquisition through participation in an early childhood program. Illustrative of this movement are criterion-referenced tests, which measure a child's performance in relation to predetermined areas of mastery (Popham, 1978), and curriculum-based assessments, which link test items to curricular goals (Neisworth & Bagnato, 1986). Major limitations of these assessment strategies include the emphasis on what children know rather than their learning potential and a general lack of attention to developmental processes and progress.

A promising development within the past decade is the Head Start Measures Battery (Bergan et al., 1984), which is designed to measure changes in developmental level through a technology known as path-referenced assessment. This is a statistical procedure for measuring development in relation to a child's position on empirically validated developmental paths or sequences (Bergan, 1980; Bergan & Stone, 1985). Research and theory in cognitive and social development were used to guide the construction of the measures in six areas: language, math, nature/science, perception, reading, and social development. Further, analyses of items were carried out regarding cultural and sociolinguistic bias. The Head Start Battery represents positive movement toward a tighter integration of developmental and psychometric theories.

The validity of an assessment of a child's competencies is improved through the integration of an array of assessment information. The analysis of performance should be *ipsative;* that is, it should emphasize individual patterning. Putting pieces of data together as in a collage can provide a more integrated picture of the child. Ipsative analyses are idiographic in concept, relying on a profile or patterned display of observations or test scores of a single individual (see Jackson & Messick, 1967). Although a detailed discussion of this approach is beyond the scope of this chapter, the main point is that evaluations of young children should grapple with the concept of a child as an integrated unit and fully realize the limitations of fragmented data such as IQ scores or reading level. An analogous argument also can be made for evaluating programs from the multiple perspectives of a range of participants (e.g., Stake, 1975).

While these are not new ideas, there appears to be growing recognition of the value of assessment information derived from multiple methods and multiple settings. For example, the NAEYC position statement on standardized testing indicates that decisions that have a major impact on children, such as retention or assignment to special classes, should be "based on multiple scores of information and should never be based on a single test score" (NAEYC, 1988, p. 44). Also, recent critiques of approaches to assessing children with special needs call for multicontextual evaluations that draw upon information from a variety of settings and informants (Achenbach, McConaughy & Howell, 1987; Cicchetti & Wagner, 1990).

INFORMING POLICY AND PROGRAM DESIGN DECISIONS

Attention to the internal and external validity of evaluations of early childhood programs has increased considerably in the past two decades as policy makers have looked to existing studies for guidance on decisions about the allocation of resources for programs of early education and care. As set forth by Campbell and Stanley (1963), internal validity pertains to whether a program (versus other uncontrolled variables) in fact contributes to outcome differences between experimental and control subjects. External validity deals with the generalizability of a study in terms of populations, settings, and the nature of program variables.

Criteria for internal and external validity often are at odds because the features that increase one may jeopardize the other (Campbell & Stanley, 1963). Research on the effects of early childhood intervention programs is illustrative of this problem. Investigations of model programs such as those included in the Consortium for Longitudinal Studies (1983; Lazar, Darlington, Murray, Royce & Snipper, 1982) tend to be high in internal validity, while studies of modal programs such as Head Start generally are low in internal validity. Conversely, the external validity of research on modal programs generally is thought to be quite high, but questions have been raised about the external validity or generalizability of research on model early intervention programs.

Many of the studies in the Consortium employed efforts to reduce the threats to internal validity, primarily through random assignment of children to program and control groups. Further, in the analyses carried out by the Consortium, studies were separated using random versus nonrandom assignment, and data analysis followed a rigorous plan that enabled the identification of robust findings. In many important ways, then, the Consortium studies exemplify evaluation research at its best, yielding strong and often unequivocal evidence regarding the effects of early education for children from low-income families.

The model programs represented in the Consortium demonstrate the benefits of early education under ideal circumstances (Datta, 1983); hence the external validity of the findings is subject to question. The initiatives were carried out with well-trained staff, close monitoring by leading researchers, sufficient financial support, and an excitement of innovation that may have contributed to a Hawthorne effect. Can the outcome results of a model effort be readily generalized to a modal program in which there are likely to be fewer support systems for maintaining quality services commensurate with those associated with the model program? Generalizability questions also can be raised regarding population validity, in that the experience of a young child living in poverty in the 1990s may differ qualitatively from the conditions of poverty in the 1960s when the Consortium interventions were carried out. Generalizability is potentially weakened by important time-period differences in environmental circumstances (e.g., youth selling and using illegal drugs) that modify or perhaps ameliorate the long-term effects of early education.

Although studies of modal programs such as Head Start are typically high in external validity, the internal validity often suffers due to a lack of random assignment to program and control group conditions. The stark realities of providing community-based early childhood programs for children and families (e.g., first-come, first-served enrollment policies) often conflict with the ideals of experimental methodology (Powell, 1987). Accordingly, there are a large number of methodologically questionable studies of Head Start and similar interventions in the literature. One of the consequences of the internal validity problems of many studies of Head Start and similar interventions is that the long-term effects on children are less impressive than the results of evaluations of model programs such as those included in the Consortium. For example, results of a meta-analysis of 76 Head Start studies, conducted as part of a Head Start Synthesis Project (McKey et al., 1985), indicate that Head Start has an immediate effect on intellectual performance, including IQ, school readiness, and achievement. These effects disappear after one to three years of school, however. Similarly, the Synthesis Project points to immediate but not long-term positive effects on such socioemotional areas as self-esteem, achievement motivation, and social behavior. There have been few studies of the long-term effects of Head Start on special education placement, retention in grade, and similar social indicators, and the existing research yields inconsistent results.

The validity of the Synthesis Project findings has been questioned because methodologically weak studies were part of the meta-analysis (Gamble & Zigler, 1989). As noted earlier, the major methodological problem of most of the Head Start studies is the noncomparability of program and comparison-group children, stemming from the lack of random assignment. A recent research report involving a reanalysis of data involving nearly 1,000 Head Start and control-group children suggests that estimates of Head Start effects can be underestimated through the use of noncomparable control groups. Lee, Brooks-Gunn, and Schnur (1988) found that the Head Start sample included a higher proportion of African-American children, mothers with less formal education, father-absent households, larger families, and children with lower preintervention test scores of cognitive functioning than the sample in the control groups. The lack of impressive long-term results of Head Start may not be solely attributable to internal validity problems, however. Haskins (1989) reminds us that a more carefully designed study of Head Start (Miller & Bizzell, 1983) did not yield long-term program effects on retention in grade or placement in special education, unlike the other (non-Head Start) studies in the Consortium.

In view of the contrasting strengths and limitations of research on model and modal early intervention programs, is it reasonable to use model program data to argue for an expansion of the number of preschool programs for children from economically disadvantaged children, or, in light of less powerful results from modal programs, do we postpone a decision about program expansion until further research is carried out on Head Start and similar community-based initiatives? Clearly such decisions can be made on ideological grounds pertaining to issues of equity and the moral responsibilities of a democratic society. From the perspective of available research evidence, however, the logical direction of decisions about the expansion of early intervention programs is less clear. There are ill-defined parameters of the uses and misuses of generalizing about the extant research literature on early childhood programs, creating an ethical dilemma for social scientists and policy makers that is heightened by a political context of growing interest in early childhood programs as part of widespread national concern regarding school reform and families' child care needs.

We have used the early intervention literature to illustrate problems stemming from inadequate attention to external and internal validity. The issues obviously extend to other domains of research on programs for young children, such as the propensity to ignore the level of program quality in studies of the effects of nonfamilial child care (see Phillips, 1987). With regard to external validity, inappropriate extrapolations have included generalizing about data from one type of setting (e.g., center-based child care) to other settings (e.g., family child care), from one type of program (e.g., the High/Scope curriculum) to other programs (e.g., all preschool curricula), and from one type of population (e.g., low-income African-American children) to other populations (e.g., low-income Hispanic children).

The generalizability of research findings across populations is an increasingly important topic as early childhood programs aimed at non-Anglo children are expanded or launched. In a thoughtful paper on population generalizability, Laosa (1990) indicates that it cannot be assumed that an outcome of a particular program will be the same when the program is implemented with different populations, especially in view of sociocultural differences in how children respond to the performance demands of classrooms (Tharp, 1989; Trueba, 1988). A top priority for research should be investigations surrounding culturally responsive forms of early childhood programs, including the effects of particular program approaches on socioculturally diverse populations.

Questions about external validity are never completely answered (Campbell, 1984), and the replication of social programs is far from being a science. One of the important lessons of the planned variation experiments involving Head Start and Follow Through is that community factors play a central role in shaping a program (Halpern & Larner, 1988). It is folly to define replication as program duplication in the field of early childhood education. Compared to questions about external validity, those about internal validity are easier to answer and are more important to consider, because questions about generalization become moot if program effects are rendered highly equivocal due to internal validity problems. The first and foremost research need, then, is to improve the internal validity of research on community-based early childhood programs.

CONCLUSION

Some progress has been made recently in the search for validity in evaluations of young children and early childhood programs. Advances have come primarily in the form of increased awareness, as evidenced by position statements and publications calling for greater sensitivity to the limits of conventional assessment procedures and the need for alternative strategies of evaluation. Movement away from dependence on IQ measures as a sole indicator of early childhood program outcomes also represents progress. At the same time, some practices continue to exhibit a blatant disregard for the importance of validity, especially in the use of school readiness tests. Major challenges remain. Little progress has been made toward the resolution of persistent issues surrounding the mismatch between developmental processes and the assumptions regarding continuity, representativeness, and context inherent in traditional approaches to assessing young children. Further work also is needed in designing evaluations of community-based early childhood initiatives that improve the frequent problem of low internal validity. The link between social policy and the search for validity is increasingly tight, in view of the rapidly growing use of assessment tools and questions about the benefits of various programs for young children. Because the stakes are high for the individual and for society, a commitment to seeking viable solutions should be deemed a priority by professionals and responsible human beings.

NOTE

This chapter is an expanded and updated version of the following paper: Sigel, I. E. (1975). The search for validity or the evaluator's nightmare. In R. A. Weinberg and S. G. Moore (Eds.), *Evaluation of educational programs for young children: The Minnesota Round Table on Early Childhood Education I* (pp. 53–66). Washington, DC: The Child Development Associate Consortium.

REFERENCES

Achenbach, T. M., McConaughy, S. H., & Howell, C. T. (1987). Child/ adolescent behavioral and emotional problems: Implications of cross-informant correlations for situational specificity. *Psychological Bulletin, 101*, 213–232.

Ainsworth, M. D. S., Blehar, M., Waters, E., & Wall, S. (1978). *Patterns of attachment: Observations in the Strange Situation and at home.* Hillsdale, NJ: Erlbaum.

American Psychological Association. (1985). *Standards for educational and psychological tests and manuals.* Washington, DC: Author.

Anderson, S., & Messick, S. (1974). Social competency in young children. *Developmental Psychology, 10,* 282–293.

Barker, R. G. (Ed.) (1963). *The stream of behavior.* Englewood Cliffs, NJ: Appleton-Century-Crofts.

Bergan, J. R. (1980). The structural analysis of behavior: An alternative to the learning hierarchy model. *Review of Educational Research, 50,* 225–246.

Bergan, J. R., & Stone, C. A. (1985). Latent class models for knowledge domains. *Psychological Bulletin, 98,* 166–184.

Bergan, J. R., et al. (1984). *Head Start Measures Battery.* Tucson, AZ: University of Arizona.

Berreuta-Clement, J. R., Schweinhart, L. J., Barnett, W. S., Epstein, A. S., & Weikart, D. P. (1985). *Changed lives: The effects of the Perry Preschool Program on youths through age 19.* Ypsilanti, MI: High/Scope Press.

Bronfenbrenner, U. (1979). *The ecology of human development: Experiments by nature and design.* Cambridge, MA: Harvard University Press.

Bronfenbrenner, U. (1989). *Ecological systems theory. Annual of child development* (Vol. 6, pp. 187–249). Greenwich, CT: JAI Press.

Bronson, M. B. (1975). *Executive competence in preschool children.* Paper presented at the annual meeting of the American Educational Research Association, Washington, DC. (ERIC Document Reproduction No. ED 107 378)

Bronson, M. B. (1985). *Manual for the Bronson Social and Task Skill Profile.* Chestnut Hill, MA: Boston College.

Campbell, D. T. (1984). Can we be scientific in applied social science? In R. F. Connor, D. G. Attman & C. Jackson (Eds.), *Evaluation studies review annual* (pp. 26–48). Beverly Hills, CA: Sage.

Campbell, D. T., & Stanley, J. C. (1963). Experimental and quasi-experimental designs for research on teaching. In H. L. Gage (Ed.), *Handbook of research on teaching* (pp. 94–172). Chicago: Rand McNally.

Ceci, S. J. (in press). *On intelligence: A bioecological view of intellectual development.* Cambridge, MA: Harvard University Press.

Ceci, S. J., & Bronfenbrenner, U. (1985). "Don't forget to take the cupcakes out of the oven": Prospective memory, strategic time-monitoring, and context. *Child Development, 56,* 150–165.

Ceci, S. J., Bronfenbrenner, U., & Baker, J. G. (1988). Memory in context: The case of prospective memory. In F. Weinert & M. Perlmutter (Eds.), *Universals and change in memory development* (pp. 243–256). Hillsdale, NJ: Erlbaum.

Ceci, S. J., & Liker, J. (1986). A day at the races: IQ, expertise, and cognitive complexity. *Experimental Psychology: General, 115,* 255–266.

Cicchetti, D., & Wagner, S. (1990). Alternative assessment strategies for the evaluation of infants and toddlers: An organizational perspective. In S. J. Meisels & J. P. Shonkoff (Eds.), *Handbook of early childhood intervention* (pp. 246–277). New York: Cambridge University Press.

Clarke-Stewart, K. A. (1988). The "effects" of infant day care reconsidered. *Early Childhood Research Quarterly, 3,* 293–318.

Clarke-Stewart, K. A., & Fein, G. G. (1983). Early childhood programs. In M. M. Haith & J. J. Compos (Eds.), P. H. Mussen (Series Ed.), *Handbook of child psychology: Vol. 2. Infancy and developmental psychobiology* (pp. 917–1000). New York: Wiley.

Consortium for Longitudinal Studies (Ed.). (1983). *As the twig is bent: Lasting effects of preschool education.* Hillsdale, NJ: Erlbaum.

Cronbach, L. J., & Meehl, P. E. (1967). Construct validity in psychological tests. In D. M. Jackson & S. Messick (Eds.), *Problems in human assessment.* New York: McGraw-Hill.

Datta, L. (1983). Epiloque: We never promised you a rose garden, but one may have grown anyhow. In Consortium for Longitudinal Studies (Ed.), *As the twig is bent: Lasting effects of preschool education* (pp. 467–479). Hillsdale, NJ: Erlbaum.

Emmerich, W. (1966). Continuity and stability in early social development: II. Teacher ratings. *Child Development, 37,* 17–27.

Forman, G. E., & Fosnot, C. T. (1982). The use of Piaget's constructivism in early childhood education programs. In B. Spodek (Ed.), *Handbook of research in early childhood education* (pp. 185–211). New York: Free Press.

Gamble, T. J., & Zigler, E. (1989). The Head Start Synthesis Project: A critique. *Journal of Applied Developmental Psychology, 10,* 267–274.

Graue, M. E., & Shepard, L. A. (1989). Predictive validity of the Gesell School Readiness Test. *Early Childhood Research Quarterly, 4,* 303–315.

Halpern, R., & Larner, M. (1988). The design of family support programs in high risk communities: Lessons from the Child Survival/Fair Start Initiative. In D. R. Powell (Ed.), *Parent education as early childhood intervention: Emerging directions in theory, research and practice* (pp. 181–207). Norwood, NJ: Ablex.

Haskins, R. (1989). Beyond metaphor: The efficacy of early childhood education. *American Psychologist, 44,* 274–282.

Howes, C. (1980). Peer play scale as an index of complexity of peer interaction. *Developmental Psychology, 16,* 371–372.

Howes, C. (1987). Social competence with peers in young children: Developmental sequences. *Developmental Review, 7,* 252–272.

Ilg, F. L., & Ames, L. B. (1972). *School readiness.* New York: Harper & Row.

Ilg, F. L., Ames, L. B., Haines, J., & Gillespie, C. (1978). *School readiness: Behavior tests used at the Gesell Institute.* New York: Harper & Row.

Jackson, D. N., & Messick, S. (Eds.). (1967). *Problems in human assessment.* New York: McGraw-Hill.

Kagan, J. (1969). The three faces of continuity in human development. In D. A. Goslin (Ed.), *Handbook of socialization theory and research* (pp. 983–1002). Chicago: Rand McNally.

Laosa, L. M. (1982). The sociocultural context of evaluation. In B. Spodek (Ed.), *Handbook of research in early childhood education* (pp. 501–520). New York: Free Press.

Laosa, L. M. (1990). Population generalizability, cultural sensitivity, and ethical dilemmas. In C. B. Fisher & W. W. Tyron (Eds.), *Ethics in applied developmental psychology: Emerging issues in an emerging field* (pp.

227–251). Norwood, NJ: Ablex.

Lazar, I., Darlington, R., Murray, H., Royce, J., & Snipper, A. (1982). Lasting effects of early education: A report from the Consortium for Longitudinal Studies. *Monographs of the Society for Research in Child Development, 47* (2–3, Serial No. 195).

Lee, V. E., Brooks-Gunn, J., & Schnur, E. (1988). Does Head Start work? A 1 year follow-up comparison of disadvantaged children attending Head Start, no preschool, and other preschool programs. *Developmental Psychology, 24,* 210–222.

Lewin, K. (1951). *Field theory in social science.* New York: Harper & Row.

McClelland, D. C. (1973). Testing for competence rather than for "intelligence." *American Psychologist, 28,* 1–14.

McKey, R. H., Condelli, L., Ganson, H., Barrett, B. J., McConkey, C., & Plantz, M. C. (1985). *The impact of Head Start on children, families and communities* (DHHS Publication No. 85-31193). Washington, DC: CSR, Inc.

Meisels, S. J. (1984). Prediction, prevention and developmental screening in the EPSDT program. In H. W. Stevenson & A. E. Siegel (Eds.), *Child development research and social policy* (pp. 267–317). Chicago: University of Chicago Press.

Meisels, S. J. (1985). *Developmental screening in early childhood: A guide.* Washington, DC: National Association for the Education of Young Children.

Meisels, S. J. (1987). Uses and abuses of developmental screening and school readiness testing. *Young Children, 42,* 4–73.

Messick, S. (1974). *The standard problem: Meaning and values in measurement and evaluation* (Research Bulletin RB-74-44). Princeton, NJ: Educational Testing Service.

Miller, L. B., & Bizzell, R. P. (1983). The Louisville experiment: A comparison of four programs. In Consortium for Longitudinal Studies (Ed.), *As the twig is bent: Lasting effects of preschool programs* (pp. 25–90). Hillsdale, NJ: Erlbaum.

National Association for the Education of Young Children. (1988). NAEYC position statement on standarized testing of young children 3 through 8 years of age. *Young Children, 43,* 42–7.

Neisworth, J. T., & Bagnato, S. J. (1986). Curriculum-based developmental assessment: Congruence of testing and teaching. *School Psychology Review, 15,* 180–189.

Phillips, D. (Ed.). (1987). *Quality in child care; what does research tell us?* Washington, DC: National Association for the Education of Young Children.

Popham, W. J. (1978). *Criterion-referenced assessment.* Englewood Cliffs, NJ: Prentice Hall.

Powell, D. R. (1987). Conceptual and methodological problems in research. In S. L. Kagan, D. R. Powell, B. Weissbourd & E. Zigler (Eds.), *America's family support programs: Perspectives and prospects* (pp. 311–328). New

Haven, CT: Yale University Press.

Seitz, V., Abelson, W. D., Levine, E., & Zigler, E. (1975). Effects of place of testing on the Peabody Picture Vocabulary Test scores of disadvantaged Head Start and non-Head Start children. *Child Development, 46,* 481–486.

Seppanen, P. S., & Love, J. M. (1990). *Observational study of preschool education and care for disadvantaged children: Recommendations for measuring cognitive and social-emotional outcomes among Chapter 1 children.* Hampton, NC: RMC Research Corp.

Siegel, L. S. (1982). Reproductive, perinatal, and environmental factors as predictors of the cognitive and language development of preterm and full-term infants. *Child Development, 53,* 963–973.

Stake, R. E. (1975). *Program evaluation, particularly responsive evaluation.* Paper presented at a conference on "New Trends in Evaluation," Goteborg, Sweden.

Tharp, R. G. (1989). Psychocultural variables and constants: Effects on teaching and learning in schools. *American Psychologist, 44,* 349–359.

Thompson, R. A., Lamb, M. E., & Estes, D. (1982). Stability of infant-mother attachment and its relationship to changing life circumstances in an unselected middle-class sample. *Child Development, 53,* 144–148.

Travers, J. F., & Light, R. J. (Eds.). (1982). *Learning from experience: Evaluating early childhood demonstration programs.* Washington, DC: National Academy Press.

Trueba, H. T. (1988). Culturally based explanations of minority students' academic achievement. *Anthropology and Education Quarterly, 19,* 270–287.

Wohlwill, J. (1973). *The study of behavioral development.* New York: Academic Press.

Wood, C., Powell, S., & Knight, R. C. (1984). Predicting school readiness: The validity of developmental age. *Journal of Learning Disabilities, 17,* 8–11.

Zigler, E., Abelson, W., & Seitz, V. (1973). Motivational factors in the performance of economically disadvantaged children on the Peabody Picture Vocabulary Test. *Child Development, 44,* 294–303.

Zigler, E., & Trickett, P. K. (1978). IQ, social competence, and evaluation of early childhood intervention programs. *American Psychologist, 33,* 789–799.

CHAPTER 11

Trends in Early Childhood Education and Development Programs

PERSPECTIVE FROM THE DEVELOPING WORLD

Cassie Landers

International organizations, private voluntary organizations, and nongovernmental organizations have long been concerned with the survival and protection of children in developing countries. These efforts have contributed to the remarkable reduction of child mortality rates and increased protection of children in exceptionally difficult circumstances. Programs directed toward these aims must continue with increased commitment, and policy makers must expand their vision and recognize the importance of ensuring the survival of children's emotional, social, and cognitive development. Although it has been accepted that good health and adequate nutrition are necessary for the psychological and social development of young children, it is less widely recognized that early childhood education and development programs have a direct and measurable impact on both the health and the nutritional status of children. Although the implications of the synergistic effect of health, nutrition, and psychosocial development on program planning are manifold, they have been generally overlooked.

It is anticipated that comprehensive early childhood education and development programs might receive greater international and national attention as a result of the following major demographic, economic, social, and political changes that have occurred in the last several decades (Myers, 1989):

• In 1990, more than 12 of every 13 children born will live through their first year (compared with 5 of 6 in 1960). By 2000, 19 of 20 children born are expected to survive. Many of these surviving children live at risk of impaired physical, mental, social, and emotional development.

• Urbanization, the disruption of stable family units, the erosion of traditional child care practices, and the difficulty of adopting new practices have a negative effect on development.

• The increase in participation by women in the labor force, combined with changes in family structures, result in increasing need for child care services.

• Lingering effects of the worldwide recession of the 1980s have left families living at the margin.

Investments in programs that enhance development in the early years of life have a compelling set of scientific, social, and economic arguments:

• Scientific research demonstrates that the early years are critical to children's social, emotional, and cognitive development. Children exposed to consistent and responsive environments have enhanced nutritional and health outcomes. Finally, research has demonstrated the positive impacts of early intervention programs on children's enrollment, progress, and performance in primary school.

• Children have a right to develop to their full potential. The 1959 Declaration of the Rights of the Child and the 1989 Convention are the most convincing and fundamental forces supporting early childhood education and development programming.

• The transmission of moral and social values that will guide the future of our children begins in the earliest months of life. Early childhood education and development programs can support parents and communities, thus providing environments that reinforce positive cultural values.

• Stressful conditions that inhibit development in the early years affect the poor more than the rich, reinforcing social inequities. In many countries, gender-linked disparities in patterns and practices of child rearing in the early years work against girls' development and educational opportunities. Early childhood education and development programs can help correct such discrepancies.

• Society benefits through increased productivity and cost savings associated with enhanced early child development. Preventive programs reduce the need for expensive curative health care; improve the efficacy of education systems; reduce the drop-out and repetition rates; and reduce the incidence of juvenile delinquency, drug and alcohol abuse, and other forms of harmful social behavior.

• Efforts to improve the educational level of girls and women will have a strong intergenerational effect on fertility. Early childhood education and development programs, linked to parental education and increasing girls' school attendance, can play a role in promoting family planning and the decline of fertility rates.

• The effectiveness of health, nutrition, education, and income-generating programs can be improved through integration with programs of child development. Early childhood education and development programs are often an important entry point for community development and health care activities.

PROGRAM POLICIES, STRATEGIES, AND REALITIES

The early development of children is promoted by a continuous interactive process between the developing child and the people and objects in a constantly changing environment. Recognizing this process's wide variation both between and within developing countries has led to the development of five complementary program approaches (Myers & Landers, 1989):

1. *Delivering a service.* Enhancing child development by attending to the immediate needs of children in centers organized outside the home.
2. *Educating caregivers.* Educating and "empowering" parents and alternative caregivers to improve their care of children and enrich their environments.
3. *Promoting community development.* Improving the physical environment, knowledge, and practices of community members and the organizational base for political and social negotiations.
4. *Strengthening national resources and capacities.* Planning, organizing, and implementing innovative techniques and models.
5. *Advocating to increase demand.* Producing and distributing knowledge to create awareness and demand.

Each has different immediate objectives and is directed toward a different audience or group of participants. Table 11.1 summarizes the beneficiaries, objectives, and illustrative models for each approach. The emphases to be given within the overall strategy will vary considerably, depending on the setting in which the program is being developed. The main goal of early childhood education and development programs is to enhance the competence of children to

Table 11.1   Programming for Child Development:
                   Complementary Approaches and Models

Program Approach	Participants/ Beneficiaries	Objectives	Models
Deliver a service	The child 0–2 years 3–6 years 0–6 years	Survival Comprehensive development Socialization Rehabilitation Improvement of child care	Home day care Integrated child development centers "Add-on" centers Workplace Preschools: formal/ nonformal
Educate caregivers	Parent, family Sibling(s) Public	Create awareness Change attitudes Improve/change practices	Home visiting Parental education Child-to-child programs Mass media
Promote community development	Community Leaders Promoters Members	Mobilize for action Change conditions	Create awareness Technical mobilization Social mobilization
Strengthen national resources, capacities	Program Personnel Professionals Para-profes- sionals	Create awareness Improve skills Increase material	Training Experimental, demonstration projects Strengthening infrastructure
Advocate to increase demand	Policy makers Public Professionals	Create awareness Build political will Increase demand Change attitudes	Social marketing Ethos creation Knowledge dissemination

adjust to, perform in, and transform their own surroundings. In some cultures, this means greater emphasis on independence; in others, greater emphasis on group solidarity.

Three sets of considerations are helpful in avoiding a piecemeal approach (Myers, 1989):

1. One must consider the five types of program strategies.
2. Programs should seek to be integrated, participatory, cost-effective, and extended over as wide a population of at-risk children as possible (UNICEF, 1984).
3. A program should target specific age groups with developmentally appropriate interventions. The tendency to restrict programs for child development to a particular age group and to emphasize the simultaneous character of survival, growth, and development is counteracted by the need for programs to cover development from the prenatal period through the early childhood period.

Innovative programming efforts incorporating these dimensions are numerous. UNICEF, the United Nations Educational, Scientific & Cultural Organization (UNESCO), the World Health Organization (WHO), the United States Agency for International Development (USAID), and the World Bank have contributed to this mix of complementary strategies, along with The Bernard van Leer Foundation, Save the Children Foundation, Aga Kahn Foundation, and others.

CRITICAL ISSUES IN PROGRAM IMPLEMENTATION

One of the major issues challenging the implementation of early childhood education and development programs is the need to respond to the rapidly growing interest in high-quality and affordable programs that can reach a significant number of children and families.

Increasing Program Coverage

The problems associated with the process of program expansion can be classified into four general categories: (1) lack of adequate resources; (2) absence of political will; (3) weak demand for services; and (4) inefficient organization, implementation, and management systems. Child development projects and programs vary widely, depending on the social and economic conditions, the mix of program components, the age group involved, the institutional structure for planning and implementation, the degree of community involvement, and the methods used to deliver the program. Expansion of a program that focuses on physical development and immunization in a small country with a high literacy rate will be vastly different from expansion of a program that attempts to build a sustained community-based service including health, nutrition, and psychosocial components in a large country with a relatively low literacy rate. Thus, there is no one formula for programming that is equally applicable in all locations. An additional set of constraints in program expansion stems from the fact that early childhood education and development programs, particularly those focusing on children under two years of age, do not require large investments in institutionalized structures and are therefore less attractive to politicians than building large-scale social service institutions.

More challenging than citing reasons for failure, however, is the systematic identification of components that account for a program's successful efforts to move to scale. Three strategies for achieving scale have been distinguished: expansion, explosion, and association (Myers, 1984). Expansion entails a "learning process approach" in which program development proceeds through three distinct stages. In the first stage, the major concern is learning to be effective; the second stage is focused on learning to be efficient; the third stage is concerned with expanding the organizational infrastructure needed to carry out the program objectives.

Increasing coverage through "explosion" circumvents the pilot stage. Implementation starts on a large scale, usually with one model serving many distinct geographic and cultural groups. This approach is usually the outcome of a national political decision that is motivated by politicians' desire to attract broad political support. An example of the explosion approach is the Bienestar program in Colombia, in which the same model is applied to all parts of the country and maximum coverage in the shortest period of time is the primary objective.

In an association model, program coverage is accomplished through independently initiated or coordinated but distinct small-scale projects, each of which responds to the needs of a given target population. In countries characterized by a loose confederation of distinct cultural groups, achieving a large-scale program by association may be desirable, since it allows each program to respond and adjust to the particular needs of a homogeneous target group.

Analyzing these three approaches forces planners to consider the various elements and preconditions involved in the complex process of expanding program coverage. Interest in child development programs is growing, simple technologies are under way, and a wide range of alternative delivery systems is being implemented. The systematic appraisal of present initiatives provides a critical opportunity to plan for expansion, and in the process, it raises the consciousness of both national governments and international organizations.

Any discussion of expanding the coverage of early childhood education and development programs necessarily raises a number of related issues, including analyzing costs and financing, creating political will, utilizing the media, achieving quality control, training personnel, and monitoring and evaluating the program.

Analyzing Costs

The prospects for expanding the coverage of early childhood education and development programs are determined to a large degree by the availability of financial resources. Cost analysis is often a particularly weak element of the early child development (ECD) policy analyses and program evaluations.

In these economically volatile times, there is no easy answer to how to mobilize resources for early child development activities. Early child development is particularly vulnerable to the economic and political forces at play, since children do not wield political power. Moreover, the services included in early childhood education and development programs cross many bureaucratic lines, and no one sector is held responsible.

Unfortunately, magical sources of revenue are not likely to be discovered; we must look widely for alternative sources. At the family level, for example, contributions by mothers, fathers, and other caregivers in the provision of children's health, nutrition, and education services must be considered. Potential community sources of revenue include contributions of space, facilities, and provision for safety and maintenance. Often untapped is the potential energy behind community solidarity efforts, including family support networking and promotion of traditional child-rearing patterns and practices. One must consider, however, the degree to which these cost-sharing mechanisms are feasible, given the growing demand for early preventive approaches and the need to increase the quality of services.

In creating resources committed to financing early childhood education and development programs, nongovernmental organizations are sometimes potential funders of recurrent costs. Collaboration among nongovernmental organizations and international assistance agencies is required in response to different financial requirements at different levels of project development.

Finally, public- and private-sector commitment must be reenergized. Economists have illustrated the play of forces affecting public-sector revenue for child care and development, including the national economic growth rate, inflation rates, competing demands of politically powerful sectors, and the diversity and elasticity of early child development revenues in relation to changes in the national economy. In the search for financial partners, the need for clear and understandable cost analysis becomes ever more critical. The main objectives of the proposed cost analysis are to determine (1) costs associated with expansion and sustainability; (2) relationship of costs to benefits, as compared with other possibilities for resource allocation; (3) potential opportunities for cost reduction; (4) ways to enhance program efficiency; and (5) alternative sources of revenue. The effective application of cost analysis may help to demystify the unknown costs associated with early childhood education and development programs (Myers & Hertenbert, 1987).

Creating Political Will

An overall strategy for early child development must include attention to the political and social commitment needed. Politicians and policy makers have the power to make budgetary decisions affecting the rate and process of program expansion; bureaucrats must be convinced of the value of child development strategies to ensure sustainability; and professionals must be encouraged to improve quality through the application of innovative techniques. In addition, it is important to capture the popular will of the community. A comprehensive and convincing rationale for investing in early childhood education and development programs, tailored specifically to the information needs and level of responsibility of the audience, must be established. Government officials must be convinced of the positive long-term benefits of prevention programs resulting in cost savings. Advocacy campaigns must have a clear sense of objectives, implementation strategies, and expected outcomes.

Successful advocacy campaigns must be based on a sensitive understanding of traditional beliefs, modern desires, and the social and economic realities determining the achievability of these aspirations. The mode of communication, the choice of content, and the form of presentation are dependent on the perceptions and perspectives of potential communicators and their audiences. Such an assessment identifies potential allies and collaborators as well as those whose collaboration may be detrimental to the achievement of the program objectives.

A particularly disturbing outcome of successful advocacy campaigns occurs when the "supply side" is unable to meet the expectations or deliver the services created by the demand. Government promises made to stir enthusiasm, mobilize demand, and spur action bring with them a responsibility to mount the sustained operations necessary to accomplish the proposed objectives. If that does not occur, successful and inspiring communication efforts can be interpreted as hollow public relations ploys—a situation all too familiar to expectant recipients.

Using the Media to Promote Early Child Development

The international expertise to focus national and international attention on children's survival needs must be transferred to the area of child development. Important to consider are the ways in which survival and development efforts could be mutually strengthened by simultaneous consideration through selected media channels. In using media to create political will, one could consider, for example, developing a "documentary series" that features child development as a global issue.

In addition to political will and national awareness created through the media, caregiver education can be enhanced through the selection and use of appropriate media channels as well as content and format. There should be a focus on local needs and the presentation of appropriate and available solutions in a compelling, practical, and demystifying fashion (Israel, Foote & Tognetti, 1987). It is firmly established, however, that applications of media techniques to educate caregivers will be successful only if audience involvement is maximized through both on-air techniques and related follow-up activities. Creative experimentation and field trials are required in the design of effective interactive media that encourage active viewer or listener involvement.

Program developers must also be aware of the increasing potential of media techniques designed to directly enhance children's development. "Sesame Street" (Polsky, 1974), developed by the Children's Television Workshop in the United States, is one example of a program that has been successfully adapted in developing countries; it is not only respected by parents, but is able to attract and sustain the active attention of preschool children. Program design should be flexible in order to respond to developmental needs at a range of developmental levels.

Achieving Quality Control

Although high-quality child care programs do positively affect development, a more complex concern is the potential for a negative impact by poor quality programs. Quality is a complex, culturally defined, and relative concept, and program planners and policy makers must begin to generate standard categories and components of quality against which programs can be measured. Without some grasp of quality and its associated costs, efforts to move forward on issues of regulation and standard setting will be curtailed.

In the past, issues of quality in early childhood education and development programs have been assessed according to three lines of investigation: (1) global assessments of a program's overall climate; (2) specific dimensions of an early childhood education and development program—including structural program aspects, such as group composition and staff qualifications; dynamic program aspects that capture children's experiences; and contextual program aspects, such as type of setting and staff stability; and (3) a relatively new line of investigation, a program's interactive effects—the relation between child care quality and children's family environments (Phillips & Howes 1987).

Assessments of the structural dimensions of child care, including adult-child ratio, group size, and caregiver training and experience, have generated greater insights into the relative impact of different program components. Contextual features of child care, such as staff stability, provide a measure of the quality important for a developmental issue such as attachment to primary caregivers. More recently, quality of child care has been assessed in terms of the joint effects of care received in a program and care received in the home. In summarizing the essential components of high-quality care generated by the large body of existing data, several components have been consistently indicated (Schweinhart, 1987):

- Developmentally appropriate curriculum that features child-initiated learning activities within a supportive environment.
- Careful selection of staff, with an ongoing strategy for in-service and on-site training.
- Attention to appropriate staff-child ratios.

- Ability of programs to engage in and establish a partnership with parents and the community.
- Strong administrative support, including comprehensive services such as health and nutrition.
- Effective evaluation and monitoring procedures allowing staff to monitor and observe children's progress.

The data suggest that quality is best understood as a blending of specific ingredients.

It is also important to assess the work environment of the child care setting. Child care environments have been largely studied as a developmental environment for young children, while the quality of the work environment for caregivers has been largely ignored—despite well-known high staff turnover rates. Efforts to understand the factors that affect staff turnover rates and the resulting negative consequences for children must also be undertaken.

Presently, child care in both the developed and developing worlds consists largely of unregulated environments. The growing pressure to expand supply exists without attention to regulation of quality. Without attention to the quality of care, enrollment statistics are of little significance. Policy analysis must provide insights into the range of possibilities for, as well as the essential characteristics of, high-quality child care; it must determine what these essential characteristics will cost (Clarke-Stewart, 1987).

Training Child Development Personnel

The training component is perhaps the most important factor associated with implementing and sustaining high-quality programs. In spite of its importance, training is often the first area to be cut as administrators struggle with decreasing resources; ineffective learning materials; didactic and sterile methodologies; lack of adequately trained trainers; and an infrastructure incapable of providing needed in-service training, follow-up, and supervision.

Effective training strategies for providers of early childhood education and development programs must enable learners to acquire skills and knowledge transferable to their particular tasks and roles. Successful training programs recognize what people know and begin by integrating the required new skills and knowledge into an existing knowledge base. The acquisition of new knowledge and skills is followed by opportunities for continued reflection and recognition of relevance for the learner's particular needs.

A successful training strategy for early child development personnel is one that emphasizes the learners' strengths rather than weaknesses, applies active and participatory training methods, perceives trainers as facilitators rather than directors, and fosters a cooperative rather than a competitive training environment. It is essential that training be a continual process providing a balanced mix of structured sessions with opportunities for follow-up and individually tailored supervision that reinforces, supports, and strengthens the learning process. If the goal is to create sustainable, high-quality systems of care, then the training approach described here is essential.

The content of the training program must respond to the strengths and limitations of a particular group of learners. It should include a balance between theory and practice. Theory should be incorporated into experience in a way that fosters continuous, systematic analysis. Opportunities for analyzing need to be integrated into the training process. With the implementation of continuous training schemes, however, new information can be phased in over time, gradually building on the learner's existing knowledge base. The development of effective curricula and training strategies based on techniques of experiential learning is encouraging. Planners would benefit from reviewing existing materials and identifying ways in which the available training materials can be adapted and adjusted (Torkington, 1989).

Monitoring and Evaluating Programs

The monitoring and evaluation of early childhood education and development programs have been hampered by the lack of available expertise, lack of widely acceptable child development instruments and measures, lack of clearly conceived program objectives, and lack of financial resources. The need for strong well-designed evaluations of early childhood education and development programs is underscored when one considers the potential applications of these results. Program evaluations can identify which factors are fundamental to achieving program objectives and are necessary components of standards for quality control. In addition, systematic attention to evaluation encourages comparisons both within and among countries of the relative effectiveness of alternative programming strategies. The information obtained from the application of effective monitoring systems can be used to guide the adaptation and refinement of program goals and objectives.

As in all fields of scientific inquiry, investigations must rely on both qualitative and quantitative data-collection methods. The multifaceted nature of early childhood education and development programs provides a range of opportunities for the simultaneous application of both qualitative and quantitative techniques, including, for example, creating new variables as well as replicating old measures, assessing process as well as outcome, and generating as well as testing hypotheses. If an early childhood education and development program is successful, it is important to determine how and why; if it is not, a similar line of inquiry is required.

Any discussion of program monitoring and evaluation must confront the complex and culturally sensitive issues regarding the identification and selection of indicators. The failure to use appropriate measures can cause considerable damage to children and families, and it is critical to assure that instruments possess the characteristics necessary to function adequately within the context for which they are developed.

The results of considerable efforts to measure early child development have led to the classification of four major categories of indicators: (1) description or diagnosis of the child's developmental level, (2) detection or screening for developmental disabilities, (3) periodic monitoring of a child's development, and (4) program evaluation (Atkin, 1989). If the need to develop instruments to measure children's development is taken seriously, criteria for developing new or evaluating existing instruments must be proposed.

A primary criterion is that the purpose of the instrument be specified and the instrument's characteristics be congruent with this stated purpose. A second criterion is the need to clearly define what aspects of development the instrument is attempting to measure. A third criterion requires that instruments be culturally appropriate, which is an issue of extreme importance and complexity. Fourth, the instruments should have adequate concurrent and predictive validity. Although greater attention has been given to issues of interobserver reliability, continued efforts are needed to assure adequate reliability among practitioners. In addition, little attention has been focused on the predictive validity of indicators, which is particularly relevant for detection and screening instruments. A final criterion in the selection of indicators relates to the ease with which instruments can be incorporated into programs. Instruments have been developed that have simple, attractive formats, easy-to-produce materials, and both practical and simple ways of reporting results. The remarkable and painstaking efforts thus far to develop simple measurement alternatives have shown that it is feasible to incorporate such tools into a variety of community-based programs.

SUMMARY AND POLICY IMPLICATIONS

The scientific evidence accumulated during the past decade demonstrates the importance of the early years of children's lives and the long-term benefits associated with increased investments in well-conceived and properly managed programs. In addition to having the confidence provided by scientific evidence, those involved in the translation of theory into action should have a sense of optimism. In the past, policy makers have been forced to rely on data from the industrialized world to justify their investments in early child development activities. More recently, a growing body of data from the developing world indicates the long-term benefits to children and their families, as reflected by increased primary school enrollments and enhanced primary school progress and performance. These data reinforce the assumption that similarly positive effects of early interventions are possible in the developing world; in fact, the potential for bringing about improvements may be greatest when social and economic conditions are more severe.

Since the International Year of the Child (1979), hundreds of demonstration programs and projects have underscored the possibilities for early childhood education and development programs to increase and foster children's abilities to cope with and creatively adapt to their environments. The expansion of early childhood education and development programs over the last decade has been dramatic.

Several critical factors can be identified in the rapid expansion of these successful initiatives. Of primary importance is a strong political commitment that enables the identification of the resources needed to achieve a set of clearly specified program goals and objectives. Political support is also critical to ensure stability, commitment, and continuity of program leadership. Additional characteristics of these programs include the application of media channels to create demand, the development of simple and efficient information systems to monitor progress and measure performance, and the implementation of flexible interactive training approaches that combine short-term instruction with ongoing field-level supervision and follow-up.

Programming success in early child development activities is consistently characterized by a well-defined set of variables that recognizes the simultaneous nature of survival and development and the interaction among children's physical, mental, social, and emotional capabilities. Another characteristic defining success is the emphasis placed on empowering caregivers and communities with the knowledge and skills needed to provide for the survival and developmental needs of their children. Successful programs encourage a level of participation beyond the formal definitions of community participation and include the child as an active participant in the creation of its own knowledge.

In spite of growing experience, millions of children and families are without services. The factors influencing national policies on child development are many and complex, reflecting unique historical conditions, widely differing national attitudes, and a variety of political and economic realities. Although considerable progress has been made in many countries in Latin America and Asia, programs are nonexistent in many parts of Africa. Many innovative programs find themselves unable to secure sustainable sources of revenue necessary to expand coverage while maintaining program quality. Often the quality of existing programs is so poor that positive benefits to children are minimal, and in some instances negative outcomes may be apparent. Moreover, the current set of strategies is unsuccessful in reaching high-risk mothers and infants from the prenatal period through the first two years of life with integrated programs that provide the appropriate balance of health, nutrition, and psychosocial components.

The challenges are set before us. We will continue to face economic questions that require a major adjustment in the allocation of resources, counteracting the present tendency for governments and other social services to meet economic pressures by cutting spending in these sectors. A second issue confronting policy makers and planners is the growing economic and social disparity among nations, which in turn polarizes the opportunities for children to reach optimal patterns of growth and development. A third major challenge relates to startling social and demographic changes, including increasing female labor force participation, rapid urbanization, and the erosion of stable family units.

These challenges require long-term commitment by professionals across many disciplines to address issues related to actual rather than theoretical integration and convergence of services. How and when to involve governments in the complex process of expansion and how to define the critical components in program quality are pressing concerns. Utilizing the advances in media technology, we must continue in our efforts to create flexible training strategies that are able to respond to the diversity of skills and needs reflected by early child development personnel. Without our commitment to the infrastructure needed to supplement intensive training courses with ongoing supervision and follow-up, the kind of programs we expect will remain an ideal. The frustrations resulting from inefficient monitoring systems must be assuaged by effective information management systems, enabling projects to adjust to a changing array of circumstances. Finally, we must continue to allow for the systematic interaction among families, children, and communities. Programs should not only incorporate and build upon parental wisdom, but must begin to identify the culture-specific opportunities for partnerships with parents that are open to us for a brief amount of time as children pass through infancy and early childhood.

The development of children in both the developed and developing worlds is jeopardized by a complex set of interlocking forces. It is a worldwide phenomenon calling for a worldwide response. Perhaps UNICEF and its partners' greatest contribution to the promotion of early child development activities could be to harness the commitment of governments, nongovernmental agencies, international donors, and public and private interest groups in an alliance for children—an alliance that is ready to recognize, understand, and respond to the integrated needs of children, families, and communities. Their collective voices, crying for help, demand sustainable programmatic responses that are capable of preventing the intergenerational perpetuation of failure by providing opportunities that foster self-esteem and confidence. It is a cry the societies of the world can no longer afford to ignore.

REFERENCES

Atkin, L. (1989). *Analysis of instruments used in Latin America to measure psychosocial development and environmental risk in children from 0 to 6 years of age.* Unpublished paper prepared for the Consultative Group on Early Childhood Care and Development, UNICEF, New York.

Clarke-Stewart, K. A. (1987). In search of consistencies in child care research. In D. A. Phillips (Ed.), *Quality in child care: What does research tell us?* (pp. 105–121). Washington, DC: National Association for the Education of Young Children.

Israel, R., Foote, D., & Tognetti, J. (1987). *Operational guidelines for social marketing projects in public health and nutrition* (Nutrition Education Series Issue No. 14). Paris: UNESCO.

Myers, R. (1984). *Going to scale.* Unpublished paper prepared for the Consultative Group on Early Childhood Care and Development, UNICEF, New York.

Myers, R. (1989). *The twelve who survive.* New York: Consultative Group on Early Child Development, UNICEF.

Myers, R., & Hertenbert, R. (1987). *The eleven who survive: Toward a re-examination of early child development programme options and costs* (Education and Training Series, Report No. ED169). Washington, DC: The World Bank.

Myers, R., & Landers, C. (1989). *UNICEF programme guidelines: Vol. 5. Early childhood development* (CF/PROG/IC/87-37).

Phillips, D. A., & Howes, C. (1987). Indicators of quality in child care: Review of research. In D. A. Phillips (Ed.), *Quality in child care: What does research tell us?* (pp. 1–21). Washington, DC: National Association for the Education of Young Children.

Polsky, R. M. (1974). *Getting to Sesame Street: Origins of the Children's Television Workshop.* New York: Praeger.

Schweinhart, L. (1987). *When the buck stops here: What it takes to run good early childhood programmes.* Ypsilanti, MI: High/Scope Resource.

Torkington, K. (1989). Training: A process of empowerment. *Bernard van Leer Foundation Newsletter, 55.*

UNICEF. (1984). *Early childhood development: Policy review* (E/ICEF/L.1). New York: Author.

CHAPTER 12

Curriculum Alternatives for the Future

Olivia N. Saracho

Bernard Spodek

Throughout this century, fundamental issues about the education of young children have been raised. During this period, early childhood programs have faced many challenges and criticisms. Some of the approaches to early childhood curriculum that existed at the beginning of the century have continued unchanged, while others have been revised and modified. In addition, new early childhood curriculum approaches have been developed, some of which have been sustained while others have faded from the scene.

There is a dynamism to the field of early childhood education and a willingness to respond to continuous societal transformations. This dynamism is reflected in the new organizational arrangements that have evolved to provide education for young children during this century as well as in the process of innovating and modifying programs.

Currently, there are many calls heard for changes in early childhood programs, both in structure and in curriculum. It is easy to respond to immediate pressures and create inappropriate short-range decisions that might lead to long-range turmoil. It is more difficult, though more responsible, to carefully analyze developing conditions in order to determine what kinds of programs might be developed in the best interests of young children.

FUTURE PERSPECTIVES

It is difficult to predict the future of early childhood curriculum development in the United States. Ultimately, there are numerous possible futures. Early childhood educators will have opportunities to create new educational environments for young children. In organizing educational programs, curriculum designers must present the familiar to young children while helping them go beyond the familiar to create and acquire new knowledge reflecting society's needs and values.

The chapters in the book explore curriculum issues from a comprehensive vantage point to assist the reader in perceiving curriculum development as a means of working with young children in appropriate ways. Bernard Spodek's chapter identifies the process of change that early childhood curriculum has undergone in response to changes in the knowledge base of society. One can expect that the requirements for being an educated person will change in the future. With such changes, along with changes in the knowledge available to society, will come changes in the curriculum of early childhood. Harriet K. Cuffaro's chapter demonstrates how the materials of early childhood education and their uses have similarly changed. We could predict that future changes in early childhood curriculum will lead to changes in the materials that will be made available to children within programs as well as in how these materials will be used.

The increasing diversity in the population served by early childhood programs that Herbert Zimiles identified will likely continue in the future. Early childhood education has always concerned itself with individual differences among children. Educators have become more sensitive to gender differences and to cultural and linguistic differences among groups of children as well. This suggests that early childhood programs will need to be increasingly flexible in their design and modifiable to respond to the educational needs of diverse populations. Traditional methods of early childhood education such as play, as presented by Olivia N. Saracho, along with methods reflecting the changes in levels of technology, as suggested by Douglas H. Clements, will continue to evolve within the context of newer programs. Teachers will need to become more aware of how to use methods and materials, both those that reflect high technology and those that reflect low technology. It may become more difficult to avoid direct instruction with young children as increased demands for knowledge are placed on them. It is important, though, that children continue to have a degree of control over their learning.

Early childhood programs of the future will have to respond to the social context in which they are implemented. Concerns about early childhood education in developing countries can provide lessons for program developers in developed countries. The need to assess these programs in the context of culture and the need to provide support for program dissemination as well as program development, as described by Cassie Landers, are as real in our society as in less developed ones. As we continue to amass evidence regarding the importance of the early years of life, we are becoming more aware that programs of early childhood education and development are an important avenue for social change. The needs of children, families, and communities will have to be met in an integrated, programmatic way.

The fact that young children will be enrolled in multiple programs means that curriculum developers will need to attend to issues of continuity and transitions among programs. Sharon L. Kagan suggests guidelines for creating increased integration and continuity in the lives of all children. But children are not the only clients of early childhood programs; the needs of parents for education and support will also have to be considered in the move to increase program integrity. Joseph H. Stevens's studies illustrate the need for parents' support systems in early childhood education. Such systems will use group learning strategies as networks of parents are created surrounding early childhood programs. Our knowledge of social learning strategies can help us build programs that allow us to transmit social skills to parents.

Early childhood programs of the future will also need to make use of new knowledge regarding children's learning and development as well as new knowledge of the consequences of varying educational techniques and structures on children's learning. The current concepts of development that Anthony D. Pellegrini and Janna Dresden have identified can be used to guide programs, but these programs will need to be carefully assessed.

Lorrie A. Shepard's chapter provides a warning that the use of standardized tests in evaluating children's learning can distort the programs in which young children are enrolled. Douglas R. Powell and Irving E. Sigel demonstrate the difficulty in assessing new early childhood programs. The problem of the validity of measures used for such assessment is one that will probably not be easily solved in the near future. Yet increasing our knowledge regarding the impact of early childhood programs is essential if we are to use our knowledge to inform social policy about what constitutes worthwhile programs for young children in the future.

The twenty-first century can offer early childhood education a bewildering assortment of options for curriculum development. Leaders in early childhood education must define the role of education in general and early childhood education in particular in our society.

They must:

1. Determine the directions that are most likely for American society and the implications for educational goals.
2. Identify the value structure to be the basis for curriculum.
3. Determine the possible learning alternatives that are available to achieve the desired educational goals.
4. Determine the most appropriate and timely strategies to enhance children's learning.
5. Involve the perspectives of others in planning a curriculum for the future.

THE FUTURE ITSELF

In the final decade of the twentieth century, American society is presenting us with the possibilities of an unknown future. Even as this book was written, we saw the hopes for universal peace, generated by the opening of Eastern Europe, dashed in the turmoil of a Middle East crisis. A year before that, political conflict in Tienanmen Square changed our relations with the People's Republic of China. Such situations seriously influence early childhood education programs. Societies can become less open when threatened. Governments must rechannel resources from domestic to international programs during periods of crisis. In addition, people's willingness to accept certain programs may change as they see their security threatened.

In spite of the pitfalls of predicting the future, one still must prepare for it. Although we cannot be sure of what the future holds in store, we can make some best guesses. We can also be flexible so that our plan for the future can be modified as the future unfolds. Planning for the future cannot be linear; it must be open-ended and flexible. Educational futurists acknowledged the problems of linear reformation. Shane (1971) suggests that the future be construed as a fan-shaped array of possible alternative futures, rather than a linear one.

Curriculum developers in early childhood education must identify educational goals in relation to a transforming society. Education in the United States, and in other nations, has always delayed in responding to changing social, cultural, technological, and economic conditions. Some delays are due to the process of cultural diffusion. But schools must learn to respond more rapidly to change.

A consequence of the rapid social change in our society has been the condition called transience, a mood or sense of impermanence in the relationships among people, things, places, organizations, and information. Extreme transience jeopardizes social stability by diminishing the cultural preservation and transmission framework. The historic role of early childhood programs and society's conforming stratagem is challenged in a culture where impermanence is a periodic state. Yet we must learn to accommodate to this change.

SUMMARY

American society has experienced tremendous transformations in the twentieth century that will continue into the twenty-first century. Impermanence in our society, cultural delay in educational institutions, and the inadequacy of traditional linear predictions of the future challenge the future of curriculum development.

Educators have provided multitudinous reasons to describe the future education of young children. Decentralized programs have been proposed for the individual or specific audiences in American society. Centralized programs serving the state have also been contemplated.

The thoughts and work of curriculum specialists will determine the disposition of educational programs in the United States in the future. This is a challenge to early childhood curriculum specialists, who will need to create more varied and more accessible learning alternatives for young children.

REFERENCE

Shane, H. G. (1971). Future-planning as a means of shaping educational change. In R. M. McClure (Ed.), *The curriculum: Retrospect and prospect, 70th yearbook: Part I. National Society for the Study of Education* (pp. 185–215). Chicago: University of Chicago Press.

About the Editors
and the Contributors

Douglas H. Clements is an associate professor at the State University of New York at Buffalo. He received his doctorate at the University of Buffalo and was an assistant professor at Kent State University. He has conducted research and published in the areas of computer applications in education, early development of mathematical ideas, and the learning and teaching of geometry. His recent research has dealt with the effects of certain Logo computer programming environments on children's metacognitive ability, creativity, and geometric conceptualizations and, through a National Science Foundation grant, has codeveloped an elementary geometry curriculum based on Logo (published by Silver Burdett). His recent books are *Computers in Elementary Mathematics Education* (Prentice Hall, 1989) and *Computers in Early and Primary Education* (Prentice Hall, 1985).

Harriet K. Cuffaro is a member of the graduate faculty at Bank Street College of Education, where she teaches courses in the foundations area and curriculum and supervises teachers. As a curriculum specialist, she has contributed to the development of nonsexist and multicultural programs and materials. Her publications and research reflect her interests in issues of equity, the history of early childhood curriculum, and young children's dramatic play and block building.

Janna Dresden is a Ph.D. student in educational psychology at the University of Georgia. Her interests are in children's cognitive development and the development of numeracy.

Sharon L. Kagan is associate director of the Bush Center in Child Development and Social Policy at Yale University. She has written extensively on child care and early education policies and practices, the role of public schools in the delivery of human services, the role of parents in their children's development, the similarities and differences in profit and nonprofit child care, and strategies for collaboration among institutions that serve young children. Dr. Kagan is coeditor of *Children, Families and Government, America's Family Support Programs, and Early Schooling: The Great Debate*. She is editor of the 1991 yearbook of the National Society for the Study of Education.

Cassie Landers is the coordinator of the Consultative Group on Early Child Care and Development (UNICEF, New York), which focuses on the developmental needs of young children in the developing world. She earned her doctorate in education from Harvard University and was a clinical instructor at the Katurba Medical College (Karnatake, India) and senior research scientist at the American Health Foundation (New York City). Among Dr. Landers's publications are "A Cry for Help: UNICEF's Response to Street Children in the Third World" (1988), "A Psychobiological Study of Infant Development in South India" (1989), and *Summary Report: Innocenti Global Seminar on Early Child Development* (1990). Dr. Landers is also editor of *The Coordinators' Notebook,* an international resource guide on early childhood development issues.

Anthony D. Pellegrini received his Ph.D. in early childhood education from Ohio State University. He is currently a professor of early childhood education at the University of Georgia as well as a research fellow at the Institute for Behavioral Research at that university. His research interests are in children's play and observational methods. He is coauthor of the chapter on play in the forthcoming *Handbook of Research on the Education of Young Children* (Macmillan).

Douglas R. Powell is a professor in the Department of Child Development and Family Studies at Purdue University. He is editor-elect of the *Early Childhood Research Quarterly* and serves on the editorial board of four other scholarly journals. He is the author of more than fifty scholarly articles and chapters and the editor and author of four books. Professor Powell serves as a consultant to major philanthropic foundations and is an advisor to the U.S. Department of Education.

Olivia N. Saracho (Editor) is professor of education in the Department of Curriculum and Instruction at the University of Maryland. She completed her Ph.D. in early childhood education at the University of Illinois. Prior to that, she taught Head Start, preschool, kindergarten, and elementary classes in Brownsville, Texas, and was director of the Child Development Associate Program at Pan American University. Her current research and writing are in the areas of cognitive style, academic learning, and teacher education in relation to early childhood education. Dr. Saracho's most recent books are *Cognitive Style and Early Education* (Gordon & Breach, 1990); *Professionalism and the Early Childhood Practitioner,* edited with Bernard Spodek and Donald J. Peters (Teachers College Press, 1988); and *Foundations of Early Childhood Education* with Bernard Spodek and Michael J. Davis (Prentice Hall, 1987, 1991). Dr. Saracho is coeditor of *Early Childhood Teacher Education,* the first volume of this series, which was published in 1990.

Lorrie A. Shepard is professor of education at the University of Colorado at Boulder. She earned her doctorate in research and evaluation methodology at the University of Colorado. Her work in educational policy research has focused on the uses of tests for special school placement—for example, identification of learning disabilities, grade retention, and kindergarten screening—and on the effects of testing on teaching and student learning. Her recent book with Mary Lee Smith is entitled *Flunking Grades: Research and Policies on Retention.* Dr. Shepard has served as president of the National Council on Measurement in Education, vice-president for Division D of the American Educational Research Association, editor of the *Journal of Educational Measurement,* and editor of the *American Educational Research Journal.*

Irving E. Sigel is a distinguished research psychologist at Educational Testing Service. His primary research interest is in the field of developmental psychology. He received his Ph.D. in human development from the University of Chicago. His earlier work involved investigations of children's intellectual development. He later studied the impact of preschool and family on children's intellectual growth. He has published widely on such topics as parent-child relationships and cognitive development. He is coauthor, with Carol Copple and Ruth Saunders, of *Educating the Young Thinker: Classroom Strategies for Cognitive Growth* (Erlbaum, 1984; originally published 1979). In addition to writing and research, Dr. Sigel has also directed preschool programs while at SUNY-Buffalo and at Educational Testing Service.

Bernard Spodek (Editor) is professor of early childhood education at the University of Illinois, where he has taught since 1965. He received his doctorate in early childhood education from Teachers College, Columbia University, then joined the faculty of the University of Wisconsin-Milwaukee. He has also taught nursery, kindergarten, and elementary classes. His research and scholarly interests are in the areas of curriculum, teaching, and teacher education in early childhood education. Dr. Spodek has lectured extensively in the United States, Australia, Canada, China, England, Israel, Japan, Mexico, and Taiwan. From 1976 to 1978 he was president of the National Association for the Education of Young Children, and from 1981 through 1983 he chaired the Early Education and Child Development Special Interest Group of the American Educational Research Association. He is widely published in the field of early childhood education. Dr. Spodek's most recent books are *Professionalism and the Early Childhood Practitioner,* edited with Olivia N. Saracho and Donald J. Peters (Teachers College Press, 1988); *Foundations of Early Childhood Education,* with Olivia N. Saracho and Michael J. Davis (Prentice Hall, 1987, 1991); and *Today's Kindergarten: Exploring Its Knowledge Base, Expanding Its Curriculum* (Teachers College Press, 1986). Dr. Spodek is coeditor of *Early Childhood Teacher Education,* the first volume of this series, which was published in 1990.

Joseph H. Stevens, Jr., is professor of early childhood education and educational foundations at Georgia State University. He completed his Ph.D. at George Peabody College of Vanderbilt University, where he worked with the Demonstration and Research Center for Early Education. He has been director of the Prekindergarten Program in the White Plains (NY) public schools and on the faculty of Teachers College, Columbia University, and the University of Washington. His recent research has focused on the social support systems of mothers with young children, particularly the support systems of very young mothers during the transition to parenthood.

Herbert Zimiles is professor of early childhood education at Arizona State University. Formerly he chaired the Research Division at Bank Street College of Education. A developmental psychologist, he received his Ph.D. in experimental psychologist at the University of Rochester. His major interests are in the child development underpinnings of education, especially those that are affected by social and technological change. He is coauthor of *The Psychological Impact of School Experience* (Basic Books, 1969) and coeditor of *Thought and Emotion* (Erlbaum, 1986).

Index

EP14 ②